THE MORAL AUTHORITY OF GOVERNMENT

THE MORAL AUTHORITY OF GOVERNMENT

Essays to Commemorate the Centennial of

THE NATIONAL INSTITUTE OF SOCIAL SCIENCES

Editors

MOORHEAD KENNEDY

R. GORDON HOXIE

BRENDA REPLAND

Introduction by REV. THEODORE M. HESBURGH, C.S.C.

transaction

TRANSACTION PUBLISHERS

New Brunswick (U.S.A.) and London (U.K.)

Library of Congress Catalog Number: 99-046674
ISBN: 0-7658-0024-1
Printed in the United States of America

Library of Congress Cataloging-in-Publication Data

The moral authority of government : essays to commemorate the centennial of the National Institute of Social Sciences / editors, Moorhead Kennedy, R. Gordon Hoxie, Brenda Repland ; introduction by Theodore M. Hesburgh.

    p. cm.
Includes bibliographical references.
    ISBN 0-7658-0024-1 (cloth : acid-free paper)
    1. Political leadership. 2. Authority. 3. Reason of state. 4. United States—Politics and government. I. Kennedy, Moorhead. II. Hoxie, R. Gordon (Ralph Gordon), 1919– III. Repland, Brenda. IV. National Institute of Social Sciences (U.S.)
JC330.3 .M67 2000
303.3′4—dc21   99-046674

Table Of Contents

SECTION FOUR

INTERNATIONAL AFFAIRS

SECTION FIVE

PHILANTHROPY AND SCIENCE

Foreword

THE NATIONAL INSTITUTE OF SOCIAL SCIENCES is an honorary society of mostly American individuals of notable achievement, devoted by service and philanthropy to the public weal.

It had its origins in the awakening perception of social needs as Reconstruction began after the Civil War. In October, 1865, on a call by the Massachusetts Board of Charities, a meeting of some 300 public-spirited citizens, chaired by the Governor, John A. Andrew, established the American Social Science Association, to plan measures of public improvement. It was modeled on the British Social Science Association founded nine years earlier, and organized into four departments: education, health, jurisprudence and finance. A fifth, social economy, was added nine years later.

Out of the American Social Science Association, leading American professional organizations were spawned and spun off: the American Bar Association, the American Historical Association, the National Conference on Social Welfare, the American Public Health Association and the National Prison Reform Association.

In 1899, the Association was incorporated by an Act of Congress as the present-day National Institute of Social Sciences, "for the purpose of promoting studies and researches in social science." This effort was led by James B. Angell, president of the University of Michigan, Daniel Coit Gilman, first president of Johns Hopkins University, and Andrew D. White, first president of Cornell University.

Our mission is to honor, recognize, and hear from a very select group of people who have made significant strides in advancing or maintaining the quality of American society.

Each year, the Institute presents its Gold Medal Honor Award to several such individuals. Their fields of accomplishment range from government, education, philanthropy, and the arts, to medicine, science, literature, and industry.

Those honored have included many famous names, such as William Howard Taft, Marie Curie, the Rockefeller Family, and Madeleine Albright; and also a list of "quiet achievers" such as Oseola McCarty (philanthropy) and Helen Nauts (immunotherapy).

The Institute is a nonpartisan organization that does not itself advocate or support any particular point of view. But upon accepting our awards, our honorees speak strongly on current issues and problems.

In this, our centennial year, it has seemed most appropriate to ask our past honorees and other distinguished representatives from the learned professions to come forward, to make statements and present their views on the issues and problems which face us all in the next century—because what these people say and do can affect these issues and problems.

The result has been this modest volume, and we have chosen as its unifying theme a subject which pervades and deeply concerns all segments of our society today, *The Moral Authority of Government.*

It is a subject which provokes a diversity of ideas, but which we think most Americans will agree has become central to our health and progress as a nation. Our contributors to this book have spoken out forcefully on it—in unison but not necessarily in agreement!

However, where possible, we will attempt to derive a clear message from their statements, on the accountability of government and what government can do in a leadership role to find new and more effective approaches to solving our problems.

BRUCE E. BALDING   WILLIAM H. BRINCKERHOFF
Chairman   *President*

National Institute of Social Sciences

Preface

The Moral Authority of Government reflects the best thinking of 45 contributors, who represent achievement in a number of fields.

Their essays have grouped themselves naturally into five chapters. In other words, the moral authority of government is exercised directly through *Presidential Leadership*, and the *Rule of Law*. Moral authority raises issues of *Character and Integrity*, and distinct dilemmas in *International Affairs*. Other institutions, notably foundations and the scientific community, exercise moral authority similar to that of government, and this is discussed under *Philanthropy and Science*.

Each of these chapters contains an introduction, which summarizes the constituent essays. It serves as a key for the reader looking for topics of special interest, as well as a road map through the individual chapter.

What we are talking about is both governmental and nongovernmental conduct. On the governmental side, perhaps Hamilton and Madison in 1788 said it best. In *Federalist No. 1*, Hamilton observed, "it seems to have been reserved to the people of this country, by their conduct and example, to decide the important question, whether societies . . . are really capable or not, of establishing good government from reflection and choice." And to that Madison added his own wisdom, "In framing a government . . . the great difficulty lies in this: you must first enable the government to control the governed; and in the next place oblige it to control itself."

The purpose of this general introduction is to identify some of the broader themes that run through more than one chapter. The principal theme of the book is that of "presidential leadership." The president personifies governmental authority, including its moral authority. Moreover, public concern over the *weakening* of the moral authority of government is often the result of *presidential* wrongdoing, whether the peccadilloes of the present incumbent, or the wrongdoing of President Nixon. Most of the essayists in *Presidential Leadership* argue that the moral authority of the leader depends on high personal standards as well as achievement.

As in *Presidential Leadership*, the materials grouped under *Rule of Law* and *Character and Integrity* frequently allude to the moral authority exercised by the example of Washington and the profound thinking of Lincoln. Similarly, when essayists in *Character and Integrity* as well as *Presidential Leadership* wrestle with the question of whether one judges a leader primarily by character, or by accomplishments, they, too, are usually referring to the president. And, of course, the president has primary responsibility for the management of international affairs.

Having said that, *Rule of Law* and *Character and Integrity* raise important issues not limited to the presidency. Is character, and the moral authority that derives from it, demonstrated most effectively not by what someone does in his or her personal life, but in the moral worth of the causes espoused, and effectiveness in pursuing them? If, as one of the essays cites, "everyone has different moral standards," then moral standards must be purely subjective. Accordingly, the private life of a government official, or any leader, is by some deemed irrelevant to his or her moral authority.

Essayists in *Rule of Law* and *Character and Integrity* promote or attack this view. The attackers argue that moral standards and authority stem transcendental truths, often of religious derivation, and always the product of centuries of development. They further argue that if there are no absolutes, then of what meaning and use are such concepts as "justice" and "liberty"? Just as moral standards cannot be subjective, continue the attackers, then, too, there must be higher laws, which are not to be altered by legislatures. This is the basis of constitutional theory, and the ultimate moral authority of Law.

Essayists in *Presidential Leadership, Character and Integrity,* and *International Affairs* all wrestle with the moral and constitutional exception known as "reasons of state." Under what circumstances, for example, is it morally acceptable for a leader, or a government, to practice deception upon the citizenry, to overthrow other governments, or to bomb civilians? While most essayists accept the necessity of such exceptional actions in an imperfect world, and agree that they do not necessarily impair the moral authority of government, one argues that deception undermines trust, and therefore moral authority.

Similarly, essayists in *Character and Integrity* and *International Affairs* raise the issue of what permits a government to take actions that would be immoral or illegal in individuals or groups?

Some would argue that if the cause is just, and the immoral or illegal behavior necessary for the cause to succeed, then government is justified. One essayist in *Rule of Law* applies this kind of reasoning to civil disobedience. Citizens, the essay argues, are justified in violating an unjust law in order to defend a higher law. But who defines the higher law, or whether a law is indeed unjust?

The French visitor Alexis de Tocqueville in his *Democracy in America* found great hope in the voluntary associations in America, and so it continues today. The final chapter, *Philanthropy and Science*, discusses the moral authority that is exercised by nongovernmental organizations, influencing both the government and the citizenry in a number of important areas.

The Moral Authority of Government raises difficult questions, to which it does not provide easy answers. Neither, apart from the views of individual essayists, does the book take positions on public issues. Rather, like its sponsor, the National Institute of Social Sciences, it is designed to stimulate creative thinking about problems that concern us all.

MOORHEAD KENNEDY
R. GORDON HOXIE

Introduction

I WOULD LIKE TO SAY A FEW WORDS about *The Moral Authority of Government*. Basically, I think this *moral authority* derives from our fundamental documents. In the case of the United States, these are the Declaration of Independence, the Constitution, and our Bill of Rights. Thomas Jefferson, of course, deduced that authority from God Himself. As he said so brilliantly, "We hold these truths to be self evident: that all men are created equal, endowed by their Creator with certain inalienable rights, among which are life, liberty, and the pursuit of happiness."

While working on the United States Commission on Civil Rights, I often quoted this wonderful sentence, which is somewhat unusual even among the other Declarations of this age. Most of our State Constitutions speak of life, liberty, and property. It was felicitous that instead of "property," Jefferson substituted "pursuit of happiness." Minorities, who do not enjoy full civil rights, cannot pursue the happiness of which Jefferson spoke.

When the Constitution was written, Jefferson happened to be our Ambassador to France. When he received a copy of the new Constitution, he said that it was a wonderful mechanism for government, logical and well balanced, but it said nothing of the human rights that he had envisioned in his pursuit of happiness. He said that he would not approve of the new Constitution unless it included a Bill of Rights, which gave us our first ten amendments, which are constantly being quoted, even today. In fact, we have enlarged those original rights substantially by other amendments.

From these three basic documents, I believe that government is endowed with great *moral authority*, as these basic documents had to be endorsed by the citizens' leaders at the birth of the nation. They fit together beautifully, and together they enshrine all of the *moral authority* that a nation needs to exist and prosper.

I regret to say that this *moral authority* is considerably diluted today, if we look at the current operation of our government. Thomas Aquinas, in his treatise about Law, defined it quite succinctly and beautifully. He said that Law was an order of reason, propagated by those who have the proper authority in the community, and dedicated to the common good. One wonders how the "common good" is envisioned today when Washington is full of tens of thousands of lobbyists who spend billions of dollars to persuade our senators and congressmen to promote some specifically individual good, and are quite successful in the process.

I believe that the grandeur of the law, the *moral authority* of government is continually eroded as they succeed.

REV. THEODORE M. HESBURGH, C.S.C.
President Emeritus
University of Notre Dame

About the Editors

MOORHEAD KENNEDY Best known as one of the American hostages in Iran, 1979–81, he is author of several works on terrorism and a recipient of the Medal for Valor from the Department of State. He holds a J.D. degree from Harvard Law School and numerous honorary doctorates. Chairman of Moorhead Kennedy Group, he is Secretary of NISS and a Gold Medal honoree.

R. GORDON HOXIE Ph.D., Columbia University, he served consecutively 1954–95 as Founder-President, C.W. Post College, Chancellor, Long Island University, and Founder-President, Center for the Study of the Presidency. He is the author or editor of many books on the presidency and public policy, and the founder of *Presidential Studies Quarterly*, which he edited for 25 years. He served in World War II and is a retired Air Force General. He is Chairman of the NISS Centennial Committee.

BRENDA REPLAND A graduate of the University of Oregon, with graduate studies at Harvard Business School, as President and Managing Partner of Moorhead Kennedy Group she has authored and produced training videos and programs. She is the recipient of the Medal of Hayange (France) for her liaison efforts between Hayange and the 90th U.S. Army Division, its World War II liberators. She speaks French, Spanish, and Norwegian, and continues her studies of Mandarin Chinese.

About the Authors

MADELEINE K. ALBRIGHT   Ph.D. Columbia University; former United States Permanent Representative to the United Nations; now United States Secretary of State. NISS Gold Medalist.

HUGH R. K. BARBER   M.D., professor, author, lecturer; leader in the field of ovarian cancer research; author of over 400 scientific articles and editor of 20 books; listed as one of the nation's outstanding physicians and medical specialists. NISS Gold Medalist.

JUDITH A. BEST   Ph.D. Cornell University; Distinguished Teaching Professor of Political Science at the State University of New York College at Cortland. She is the author of *The Choice of the People? Debating the Electoral College*; *The Case Against Direct Election of the President*; and *The Mainstream of Western Political Thought*. Awards include the Carnegie Foundation Honor Salute for Educational Leadership.

JOHN T. CASTEEN III   Ph.D. and, since 1990, President of the University of Virginia; named the Outstanding Virginian for his work in education. Mr. Casteen received the Mishima Award for Fiction for his collection of short stories. NISS Gold Medalist.

ROBERT E. DENTON, JR.   Ph.D. Purdue University; W. Thomas Rice Chair of Leadership Studies and Director of the Virginia Tech Corps of Cadets Center for Leader Development at Virginia Polytechnic Institute and State University. He has co-authored or edited eleven books, which include *Political Communication in America, Fourth Edition*; *The 1996 Presidential Campaign: A Communication Perspective*; and *The Clinton Presidency: Images, Issues and Communication Strategies*.

ANTHONY DREXEL DUKE   Princeton graduate; Honorary Doctorates in Humane Letters from Adelphi College, Long Island University, and Drexel University. He is an educator, sociologist, philanthropist, and founder of Harbor for Girls and Boys where he is President and Treasurer. NISS Gold Medalist.

ROBERT FERRELL   Ph.D. Yale University; Distinguished Professor Emeritus of History, Indiana University. He is the author of many books, including *The Dying President: Franklin D. Roosevelt*, and *Truman and Pendergast*.

BETTY GLAD   Ph.D. University of Chicago; Olin D. Johnston Professor of Government and International Studies at the University of South Carolina; author of numerous books on the presidency and national security policy, including *Jimmy Carter: In Search of the Great White House*, and *The Psychological Dimensions of War*.

DAN F. HAHN   Ph.D. University of Arizona; visiting Professor in the Department of Culture and Communication at New York University. His most recent book, *Political Communication: Rhetoric, Government, and Citizens*, received the Everett Lee Hunt award from the Eastern Communication Association.

C. LOWELL HARRISS   Ph.D. Columbia University; Chairman, Robert Schalkenbach Foundation, Inc., Professor Emeritus of Economics, Columbia University. Formerly Economic Consultant to The Tax Foundation, Inc., and Executive Director of the Academy of Political Science, he is co-author of *American Public Finance*, and *The American Economy*.

FRANCIS H. HELLER   J.D. and Ph.D. University of Virginia; Roberts Distinguished Professor Emeritus of Law and Political Science, University of Kansas. He is author of *The Presidency: A Modern Perspective*; *The Truman White House: The Administration of the Presidency 1945–1953*; and *USA: Verfassung und Politik*.

THEODORE M. HESBURGH   STD Catholic University; President Emeritus of Notre Dame University; 124 honorary degrees 1954–92. He is the author of numerous books including *The Human Imperative: A Challenge for the Year 2000*, and Chairman, Rockefeller Foundation.

LAWRENCE R. JACOBS   Ph.D. Columbia University; Professor of Political Science at the University of Minnesota. He is the author of *Health of Nations*, and co-author of the forthcoming book, *Politicians Don't Pander*.

TRAVIS BEAL JACOBS   Ph.D. Columbia University; Fletcher D. Proctor Professor of History, Middlebury College, and author of *Ike's Columbia Crusade*.

DOROTHY BUCKTON JAMES Ph.D. Columbia University; Professor of Political Science at Connecticut College. Her published works include four books and numerous articles in the areas of the American presidency, policy analysis, and political thought. Recent awards include the Policy Studies Organization Award for "Outstanding Woman in the Field of Policy Studies."

MICHAEL KAHN J.D. Stanford University; Senior Partner of Folger, Levin & Kahn LLP. Among his publications are "Abraham Lincoln's Appointments to the Supreme Court: A Master Politician at his Craft," *Journal of Supreme Court History*.

MOORHEAD KENNEDY J.D. Harvard Law School; Chairman of the Moorhead Kennedy Group, a consulting firm. He holds honorary doctorates from, among others, University of Pittsburgh and Middlebury College. His books include *The Ayatollah in the Cathedral, Reflections of a Hostage*. NISS Gold Medalist.

FRANK KESSLER Ph.D. University of Notre Dame; Professor of Political Science, Missouri Western College. He is author of numerous works on the presidency.

THEODORE P. KOVALEFF Ph.D. New York University; Economic Research for Dirks and Company; former Assistant Dean, Columbia University School of Law. He is the editor of *The Antitrust Impulse: An Economic, Historical and Legal Analysis*.

SAMUEL LEITER L.L.B. Harvard Law School; Salem, Massachusetts attorney, whose specialties include labor law and civil rights. He is the co-author of a volume to be titled *Affirmative Action and Anti-Discrimination Law and Policy: An Overview and Synthesis*.

WILLIAM LEITER Ph.D. University of Chicago; Professor of Political Science, California State University, Long Beach. He is the co-author of a volume to be titled *Affirmative Action and Anti-Discrimination Law and Policy: An Overview and Synthesis*.

RICHARD G. LUGAR M.A. Pembroke College, Oxford University; the longest-serving United States Senator in Indiana's history. Chairman of the Senate Agriculture, Nutrition, and Forestry Committee, and past Chairman of the Senate Foreign Relations Committee, he is author of *Letters to the Next President*. NISS Gold Medalist.

PAUL J. MAURER Master of Divinity from Gordon-Conwell Theological Seminary; H.B. Earhart Fellow at Claremont Graduate University; Vice President for the National Coalition for the Protection of Children and Families. He is the author of "Media Feeding Frenzies: Press Behavior During Two Clinton Scandals."

JOHN K. MCKINLEY   M.S. University of Alabama. He holds 13 patents in chemical and petroleum processing; retired Chairman and Chief Executive Officer of Texaco, Inc. NISS Gold Medalist.

MARK L. MELCHER   Graduate of the University of South Dakota, Managing Director and Director of Washington Research at Prudential Securities. For 26 years, he has provided award-winning commentary on social, economic, and political issues and trends for the nation's large institutional investors. He is a member of the Board of the National Humanities Institute.

DAVID MERVIN   Ph.D.; a reader in Politics at the University of Warwick, Coventry, England. His publications include *Ronald Reagan and the American Presidency*, and *George Bush and the Guardianship Presidency*.

THE RT. REV. PAUL MOORE, JR.   D.D.; Retired Episcopal Bishop of New York; author of *The Church Reclaims the City* and other volumes; recipient of the Freedom of Worship Medal, Franklin and Eleanor Roosevelt Institute. NISS Gold Medalist.

RUTH P. MORGAN   Ph.D.; Provost Emeritus and Professor Emeritus of Political Science at Southern Methodist University. Her publications include *The President and Civil Rights: Policy-Making by Executive Order*, and the forthcoming *Forced Choices: The Impact of the Voting Rights Act on City Politics*.

MARIE D. NATOLI   Ph.D., J.D.; Professor of Political Science, Emmanuel College. She is the author of numerous works on the United States vice-presidency, monetary theory, business, finance, and banking.

ABBY O'NEILL   Graduate of Bradford College; Chairman and CEO of Rockefeller Financial Services, and Chairman of the Board of Rockefeller and Company, Inc. Her life has been devoted to family, philanthropy, and community service. NISS Gold Medalist.

JAMES P. PFIFFNER   Ph.D. University of Wisconsin at Madison; Professor of Government and Public Policy at George Mason University. His eight books on the presidency include *The Strategic Presidency: Hitting the Ground Running*, and *The Modern Presidency*.

HOWARD PHIPPS, JR. AB Harvard; Chairman Emeritus of the Wildlife Conservation Society, founded in 1895 as the New York Zoological Society. He is a conservationist and NISS Gold Medalist.

RICHARD M. PIOUS Ph.D. Columbia University; Ochs Professor of American Studies, Barnard College and Columbia University. Among his numerous publications are *The President, Congress and the Constitution,* and *The Presidency.*

HAROLD C. RELYEA Ph.D. The American University; Specialist in American National Government with the Congressional Research Service of the Library of Congress. He was formerly editor of the *CRS Review,* and his most recent books include *Federal Information Politicies in the 1990's,* and *The Executive Office of the President.*

STANLEY A. RENSHON Ph.D. University of Pennsylvania; Professor of Political Science at the City University of New York and a certified psychoanalyst. His psychological biography of the President, *High Hopes: The Clinton Presidency and the Politics of Ambition,* won the American Political Science Association's Richard E. Neustadt Award for the best book on the presidency and the National Association for the Advancement of Psychoanalysis' Gradiva Award for the best biography.

MICHAEL P. RICCARDS Ph.D.; President of Fitchburg State College in Fitchburg, Massachusetts. Among his books are *Ferocious Engine of Democracy: The American Presidency from 1789 to 1989,* and *The Vicars of Christ: Faith, Leadership, and the Papacy in Modern Times.*

DONALD L. ROBINSON Ph.D. Cornell University; Charles N. Clark Professor and Chairman, Department of Government, Smith College. He is the author of *To the Best of My Ability, The President and the Constitution.*

RAYMOND J. SAULNIER Ph.D. Columbia University; Professor Emeritus on the Barnard College, Columbia University faculty and was Chairman of the Council of Economic Advisers. His books include *The Strategy of Economic Policy,* and *Constructive Years: the U.S. Economy under Eisenhower.*

JEAN REITH SCHROEDEL Ph.D. Massachusetts Institute of Technology; Associate Professor and Chairman of the Department of Politics and Policy at Claremont Graduate University.

She has written extensively on Congress, the presidency, and a range of public policy issues, and her books include *Alone in a Crowd*, and *Is the Fetus a Person?*

ROBERT Y. SHAPIRO   Ph.D. University of Chicago; Professor of Political Science at Columbia University. He is co-author of *The Rational Public*, and the forthcoming book, *Politicians Don't Pander*.

BEVERLY SILLS GREENOUGH   Former coloratura soprano, she is Chairman of the Board of Lincoln Center for the Performing Arts, Inc., author of *Beverly*, and recipient of the Presidential Medal of Freedom and, among many other awards, is an NISS Gold Medalist.

WILLIAM C. SPRAGENS   Ph.D. Michigan State University; Research Director of Spragens and Skinner Associates, and Professor Emeritus of Political Science at Bowling Green (Ohio) State University. He is the author of *Electronic Magazines*, and editor-in-chief of *Popular Images of American Presidents*.

RICHARD BOIES STARK   M.D., Professor Emeritus of Clinical Surgery, Columbia University, and founder of the Plastic Surgery Department at St. Luke's Hospital in New York City. He has authored six books and numerous professional articles. NISS Gold Medalist.

FRANK E. TAPLIN, JR.   J.D. Yale Law School; he is a Fellow of the Morgan Library, former President of the Metropolitan Opera and Vice Chairman of Lincoln Center. He is the author of *A Spirit on the Wing: Edith Smith Taplin, 1883–1963*. NISS Gold Medalist.

WILLIAM J. VANDEN HEUVEL   Graduate of Cornell Law School; international lawyer and investment banker and the former U.S. Ambassador to the United Nations, Chairman of the Franklin and Eleanor Roosevelt Institute, and Chairman of the Council of American Ambassadors. He is the author of *RFK: On His Own*. NISS Gold Medalist.

SHIRLEY ANNE WARSHAW   Ph.D. Johns Hopkins University; Professor of Political Science, Gettysburg College. She is the author of numerous works on the presidency.

PRESIDENTIAL LEADERSHIP

Moral Authority and the Presidency

R. GORDON HOXIE

FOUNDER, CHAIRMAN EMERITUS
CENTER FOR THE STUDY OF THE PRESIDENCY

IN THE AMERICAN SYSTEM OF GOVERNMENT, from George Washington to the present, the presidency is the key factor in the nation's moral authority. Indeed, Washington, by his deeds and by his principles, established the moral tone of the nation. In his first inaugural address, he asserted, "The foundation for national policy will be laid in the sure and immutable principles of private morality." In his farewell address, Washington asserted, "Of all the dispositions and habits which lead to political prosperity, religion and morality are indispensable supports. . . . Virtue or morality is a necessary spring of popular government. The rule indeed extends with more or less force to every species of Free Government."

Abraham Lincoln related moral principles to slavery. His Cooper Union address in New York City in February 1860, emphasized "our moral . . . responsibilities" and made him a candidate for the presidency. His second inaugural address resonated with moral and religious tones. Frederick Douglas was the first black man invited to an inaugural reception, and Lincoln inquired of him how he liked the address. Douglas replied, it was "a sacred effort."

Washington and Lincoln contributed much to the establishment of the moral authority of the American government. This was furthered by Theodore Roosevelt who found in the presidency a "bully pulpit." His distant cousin, Franklin Roosevelt, in the depths of the nation's worst depression, declared, "The presidency is preeminently a place of moral leadership."

1

Truman succeeded to the presidency after less than three months as Franklin Roosevelt's vice president. He was soon confronted by Communist imperialism. He fervently believed that "in the long view, the strength of our free society and our ideals will prevail over a system that has respect for neither God nor man." Perceiving sources of moral and spiritual strength in the nation's churches and synagogues, he concluded that "this only hope of mankind for enduring peace lies in the realm of the spiritual." He further believed that the president, especially in times of crisis, must provide moral leadership for the nation.

In his first inaugural address, President Eisenhower began with his own prayer, "Give us, we pray, the power to discern clearly right from wrong, and allow all our words and actions to be governed thereby." In his farewell address eight years later, as president of the United States, he emphasized the need for "an alert and knowledgeable citizenry."

But has the moral leadership of the presidency—the moral authority of government—declined in these past four decades? The essays which follow indicate, with notable exceptions, that it has. In the first of these essays, Professor Richard M. Pious, Ochs Professor of American Studies, Barnard College and Columbia University, seeks to address this decline in moral authority. He asserts, "By the end of the 1990s, it was clear that any president who sought to use the 'bully good pulpit' and preach a national agenda risked becoming a parody on late night television and Sunday morning talk shows." He blames it in part on the change in White House media relations from mutual understanding to an adversarial relationship. Second, he believes that, "Presidents since Lyndon Johnson have proposed new economic and social programs based on incomplete and often inaccurate data, and on untested and unproven theoretical assumptions." Third, compromise—the essence of democratic politics—has come to be viewed as immoral. Pious believes that when presidents are "sensitive to issues of democratic accountability . . . their moral authority will increase."

In her essay entitled "The Presidency and Moral Leadership," Dr. Ruth P. Morgan, Provost Emeritus, Southern Methodist University, finds three aspects as viewed by the public: "The president should be a moral force in policy formulation; the president should set high standards of personal ethics, and the president should be an example of integrity in official conduct and set the moral tone for the administration." But presidents are measured by the climate of the times. As Walter Lippmann observed nearly 70 years ago, "It is a nice question whether a period of exposure signifies that politics has recently become unusually scandalous or that an unusually efficient prosecutor has appeared on the scene."

In his essay, "The Moral Talk of Presidents," Dr. Michael Riccards, President, Fitchburg State College, discerns from the beginnings of our nation "the Founders in both parties maintained a high regard for the association of government" with "morality and . . . religion." Riccards finds, "In the use of moral talk, there has been no more eloquent voice than Abraham Lincoln." Lincoln used "moral talk" both to save the Union and free the slaves. Riccards concludes, "Presidents use moral talk to help mobilize the nation behind great and lesser courses."

Paul J. Maurer, Claremont Graduate University, details Washington's contributions to moral authority linking morality and religion, adding Madison's qualification that religion must be separated from government. He extols Lincoln's 1858 "house divided" address, delivered when he was seeking election to the United States Senate from Illinois. Therein came his irrevocable challenge, "A house divided against itself cannot stand. I believe this government cannot endure, permanently half *slave* and half *free*." Maurer also cites President Reagan, whom he contends "spoke about morality with a frequency unmatched by any other U.S. president." He concludes that "morality is an important factor in the presidency."

Dr. Shirley Anne Warshaw, Professor of Political Science, Gettysburg College, focuses on the modern Presidency, beginning with Franklin Roosevelt, when presidents wrested from the Congress leadership of the nation in both domestic and foreign policy. As presidents have increased their authority, they have become more subject to scrutiny. In the case of Clinton, Dr. Warshaw believes, "The impeachment was a strong warning which in the future would be followed by conviction." At the same time, Dr. Warshaw concludes, "there can be no absolute tests of moral authority, only of legitimate authority."

Dr. Stanley A. Renshon, Professor of Political Science, City University of New York Graduate Center, examines presidential leadership. He asks, "Why has it been so difficult for presidents and candidates to find, and to lead from, the political center?" He finds the answer, "In part because of the mismatch between presidential ambitions and ideals on the one hand, and the contour of American politics on the other." He concludes "[leadership] makes use of and often amplifies, a president's character—his ambitions, ideals, ways of dealing with others, and of course his political skills."

The next two essays relate moral leadership and public opinion. In the first, Dr. Robert Y. Shapiro, Professor of Political Science, Columbia University, and Dr. Lawrence R. Jacobs, Professor of Political Science, University of Minnesota, posit the strong moral and religious view of Americans. They portray presidents from Truman through Reagan in their speeches to the nation emphasizing moral and religious values, and at the same time increasingly polling public opinion. This does not mean that they will comply with polls. But the authors conclude, "even if they did, presidents would exert moral authority by reflecting the public's own."

The ensuing essay by Dr. Jean R. Schroedel, Center for Politics and Economics, Claremont Graduate University, portrays gender polling and seeks to explain why on the one hand women are more disapproving than men of President Clinton's private behavior, but on the other hand are more approving than men of his job performance. She credits the higher rating on job performance to his record of reaching out more than his presidential predecessors in appointing women to the more prestigious cabinet and White House posts; and to such legislative initiatives as the 1994 Violence Against Women Act. She gives Clinton high praise for advancing what she terms "the moral legitimacy of the presidency as a representative body."

Acknowledging the moral voices from the past, Dr. Frank P. Kessler, Professor of Political Science, Missouri Western College, finds the same ingredients for moral authority in the twenty-first century: "integrity, high-minded purpose, political savvy, and a commitment to restore and retain the public trust." The "bully pulpit" which Theodore Roosevelt perceived in the presidency a century ago is alive and well, awaiting its incumbent "to mount it with confidence and trust in the ultimate good will and good sense of the historic American political culture and the American people."

Further reflecting on the past in search of greatness in the presidency, Dr. Betty Glad, Olin D. Johnston Professor of Government and International Studies, University of South Carolina, examines major decisions in the Eisenhower and Kennedy presidencies. She asserts, "the moral authority of government is rooted in its ability to meet the demands for justice and security of its people." She points out that "at critical points in our history we have been guided by statesmen who have helped us navigate safely through difficult situations." She finds this then in Eisenhower and Kennedy. In the case of Eisenhower and the Hungarian uprising in 1956, Eisenhower termed war as "stupid, cruel, and costly" and secured United Nations support for Soviet withdrawal rather than accede to the demands of many of his advisers which portended World War III. As Glad observed, "He had the self-control and the political skill that enabled him to choose and stick to a peace-making option . . ." Glad found Kennedy exercising similar prudence in the Cuban missile crisis. She concludes that Eisenhower and Kennedy, "in serving the American people well . . . contributed to their government as a source of moral authority."

Inevitably in an examination of moral authority, Eisenhower's name looms large. He was peculiarly equipped to examine moral authority both in war and in peace. Prior to becoming president of the United States, Eisenhower had served as president of Columbia University. In the next essay, Dr. Travis Beal Jacobs, Proctor Professor of Political Science, Middlebury College, portrays the Columbia years wherein Eisenhower developed and expressed many of his views on democratic citizenship and moral leadership. Shortly after coming to Columbia, he addressed a convocation at the Jewish Theological Seminary, declaring, "We believe that because men have been born with a soul, they have inalienable rights and none can take them away . . . The true purpose of the educational institution," he asserted, "is to make certain that each of us is equipped to be a citizen in a democracy . . ." At his Columbia inauguration he emphasized, "Every institution built by free men . . . must be first of all concerned with the preservation and further development of human freedom."

The concluding paper in this section is by Dr. Donald L. Robinson, Charles N. Clark Professor and Chair of Government, Smith College. He terms his paper, "The Authority of Presidents: Personal Morality and Political Effectiveness." He asks the critical question, "Is it important for a political leader to be morally good?" As a corollary, he asks, "What is the relation between personal morality and effectiveness as a political leader?"

Robinson cites Machiavelli, the sixteenth-century Florentine patriot who despaired for his State and justified acts for the Prince which conventional morality would not sanction. In this same realism, the American, Reinhold Niebuhr, in the era of German fascism, argued that our political leaders must have the craft of those who would destroy freedom. There must be a moral calculus to overcome evil. In the United States, from the nation's beginnings with Washington and its defense with Lincoln, there is virtue—that virtue to which my mentor, Carl L. Becker, referred as "the fundamental principle, the indispensable guarantee of the republican form of government."

Robinson asserts what is needed for a great leader can be discerned in "Lincoln's great virtues—prudence, to tailor high goals to practical realities, and magnanimity, to be forgiving and generous spirited toward defeated foes."

Since Robinson teaches at a great women's college, he concludes with feminine pronouns: "To achieve greatness, a president of the future must have a strategic vision, a sense of history, and keep awareness of the dangers and possibilities of her moment in political time. She must be firm in purpose, courageous and tenacious in the face of adversity. She will need great energy." And this returns us to Alexander Hamilton's observation, "Energy in the executive is a leading character in the definition of good government."

CHAPTER ONE

Moral Action and Presidential Leadership

RICHARD M. PIOUS

ADOLPH AND EFFIE OCHS PROFESSOR
BARNARD COLLEGE

GRADUATE SCHOOL OF ARTS AND SCIENCES
COLUMBIA UNIVERSITY

BETWEEN THE LATE 1960s and the end of the century, survey researchers reported ominous findings for the state of American democracy: rates of voter turnout declined in primaries and general elections; levels of apathy, cynicism, and alienation sharply increased; and public trust in government to "do the right thing" sharply declined.[1] These changes in public attitudes occurred in a period of time in which any fair-minded observer would have noted that American government *was* doing the right thing—in race and gender relations, in civil liberties protections, in anti-poverty efforts—and in which many governmental efforts were succeeding, at least by statistical measurement. Why then, are so many Americans fed up with government, receptive to appeals by politicians who run "against Washington," happy to see it "reinvented" and downsized, and less and less willing to look to government to solve problems? By the end of the 1990s, it was clear that any president who sought to use the "bully good pulpit" and preach a national agenda, risked becoming a parody on late night television and Sunday morning talk shows. "The presidency is preeminently a place of moral leadership," Franklin Roosevelt observed in the midst of the Depression; but that was then and this is now. What has changed?

We can begin with an unanticipated and ironic outcome: laws, procedures, and institutions designed to make the president more accountable and the office more transparent may actually have the opposite effect. Consider the vulnerability of presidents to scandals involving either their activities in government or their personal lives. In the traditional Washington norm, members of the Washington press corps protected those at the top and made clear distinctions between public duties and private lives. Today, an investigative stance and adversarial norms characterize White House–media relations. Tattlers are rewarded in the scandal markets, which pay a premium for exposés about politicians close to or at the top. The incentives are for those having knowledge of a scandal to "sell high"—which is just when someone achieves a presidential nomination or gains the office.

Presidents today are more vulnerable once allegations of public or private wrongdoing surface. The courts have chipped away at presidential immunity. Though a president enjoys civil immunity up to the outer limits of his office and there is as yet no settled consensus on his vulnerability to indictment while in office, he enjoys no immunity for actions taken prior to entering office, and his aides enjoy less civil and no criminal immunity.[2] Presidents cannot win their claims of executive privilege except unless the courts find significant national security concerns are involved.[3] They cannot win claims of attorney-client privilege and protective function privilege except in narrowly defined circumstances, and they no longer can use the legal resources of the institutionalized presidency to protect them in private matters.[4] First the independent counsels and now attorneys for litigants, sometimes backed by self-styled watchdog groups, can dog presidents, not only about public matters, but also about their private affairs (in both meanings of the term). Because it may cost millions of dollars to defend against lawsuits, possible indictment and even impeachment (if the House believes that the president has subverted the judicial process in which he is enmeshed), presidents and their aides now set up legal defense funds. These are not regulated under even the lax campaign finance codes, and the potential for abuse of power and conflict of interest, with regard to well-heeled contributors, exists.[5]

A second irony involves the complexities of public policy-making. Presidents since Lyndon Johnson have proposed new economic and social programs based on incomplete and often inaccurate data, and on untested and unproven theoretical assumptions. They have spent little time on implementation once programs have been approved. Because the presidential roles as "innovator in chief" and "legislator in chief" have been institutionalized, the public and media have come to expect presidents to introduce major new programs, and their passage by Congress has become a yardstick to measure their success. But presidents are caught between a rock and a hard place because their governing authority has eroded due to a perceived lack of success of programmatic initiatives over the past forty years. This creates two issues for presidents, which the American people increasingly perceive in moral terms. First, as the complex statistical science of risk management has taken hold in policymaking, presidents are increasingly vulnerable when risky business goes awry, whether it involves a space shuttle, a cost-benefit analysis of healthcare costs or energy options, and so on. The idea of weighing costs against benefits may appeal to economists, but for the general public, it may seem immoral, particularly in contexts involving health, the environment, and families. Second, all the postwar presidents—by and large weak party leaders who do not command working majorities in Congress—must spend considerable time and effort overcoming their vulnerabilities. They must consider their power stakes, maneuver between friends and adversaries, and build coalitions with all the permanence of sandcastles. Their spatial positioning is tentative, conditional, and reversible. As presidents maneuver, they are portrayed in the media as manipulators without principles or scruples. The very process by which they eventually get coalitions and compromise—in other words, the very essence of democratic politics, which is a willingness to compromise—has become characterized as immoral, if not downright evil. "Men descend to meet," Emerson once said, but an attempt to gain a meeting of minds is today often viewed quite literally by the anti-political culture as a descent to the netherworld. The predictable result in an anti-political culture is the increasing influence in the legislatures of the true believers, who claim to be in favor of moral principle over immoral political compromise.[6]

A third irony involves the characterization of presidential motivation in foreign affairs. The Wilsonian approach to foreign policy seems to have triumphed—at least in rhetorical terms—over the realpolitik approach of the foreign policy establishment, which actually dominated cold war decision making. The cold rationality possessed by the Johnson and Nixon advisers in their Vietnam calculus (our word had been given, our ability to deter was at stake, our efforts at "compellence" would work when systematically applied through escalation) gave way under the Carter and Reagan presidencies to moral appeals. We supported freedom fighters in Nicaragua whom Reagan claimed were the

"moral equivalent of the Founding Fathers"; we provided humanitarian aid to the wretched of the earth in Somalia; we attacked
terrorists in Libya and Afghanistan who had bombed the innocent; we confronted a series of would-be Hitlers in Iraq and
Serbia; we supported peacekeeping missions around the world.

A Wilsonian approach to foreign policy leads presidents into
several quagmires. First, it may mean defining a conflict as a Just
War, which then becomes difficult to extricate from, with honor,
if negotiations with the "Hitler" involved are required. Second,
presidents who "go it alone," who use intelligence assets or the
military unilaterally on their own prerogative, face questions
about their adherence to norms of international law or constitutional processes. Congress still insists on a collaborative role, and
is strongly backed by public opinion. Presidents have thus far
finessed these issues by paying lip service to the War Powers Act,
claiming to welcome the "support" of Congress, and even at times
soliciting votes applauding or authorizing their war making—
without giving up their constitutional claims.[7] There may yet be a
constitutional confrontation: when it comes, the federal courts
are very likely to give the constitutional victory to the president,
but the backlash against presidential war making power is likely
to be severe.[8] Third, and perhaps most significant, the "credibility
gap" opened up by Eisenhower with the U-2 affair, Kennedy with
the Bay of Pigs, and Johnson and Nixon with the Vietnam War,
has now grown to such proportions that presidents can even be
accused of "wagging the dog"—using the military to distract
attention from domestic issues. It is ironic that presidents who
are using the armed forces to uphold moral principles—at great
cost in American lives and treasure—must defend themselves
against charges of immoral motives, when in the nineteenth century, more traditional use of armed forces for territorial aggran-
dizement provoked no such response. A utilitarian use of force
will likely call forth a utilitarian opposition (i.e., the cost is not
worth the effort); a morally-based use of force calls forth an even
stronger moral response from the opposition, and a president
who makes such an appeal risks being considered immoral in the
very act of making the moral argument.

What can presidents do to regain moral authority? For start-
ers, one is tempted to offer presidents the same advice that senior
faculty offer to their junior colleagues about relationships with
students: "Don't get involved with anyone who has more prob-

lems than you do." One might also suggest that changes in campaign finance laws including free airtime for candidates, would reduce campaign contribution violations. But beyond lowering the likelihood of getting caught in a scandal or being charged with corruption, moral authority in the White House needs to be reestablished in its routine workings: How do we get the American people to believe that the government can be trusted to "Do the right thing?"

The answer is not rocket science. The presidency, Clinton Rossiter once wrote, operates successfully only when the president selects "ends and means that are 'characteristically American.'"[9] Prudential leadership would involve matching risks to opportunities, avoiding "normal accidents" and other organizational dysfunctions, and seeing that the public understands and supports risky business.[10] When a situation involves uncertainty (i.e., the odds cannot be specified), the president would speak honestly to the American people about what that means for public and foreign policy. Beneficial leadership would involve acting for the public good, rather than for personal or even presidential benefit. The goal of a president should not be to increase his own power, or even necessarily to guard his reputation and maintain his options. At some point, power must be expended, reputation must be put on the line, and options must give way to action. And when that point is reached, the president must be able to make the case that his decision is in the best interests of the nation. Finally, moral authority can be restored by resilient leadership. Washington, Lincoln, and Franklin Roosevelt were exceptional leaders, not by avoiding policy failures, but rather by learning from them, by modifying their approaches, and by having the will to endure and prevail.[11]

Moral authority is a relationship between ruler and ruled, between the president and the American people. Maintaining it is not a matter of leading a "moral life" or bloviating about moral values. It is not a matter of exhorting the American people, of blaming them (or their blaming the president) for moral shortcomings. It is not a matter of substituting some new ideology, religious or natural law, or even scientific and technological imperatives in government. It is not a matter of courting popularity by giving the people what they want. It is not about spinning to create new values, or of wheeling and dealing to keep the game going.[12] When presidents talk excessively about values and moral leadership, it's a pretty good bet they are not exercising it. *Moral leadership in the White House is not moralism:* instead, it is a day-to-day matter of incumbents in the Oval Office thinking and acting presidentially. It involves determining the causes that compel government action, of leading by personal and political example, and of sharing common values and feelings and reworking their meaning to fit the exigencies of the hour.

When presidents are seen to sustain the legitimacy of the office (by adhering to statutory and constitutional law), when they enhance the intellectual authority of the office (by proposing programs based on sound data and theories, with due appreciation for risk and uncertainty), and when they remain sensitive to issues of democratic accountability (by minimizing corruption and conflicts of interest), their moral authority will increase. At that point, we will no longer have a divergence between high levels of presidential popularity and low assessments of presidential character, nor these ironies of presidential policymaking.

The Presidency and Moral Leadership

RUTH P. MORGAN

PROVOST EMERITUS
SOUTHERN METHODIST UNIVERSITY

PRESIDENTS OF THE UNITED STATES, as well as party orators, journalists, and academicians, consider "moral leadership" to be a role vital to a successful presidency. However, few commentators specify the standards they expect of presidents in carrying out this role. Furthermore, the public is fickle and ambiguous as to the standards of ethical behavior it expects of presidents.

In my survey of the extant literature on the subject, I discerned three aspects to this presidential role expectation— namely, the president should be a moral force in policy formulation, the president should set an example of integrity in official conduct, and he should set the moral tone for the administration.

Surprisingly, the intense periodic interest in scandal and corruption has generated little systematic research. Some years ago. Walter Lippman admitted trying to catalogue corrupt acts, without success, and later wrote:

> It would be impossible for an historian to write a history of political corruption in America. What he could write is the history of the exposure of corruption. Such a history would show, I think, that almost every American community governs itself by fits and starts of unsuspecting complacency and violent suspicion. There will be long periods when practically nobody except the profession reformers can be induced to pay attention to the business of government; then rather suddenly there will come a period when every agency of investigation is prodded into activity, and the civic conscience begins to boil . . . "it is a nice question whether a period of exposure signifies that politics has recently become unusually scandalous or that an unusually efficient prosecutor has appeared on the scene."[1]

13

CRITERIA FOR ESTABLISHING STANDARDS
OF PRESIDENTIAL BEHAVIOR

Participants and spectators use at least three criteria separately or in combination in their attempts to establish standards of presidential behavior: interpretation of legal norms, public opinion regarding ethical norms, and perceptions of public interest. In each instance, the criterion is an essentially normative one.

1. Legal Norms

In the two recent cases in which charges were brought against presidents, articles of impeachment included criminal violations of statutory law in the case of Richard Milhous Nixon and unlawful perjury before a grand jury and obstruction of justice in the case of William Jefferson Clinton. In both cases, the allegations also included violation of the presidential oath of office and of the constitutional duty to take care that the laws be faithfully executed. On the latter and broader issue of oath of office and constitutional duty, what the president may or may not do in specific instances remains unclear, as individuals typically view such constitutional questions through the lens of their policy preferences. Indeed, presidents who have claimed obedience to the word and letter of the Constitution, such as James Buchanan or William Howard Taft, are considered "literalist" or "weak" presidents.

The investigations of possible violations of legal norms by presidents Nixon and Clinton, both polarizing figures, proceeded quite differently. The Ethics in Government Act of 1978, which established the Office of Independent Counsel, changed the dynamics of the congressional investigation. Congressional committees played major roles in developing the evidence in public view during the Watergate investigation, which helped to mobilize public opinion for impeachment. On the other hand, the Clinton impeachment hearings depended upon information gathered in private by the Office of Independent Counsel, which caused attention to focus on Special Prosecutor Kenneth Starr and his report rather than upon the development in public view of evidence of wrongdoing.

2. Public Opinion on Ethical Norms

To use the public judgment as to whether an act is corrupt or not finds opinions divided and ambiguous. In looking at historical data for comparative and trend information, one finds that the ethical norms for official conduct are relative to the personal popularity of the president, the mood of the public, the make-up of Congress, the ingenuity of the press, and the events and circumstances of the time.

Some opponents of the impeachment of President Clinton made a distinction between his case and that of President Nixon's on the basis that impeachment should be used only in cases of official conduct that subverts the government and not for unlawful conduct that is private and unofficial. However, Federal District Judge Susan Webber Wright found the president guilty of some of the charges of which he was acquitted in the trial in the Senate—namely, providing false testimony under oath and obstructing justice in the Paula Jones case by denying information that might have helped her sexual harassment case. Judge Wright ruled on April 12, 1999, that Mr. Clinton engaged in "misconduct that undermines the integrity of the judicial system."[2] Even so, as long as Clinton's violations of law were pictured as "only lying about sex" and not about abuses of government power, the president retained his popularity with the public.

3. Perceptions of the Public Interest

After acknowledging that presidential actions should be faithful to the public interest as opposed to personal, group, or special interests, one is again confronted with a normative problem. In the earliest days of the republic, public officials were viewed as exclusively concerned for the public good. With the development of parties, political figures learned that to stay in office, they had to be loyal to the interests of their party. These conflicting roles were papered over by rationalizing that the public interest might best be pursued through party politics. Hence, Andrew Jackson pioneered using his leadership of a mass political movement to promote partisan control of government, while at the same time proclaiming himself to be the "tribune of the people."

The Watergate affair may in fact point to a distinction made by the public between the norms of conduct for party politics and those for policymaking officials. As long as the Watergate burglary was pictured as campaign politics, the public was slow to become aroused. As late as April, 1973, a Harris survey showed 73 percent of the people agreed with the claim that, "dirty campaign tactics exist among both Republicans and Democrats, and the

Nixon people were no worse than the Democrats, except they got caught at it."[3] Public attention was finally aroused only when evidence began to link important figures in the White House and in governmental agencies with abuses of government power.

INVESTIGATIONS OF CORRUPT ACTIVITIES

The vehicles for exposing scandal and corruption in the United States are congressional investigations, the efforts of the press, and investigations by special prosecutors. The 1978 Ethics in Government Act established an office of independent counsel so that on charges of wrongdoing the executive branch would not be investigating itself through the Justice Department. This law, controversial from its inception as a congressional reaction to Watergate, is but the latest attempt to find a way to investigate alleged wrongdoing that is at least perceived to be objective, independent, and nonpartisan.

While the claim to objectivity by the press is arguable, democratic theory affords a free and independent press a prominent role as the "watchdog of government." At the turn of this century, the muckraking of Lincoln Steffens and some of his contemporaries helped to establish a pattern for press condemnation of official misconduct. The crusading journalists, labeled "muckrakers" by Theodore Roosevelt, were professional writers who clearly viewed themselves as objective observers of society. Then later in the century, two *Washington Post* reporters are credited with keeping a spotlight focused on Watergate and of inspiring a generation of "investigative reporters." These later reporters, whose careers are invested in uncovering scandal, are fostering an era of "taste for political scandal production," to use Suzanne Garment's words in her acclaimed book, *Scandal: The Crisis of Mistrust in American Politics.*[4]

The long history of congressional probes into possible misconduct in the executive branch dates to the inquiry into the St. Clair expedition in 1792. The periods of most intensive congressional investigative activities were those during the Grant administration following the Civil War and following World Wars I and II and in the backwash of Vietnam. The congressional investigatory patterns have prompted two general theories of scandal exposure, the "war theory" and the "partisan theory."

The former theory suggests that following sustained periods

of war, disillusionment sets in and there are moral relapses. Furthermore, Congress is restless after wars and vehemently assertive of its prerogatives, and frequently at odds with the executive branch. This should not be surprising, since power flows to the presidency during wartime. Following this pattern, Congress became much more assertive of its prerogatives following the Vietnam war and, among other things, passed the War Powers Act with the intention of restricting the president's war-making authority.

Others have pointed to the conflicting political forces that have had an impact on congressional investigations. The last years of the Grant administration and the periods immediately following the two world wars coincided with shifts of congressional majorities to a party long in the minority. During Grant's tenure from 1869 to 1877, there were rumors of corruption, but it was not until the Democrats recaptured control of the House in the 1874 elections that the number of investigations soared. The Republicans, on the other hand, gained control of the House in the 1918 election and conducted a series of studies of World War I mobilization under President Wilson, a Democrat. Committees of the Republican Eightieth Congress, elected in 1946, studied closely World War II mobilization and reported infiltration of the government by Communists during the administrations of Democratic Presidents Roosevelt and Truman.

Proponents of this theory can also point to the surprisingly slight inclination on the part of the Democratic Congress to probe the conduct of the war in Vietnam, even though a majority of the public considered American involvement in Vietnam as "morally wrong," according to a Harris survey in 1971.[5] Rather, Nixon became the casualty of events that stemmed from the Cold War/Vietnam environment. Furthermore, those directly involved as participants and those indirectly involved as journalists have pointed to the Pentagon Papers as the "pivotal point" for Watergate. Ironically, when the Pentagon Papers appeared, Nixon "saw the documents chiefly (and rightly) as a rebuke to the previous Democratic administrations."[6]

President Clinton's experience following the Republican takeover of Congress in the mid-term elections during his first term also gives some credence to the partisan theory. In addition, however, the congressional hearings on charges of unlawful conduct by President Clinton reinforce the fact that the American political system is suffering serious fallout from the erosion of the political middle ground.

ELECTORAL IMPACT OF SCANDALS

Repeatedly in American history, reform issues have shown a tendency to be short-lived. This was the case, for example, when the public turned to Grover Cleveland as a deliverer from corruption. His honest administration and civil service reforms, however, were insufficient to overcome tariff as the principal issue in the election of 1888.

Since 1939, The Gallup Poll has been measuring issue orientation through responses to unstructured questions concerning the most important problems facing the country. In the 1950s, corruption as a "main concern" for the public peaked at 3 percent. Even so, in 1952, Dwight Eisenhower mounted an effective campaign on the issues of "Korea, Communism, and corruption." Of those who voted for Eisenhower, 42 percent said they did so because of the corruption issue, and yet corruption virtually disappeared from public comment almost immediately after the election.

In examining the trends in issue orientation as measured by The Gallup Poll, one finds that the public has in fact shown little concern over corruption as compared with their concerns over economic issues. Between 1969 and 1999 "corruption in government" as a main concern peaked at 16 percent in May 1973, but at that time economic concerns reached an all-time high of 70 to 75 percent. This pattern helps to explain the low saliency with the mass public of the Clinton transgressions during a booming economy.

The historical record of congressional investigations, press reporting, and special prosecutors does not hold out much hope for finding institutional structures that can ensure objective standards for presidential performance in terms of moral leadership. In all likelihood, periods of intense investigation of scandal and corruption will coincide more or less with the social and political climate that exists at the time. In the past, at least, contextual circumstances have had far more impact on the formulation of public attitudes than has any standard of legal or ethical political behavior against which the president has been measured and found wanting.

The Moral Talk of American Presidents

MICHAEL P. RICCARDS

PRESIDENT
FITCHBURG STATE COLLEGE

THE COUSINS ROOSEVELT had it right about the presidency. Theodore called the office "a bully pulpit" and Franklin viewed it as "pre-eminently a place of moral leadership." They were talking not about simple public policy choices, but of the broader and deeper possibilities of linking the political order with moral categories.

Such an assertion is not new. The founding fathers, using a very different vocabulary, paid special attention to the importance of character and civic education in order to safeguard the fragile form of government they created. The history of republics was not marked by long term successes, and there was no guarantee that the new Atlantic coast collection of states would fare much better.

Despite the obvious fact that there were substantial and often nasty differences of opinion on the appropriate methods of nation-building, the founders in both parties maintained a high regard for the association of government, morality, and even in some cases religion. The young George Washington compiled a long collection of personal rules of conduct by which to live. John Adams' correspondence is full of moral exhortations on every topic imaginable. While the Virginian presidents were more committed to a complete separation of church and state than many Federalists—especially Alexander Hamilton—they too emphasized the formation of character, the quality of moral judgments, and the importance of hearth, home, and school in reinforcing each other. In place of an aristocracy of birth and money, Jefferson wanted to create an aristocracy of talent and merit. They knew that in their definition of democracy some sort of an elite had to rise up and act as guardian.

In the twentieth century, the great, persistent moral issues revolved around the proper role of government in our lives and the threats from the outside. The philosopher Isaiah Berlin[1] has argued that in the West there are two concepts of liberty. The first emphasizes the critical nature of positive steps to create a community in which self expression is possible and maximized, and in which people are empowered and enriched by the actions of a benevolent state. The second type—negative liberty—is the belief that individuals should be able to live their own lives unfettered by restrictions, constraints, and paternalism.

The issue of government assistance and/or intrusion has characterized the political debates of this century. It is one of the major themes of our political discourse and it has been framed in emotive words that celebrate liberty, equality, democracy, and altruism. Theodore Roosevelt, Woodrow Wilson, and their protégé Franklin Delano Roosevelt did not just make political or social arguments for the expansion of the welfare state based on the changing times. They buttressed those realities with the clear vision that democracy, equity, fellow feeling, and basic human decency demanded an activist government. That tradition may have reached its apogee with John F. Kennedy and Lyndon B. Johnson when they dealt with the civil rights controversies in the 1960s. J.F.K. said that the issue was "as old as the scriptures . . . and as clear as the American Constitution." Lyndon Johnson's "We Shall Overcome" speech was a clear moral clarion call, given almost in the same cadences as the white Protestant clergy that so dominated the land of his youth.

The more conservative presidents of the twentieth century were not to be outdone. Calvin Coolidge and Herbert Hoover, for example, both defended capitalism, not as a way to grow rich, but as moral alternatives that were grounded in an homage to individualism and freedom. Coolidge especially seemed to value classical virtues in his defense of American institutions and the American economy.

In terms of foreign policy, modern presidents have clearly emphasized moral talk to explain the threats and anxieties posed by the outside world. William McKinley argued that the United States had to go to war in the Philippines to convert the natives to Christianity. He did not realize that they had been Catholics for centuries. However, while his successor, Theodore Roosevelt, was highly judgmental, his policies were more real politik than moralizing. But his opponent, Woodrow Wilson, reached back into his own Calvinist background to explain American foreign policy in the most compelling of idealistic expressions. He promised to end the power politics of the past and to wage war to make the troubled world safe for democracy. Franklin Roosevelt continued Wilson's rhetoric and was blessed with a great relief picture that supported his war efforts. The Nazis and their allies were so evil that few questioned the need to end their killing machines. Great enemies make for great alliances, it is said, but evil enemies make for comfortable moralizing.

The cold war presidents from Truman through Bush gave us a Manichean order that proved to be rather effective and that was probably overall a true reflection of reality. In facing the Soviet Union, these presidents used moral talk to separate United States policy objectives from those of the USSR—even when those objectives seemed to violate the very best instincts of the republic. Ronald Reagan said it most succinctly: the USSR was an evil empire, and so it fell like a decrepit roof sitting on a decaying structure.

In the use of moral talk, there has been no more eloquent voice than that of Abraham Lincoln. Personally, he was not attached to any denomination, had an agnostic streak in his youth, and was certainly not wedded to Protestant orthodoxy. But in the crucible of war, he seemed almost overwhelmed by the chaos and the slaughter around him. He tried incessantly to explain the importance of this war in terms of the preciousness of the Union and the stewardship passed on by the Founding Fathers, most of whom were both Southerners and nationalists. Those justifications became too threadbare after several years at war, and so for political and emotional reasons he raised the Union cause to a new moral plane. His second inaugural address is usually praised as the essence of magnanimity. But if one looks closely, the president is calling down the awful vengeance of God—the God of the Old Testament—on the struggle, knowing well that slavery would be judged in the balance as an abomination. His vocabulary, his allusions, his paraphrases were direct links to the major source of morality for the almost Protestant nation—the King James Bible.

Those articulate presidents—Jefferson, Lincoln, Wilson, FDR—were the high priests of the American moral order. Even Jefferson, not given to religious affiliations, spent some of his time as vice president cutting out the miracle stories of the New Testament so that he could present a book that cast Jesus of Nazareth as a great philosopher and teacher.

Although many of these men had personal situations that may not have reflected well on their individual morality, they all surely accepted the notion that American presidents were to be, in our vocabulary, role models, especially to the young.

They did accept an association between their personal conduct and their public positions. Surely some of them strayed off the straight and narrow on occasion, but they did seem more definitely to acknowledge the association of behavior, rhetoric, and effectiveness than we do.

With the Clinton sex scandals, the American people definitely made a distinction between a president's personal behavior, which most found reprehensible, and his political skill and executive leadership. Probably there are a variety of reasons for that distinction; generational change in attitudes on sexual ethics, the legitimacy conferred on Clinton by two popular elections, the ineptitude of congressional Republican critics, the questionable tactics of the special prosecutor, the unsympathetic view of many toward Clinton's accusers. Clearly the American people led the Senate and the voracious media in refusing to accept the impeachment option.

Clinton became especially vulnerable to moral attacks because of his decision to appropriate the GOP's emphasis on family values. To neutralize criticism of his policies supporting abortion on demand and toleration of gays in the military, the president enacted a series of symbolic actions and glossy statements designed to underscore his commitment to traditional family values. To his opponents such a cynical adoption of conservative themes only added to the texture of their hatred.

The Clinton controversy, however, graphically focused attention on the problem of personal versus public morality. If the national attention accepts the unity of the two, then such a view can lead to a very narrow-minded, voyeuristic style of politics that focuses on personality rather than on true character. On the other hand, if there is a serious discontinuity, one can easily be portrayed as a hypocrite and a base cynic. It is not an easy dilemma to solve or to calibrate.

Why then do presidents—mere fallible mortals as you and I— engage in moral talk? Surely many other political systems do not seem as prone to such style of rhetoric as the United States. There are at least two explanations that can be postulated. First, the American people are still comparatively a religious people; that is, they are more likely to believe in God, the immortality of the soul, the efficacy of prayer, the power of religious revivals, the centrality of neighborhood churches and chapels, and the relevance of the Scriptures. There are differences by region, age, and race, but matched up against the other Western industrialized nations, the Americans are a religious, or at least a moral, people—a people who view life somewhat in moral categories.

The second reason is a more practical consideration. The American system of government is deliberately constituted to be a disjointed and fragmented collection of power centers that prevents quick, cohesive, and concerted action. The federal system, the separation of powers, the litany of checks and balances, the complexities of the multicultural fabric, all work against centrifugal forces. Presidents use moral talk to help mobilize the nation behind great and lesser causes. They appeal over the heads of interest groups, selfish politicians, and parochial interests to a broader plane, to a different horizon in which moral talk is a shorthand—a road map—to guide an often anxious and restless republic.

The Moral Dimension of the Presidency

PAUL J. MAURER

CLAREMONT GRADUATE UNIVERSITY

RECENT EVENTS have helped revive discussion about the morality of the president of the United States. This was partly triggered by an event that took place on September 16, 1998. On that day, a beleaguered President Clinton, then struggling to save his presidency, faced questions from reporters asking if he still had the "moral authority" to lead the nation. The president replied ". . . in my view, that [moral authority] is something that you have to demonstrate every day . . ."[1]

This line of questioning is an unusual one. One rarely hears a reporter asking the president about his "moral authority" or anything else dealing with morality. This essay considers whether there is a moral dimension to the office of the presidency. Our examination is not concerned with the particulars of President Clinton, but whether those who served as United States presidents provide evidence that they considered there to be a moral dimension to the office of the presidency. To discover this, research focused on the writings, correspondence, and the public papers of the U.S. presidents.[2] Our sampling considers four presidents.

GEORGE WASHINGTON: THE PACESETTER

George Washington's thoughts on morality are quoted far more than any other U.S. president. Among presidents who cite Washington on matters of religion and/or morality are Abraham Lincoln, Dwight Eisenhower, Lyndon Johnson, Gerald Ford, and Ronald Reagan. Washington was considered during the constitutional convention to be an ideal choice for chief executive because of the outstanding combination of leadership and virtue he embodied. Many thought he would serve as president for life, but after his second term he chose to leave office. As he went back to private life, with no political agenda to fulfill, he offered the nation wise counsel in his Farewell Address. In that address and other writings of Washington, we find three key points regarding morality.

First, Washington believed that religion and morality are pillars to political prosperity. Using an interesting metaphor, he argued that morality is not only fundamental to the success of the United States, but that it holds up the political structure. He says, "Of all the dispositions and habits which lead to political prosperity, religion and morality are indispensable supports."[3] He considers religion and morality to be "great pillars of human happiness."[4] Prosperity is tied to goodness, implying that without the pillars, the entire structure will collapse. For Washington, prosperity was not merely economic. Rather, honor, virtue, truth, justice, etiquette, and respect are all necessary for national prosperity.

Second, public and private morality are related. Washington believed that private morality was relevant to public service. In his first inaugural address, Washington said, "the foundation of our national policy will be laid in the pure and immutable principles of private morality . . ."[5] Lest we think Washington was alone in his sentiment, the Senate, in an address back to Washington, affirmed his statement, then added,

> If individuals be not influenced by moral principles, it is in vain to look for public virtue. It is therefore the duty of legislators to enforce, both by precept and example, the utility as well as the necessity of a strict adherence to the rules . . .[6]

Third, Washington believed religion is necessary for morality. While being careful not to name Christianity specifically, Washington takes to task the conception that a good education is enough to create goodness. Washington exhorted,

> let us with caution indulge the supposition that morality can be maintained without religion. Whatever may be conceded to the influence of refined education on minds of peculiar structure, reason and experience both forbid us to expect that national morality can prevail in exclusion of religious principle.[7]

JAMES MADISON:
SEPARATION OF CHURCH AND STATE

James Madison, along with Thomas Jefferson, was responsible for
the disestablishment of the church in the United States. This
work was accomplished before Madison became president, but
his comments as chief executive look back at a landmark political
accomplishment dealing directly with issues of liberty, oppression, civil rights, and morality. Madison wanted to make sure we
never forget that the separation of church and state is the only
righteous path. He counseled,

> If the public homage of a people can ever be worthy the favor-
> able regard of the Holy and Omniscient Being to whom it is ad-
> dressed, it must be that in which those who join in it are guided
> only by their free choice, by the impulse of their hearts and the
> dictates of their consciences; . . . religion, that gift of Heaven for
> the good of man, freed from all coercive edits, from that unhal-
> lowed connection with the powers of this world which corrupts
> religion . . . can spread its benign influence everywhere.[8]

Madison offered an extensive and systematic argument for
disestablishment in his apologetic entitled "A Memorial and
Remonstrance."[9] The core of Madison's argument is that freedom of conscience is a natural right and cannot be properly
taken away by anyone, including the state. Denying this liberty is
especially heinous for the state to engage in, because it possesses
both the power and the potential to oppress and punish. Madison's fundamental basis is not the practical effect of the bill on
society, nor the political climate, nor toleration, nor reason, but
rather the natural right of the freedom of conscience. Madison
seems to think the church indeed plays a proper and extremely
useful role in a free and virtuous society and that the principles of
morality and religion are "the best foundation of national happiness."[10] The strength and influence of the church, thought Madison, would be best maintained if they were free of state control
and funding.

ABRAHAM LINCOLN:
FREEDOM AND EQUALITY AS MORAL PRINCIPLES

Abraham Lincoln wrote frequently and at times passionately
about morality, mostly as it related to slavery. Beginning when

Lincoln was a young man and demonstrating ironclad consistency over time, Lincoln argued that the prosperous future of our nation depended on a reverence for the law and moral decision making.

Lincoln's willingness to confront slavery was rooted in his belief that it was morally wrong.[11] Because Lincoln believed "Negroes" were human beings, he understood that the institution of slavery should not exist. The question of morality and humanity created the most basic distinction between Lincoln and John C. Calhoun, the intellectual champion of slavery, and Stephen Douglas, Lincoln's political foe.

Lincoln's moral belief about slavery became manifest in part by an experience he had at the age of thirty-two, an incident that left a lasting impression. Lincoln recounts his observation of twelve slaves who were chained six- and six-together. "A small iron clevis was around the left wrist of each, and this fastened to the main chain by a shorter one at a convenient distance from the others; so that the Negroes were strung together like so many fish upon a trot line. In this condition they were being separated forever from the scenes of their childhood, their friends, their fathers and mothers, and brothers and sisters, and many of them, from their wives and children, and going into perpetual slavery . . ."[12]

Equality is a moral concept for Lincoln and lies at the core of his argument against slavery. While there is implicit evidence that Lincoln derived his moral basis from his understanding of the Bible or natural rights, or perhaps a combination of the two,[13] he explicitly derived his understanding of equality from the Declaration of Independence.[14] In his speech on the Kansas-Nebraska Act, Lincoln said, "if the Negro is a man, why then my ancient faith teaches me that 'all men are created equal'; and that there can be no moral right in connection with one man's making a slave of another."[15]

Lincoln's concern intensified once the Dred Scott decision was handed down by the Supreme Court because the Court, like Douglas, interpreted the Declaration of Independence as not referring to Negroes. Lincoln declares "this grave argument comes to just nothing at all . . . [and does] obvious violence to the plain unmistakable language of the Declaration."[16]

Lincoln also believed the immorality of slavery was a threat to democracy and the union. In Lincoln's speech on the Kansas-Nebraska Act, he used highly passionate language to describe the "monstrous injustice" of slavery and its attack on liberty, a most fundamental principle of democracy.[17] Lincoln's most enduring statements regarding the threat of slavery to the republic came in his "house divided" speech where he argues that our republic "cannot endure permanently half slave and half free."[18]

RONALD REAGAN:
COMMUNISM AND EDUCATION

Ronald Reagan spoke about morality with a frequency unmatched by any other U.S. president. President Reagan was fond of quoting George Washington's Farewell Address where he said, "Of all the dispositions and habits which lead to political prosperity, religion and morality are indispensable supports."[19] Reagan did not hesitate to admit that religion was a guide for him, saying "to think that anyone could carry out the awesome responsibilities of this office without asking for God's help through prayer, strikes me as absurd. . . . I do not believe you can function in politics without some sense of morality."[20]

An understanding of morality provided the basis for Reagan's defense strategy as it related to the Soviet Union. Reagan believed that the oppressive, atheistic, totalitarian, and expansive doctrine of Marxism was fundamentally immoral. President Reagan was determined not only to take Marxist doctrine seriously, but rejected appeasement as a flawed strategy against an "evil empire."[21]

Reagan's moral belief about communism played a determinative role in his effort to increase United States spending on defense, ultimately resulting in the appropriation of billions of taxpayer dollars. Many believe that history has validated Reagan's defense strategy. The systematic dismantling of Marxist Communism behind the former Iron Curtain illustrates not simply that ideas have consequences, but that morality too can help change the world.

Reagan also spoke of a relationship between morality and education. Reagan spoke frequently about the need for schools to reject "value free" education,[22] reminding teachers that "you are molding each rising generation. You're working with parents to fill young minds with the knowledge and young hearts with the morality . . ."[23] Reagan's primary policy initiative along these lines was a proposed constitutional amendment that would provide for a moment of voluntary prayer in the public schools,[24] arguing that prayer in school is consistent with our national heritage and an issue of religious liberty.[25]

CONCLUSION

This essay provides a brief sketch of how four U.S. presidents integrated morality with the office of the presidency. There are many others. Teddy Roosevelt, for example, argued for the existence of a "righteous" or "moral" form of war,[26] a moral standard for immigration,[27] and a standard of morality in business.[28] President Jimmy Carter argued that presidential greatness is partly defined by making decisions that are morally correct, even when they may be unpopular.[29] Carter thought morality to be not simply a part of the office of the presidency but part of our national identity, leading him to assert that "a nation without morality will soon lose its influence around the world."[30]

Also deserving notice are the contributions of Grover Cleveland, William McKinley, Harry Truman, Dwight Eisenhower, Franklin Delano Roosevelt, and many others. Among all these Chief Executives, there exist at least three common threads.

First, there seems a common willingness to discuss some form of international morality. This concept appears while addressing issues of annexation, the threat of war, the formation and role of the United Nations, the need for peace and stability on a global level, and action against dictators who flex their despotic muscles.

Second, there appears to be a reasonably strong connection between public service and private morality. The argument that morality should only be private, with no relationship to public service, seems to be a more recent phenomenon. In addition to Washington, Madison, Lincoln, Carter, and Reagan, the connection between public service and private morality is also found in the speeches of Lyndon Johnson, Gerald Ford, and George Bush.

Third, we conclude that morality is an important factor in the presidency. Some of the most important decisions of our nation's history had a decidedly moral dimension, running contrary to some contemporary thinking that we must divorce policy from morality. Perhaps the time has come to reconsider the role that morality plays in the office of the president.

CHAPTER FIVE

The Presidency:
Legitimate Authority and Governance

SHIRLEY ANNE WARSHAW

PROFESSOR OF POLITICAL SCIENCE
GETTYSBURG COLLEGE

THROUGHOUT THE PAST TWENTY-FIVE YEARS, the American presidency has been challenged by increased public scrutiny, leading to questions about the moral authority that the president must command as the nation's highest elected official. What does the American public expect from its president and are these expectations significantly different than the constitutional responsibilities imposed on the nation's chief executive? What is the intersection of public expectation and constitutional obligation? At what point does the consent of the governed affect the legitimate authority of the president to conduct the nation's business?

Management of the nation's business is in fact a relatively recent role for the president, a role that Franklin Delano Roosevelt brought to the Oval Office and wrested away from Congress. The last fifty years of presidential governance, spanning the eleven administrations from Franklin Delano Roosevelt to Bill Clinton, have resulted in enormous changes in presidential authority in domestic and international policymaking. Presidents, rather than Congress, dominate both domestic and international policymaking. As the federal government became increasingly dominant in domestic affairs during and after the New Deal, presidents have played a key role in guiding policy decisions and overseeing the implementation of the policies. Similarly, as America's military and economic might began to dominate the international arena in the post-World War II years, presidents guided foreign policy to protect the nation's strategic and financial interests globally. These changes in presidential authority have been supported by the public as legitimate roles for the president. These legitimate roles established for the president include the president as the nation's policy leader and as the manager of the policy process, both in the domestic and international arena.

The transition from congressional government to presidential government has not been an easy one, as the current dilemma over moral authority in the presidency indicates. Congressional government was far easier for the American public to accept, for it spread governmental responsibility among a large group and diminished the power of any individual. After the struggle for independence in 1776, the American public had little tolerance for chief executives with uncontrolled power. The former colonists did not want to establish a new government that allowed the chief executive unbridled authority. The constitutional convention of 1787 endeavored to satisfy the call for control in the nation's highest office by limiting authority and by establishing a system of checks and balances with the legislative branch. Throughout the first one hundred and fifty years of the nation's history, Congress oversaw policy matters and routinely worked with the executive departments to implement those policies. With the exception of Lincoln, Wilson, and Theodore Roosevelt, presidents played a relatively minor role in guiding the nation's policy development and implementation. Congress was satisfying the expectations of the American public in this role. Public expectation was to reduce the role of the president to ensure that a king-like executive did not emerge in the evolving governmental structure. Congress willingly accepted the mantle of that responsibility.

The responsibility for policy management shifted, however, during the 1930s when Congress was unable to cope with either the crisis brought on by the stock market crash of 1929 and the subsequent depression that followed, or with the march of Hitler's armies across Europe. The newly elected president, Franklin Delano Roosevelt, began proposing legislation to reverse the economic instability of the depression in a series of plans known as the New Deal legislation. Congress supported the proposals and an economic upswing began. Soon after the economic crisis turned around, the nation was deeply involved in wars in both the European and Pacific theaters. Roosevelt was again called upon to lead the nation out of a crisis. Throughout his twelve years in office, Roosevelt changed the way the American public viewed the presidency. His success with the New Deal programs and his success in leading the war effort transformed the presidency from a secondary player in policymaking to the primary player in policymaking. Congress was now the secondary player.

This major transformation in the way the American public viewed the presidency began the scrutiny that has continued in various degrees since the 1930s. When Franklin Roosevelt pushed too hard for power with his Court-packing scheme in the mid-1930s, the American public fumed that he had become arrogant and taken his power too far. The Court-packing scheme was solidly defeated by Congress after numerous newspaper articles condemned the proposal, reflecting the public outcry against it. While the public supported increased power in the presidency, they drew clear lines as to the acceptable limits on that power.

The television age brought further scrutiny on the presidency in the 1950s and 1960s, as television cameras were able to deliver to the public the full content of speeches made by presidents. Reporters could no longer rephrase statements and press secretaries could no longer say presidents had been misquoted. The public now saw exactly what presidents said and could make judgments about both content and candor. Television was beneficial to some presidents, such as John F. Kennedy, who allowed television cameras into his personal life with pictures of his family at the family compound in Hyannisport, Massachusetts, and with pictures of his wife detailing the magnificence of the White House. But it was also detrimental to some presidents, such as Lyndon Johnson, when images of the war in Vietnam were so dramatically flashed across every living room in the nation. Public scrutiny of the presidency was dramatically changed by the rise of television and the pictures that Americans saw both of the president and of the policies that presidents initiated. Public scrutiny drove out Lyndon Johnson, as the images of a failed war continued to flash across television sets across the nation, with somber commentary by Chet Huntley and David Brinkley recounting the daily casualties.

When Richard Nixon was inaugurated in January, 1969, he entered office fully aware of the growing public scrutiny on the presidency. Not only had television become a potent force in capturing the heart and mind of the American public, but the power of the presidency had become an equally potent force. The American public routinely looked to the president rather than Congress to lead the nation. Congress had become mired down in its own size (which had peaked at 435 in the House and 100 in the Senate), the complexity of policy decisions, and the politics of catering to special interest groups. The Truman and Eisenhower years (and to a lesser degree the Kennedy years by virtue of the Cuban missile crisis) had moved foreign policymaking firmly within the reins of the presidency. The Johnson years had moved domestic policymaking, by virtue of the Great Society legislation, firmly within the reins of the presidency. Where Franklin Delano Roosevelt had initiated the transformation to presidential government, his successors confirmed the transformation.

But the transformation to presidential government was not without cost, for while the presidency increased its power over policymaking, the public increased its scrutiny over the presidency. Richard Nixon entered office committed to a wide range of international objectives, particularly his initiatives with the Soviet Union and China and ending the war in Vietnam, and to a wide range of domestic objectives, most notably his New Federalism which gave greater power to state and local governments in determining how to use federal dollars. Nixon viewed his electoral victory over Hubert Humphrey as a mandate from the American public to move his policies forward. However, Nixon's secret negotiations with Russia and China, secret bombings in Cambodia, the failure to end the Vietnam War, and a series of impoundments of congressionally-appropriated program funding led to public disillusionment with presidential leadership.

The disillusionment with presidential leadership took a variety of forms, including mass demonstrations against the president's Vietnam war policies, election of increased numbers of Democratic members of Congress, and newspaper editorials against various presidential decisions. Following the break-in at the Democratic Party's national headquarters at the Watergate complex in Washington, D.C. in 1972, the public began to question whether President Nixon had himself been involved in either the initial burglary or any aspect of later decisions regarding a cover-up. President Nixon continually denied any personal or White House staff involvement in any aspect of the Watergate break-in or with any cover-up. Had Nixon immediately acknowledged that members of the White House staff had been involved, perhaps the public would have moved on to other issues. But the failure of President Nixon to acknowledge either his role or that of his White House staff in any of the

Watergate events led to a formal investigation in the House of Representatives and the initiation of impeachment hearings.

The American public had supported the increase in power that the presidency had gained in the years since Franklin Delano Roosevelt that had transformed policymaking from the congressional to the presidential arena. The public viewed the increased power in the presidency as essential in overseeing the rapidly expanding role of the federal government at both the domestic and international level. Yet such unbridled power was not to be without consequence, and that consequence proved to be President Nixon's downfall. With power came responsibility, and to a large degree President Nixon ignored the responsibility—of the power of office, a power that often was prerogative in nature. Prerogative power is by definition extra-constitutional and without boundary, but must be used only to protect the general welfare. John Locke, who carefully articulated the prerogative power of the executive in his *Second Treatise on Civil Government,* wrote that executives should use their prerogative powers judiciously and only when necessary to protect the public and the general welfare. Although Nixon believed that he was protecting the national interest in his activities, the public viewed his activities quite differently and stripped him of his power in the summer of 1974.

The Nixon case is a classic example of the public exercising its right to ensure that the executive has the consent of the governed. When consent is lost, the public ensures either through the ballot box or legislative process (impeachment), that power is maintained within acceptable parameters. What presidents have to determine—given the elasticity of prerogative power—is the acceptable limits of that power.

Through the next two decades, four presidents carried on the work of leading the nation and managing the business of State. One president, Ronald Reagan, ran into significant public scrutiny over the foreign policy activities of White House staff in the Iran-contra affair. However, Reagan skillfully defused the issue by acknowledging that some of the activities were carried out with his approval and assuring the nation that some were not. He was remorseful for his lack of judgment for his part in the Iran-contra events, and sought the public's support in finding ways to ensure that White House staff did not act independently in the future. His presidency had been subject to severe public reproach but not irreparable damaged.

The question now arises as to how do we determine how the consent of the governed affects the legitimate authority to govern? What role does moral authority play in this equation? And, particularly, what happened in the Clinton presidency that led to President Clinton's impeachment and serious reservations about his ability to govern?

The lessons learned from the post-Roosevelt era are framed around the increased power of the president and the subsequent public scrutiny of that power. As presidents have increased their power and Congress has largely defaulted on oversight of this power, the public has increased its scrutiny of their chief executives. With power comes responsibility, and as the nation rapidly has become the world's economic and military leader in an increasingly unipolar world and as the executive branch has become the domestic and foreign policy maker, the president has become increasingly scrutinized for policy decisions. It is clearly a reasonable objective of the governed to control the power of its own government, particularly the power of the presidency. As presidential government dominates the policy process, policy oversight by the public has become more intense.

Yet public oversight of the presidency has taken new turns during the Clinton administration, as the president's personal life was called into question. The authority of the presidency was jeopardized by a public outcry at extra-marital affairs by the president, particularly one involving a White House intern, Monica Lewinsky. The issue of moral authority and the presidency was raised during this period, leading in 1998 to impeachment in the House but not conviction in the Senate. Was this public outcry around moral authority during the Clinton administration any different than the public outcry around abuse of power during the Nixon administration? The answer is probably no, for in both cases the issue was simply one of whether the president had the consent of the governed in managing the nation's affairs. In the Nixon case, the president had very little support within the nation, either among the populace at large or within Congress. Impeachment was inevitable, and President Nixon chose to resign rather than face certain impeachment and conviction. In the Clinton case, the president had only limited support in the House of Representatives and Senate but had broad-based support against impeachment among the public at large. At various times during President Clinton's impeachment hearings, he had 70%

or more support in the public opinion polls. It is important to note, however, that the public was deeply concerned about the president's personal behavior but was willing to separate that behavior from his public actions for the time being. The public allowed the House of Representatives to conduct the impeachment hearings with the understanding that the Senate did not have the votes to convict the president. However, the unequivocal message from the public to the president, and to future presidents, was that personal conduct unbecoming a president was unacceptable behavior and in the future would not be tolerated. The impeachment was a strong warning which in the future would be followed by conviction.

In summary, presidents must have the consent of the governed in order to carry out the roles and responsibilities of the presidency. The emergence of presidential government during the Roosevelt administration brought enhanced power to the office of the president but also enhanced public scrutiny of each of the office holders. Power is not without obligation. The obligation of the president is to the governed. When the governed feel that the legitimate authority of the president to govern has been violated, whether through official or personal conduct, that authority is compromised. Power can only be maintained when the consent of the governed provides legitimate authority. The question of "moral authority in government," I believe, should be reframed around the question of legitimate authority. Presidents govern with the consent of the governed, a consent which is constantly redefined by changing times and changing values and changing expectations of leadership. As long as presidents meet the Lockean concept of ruling within the precepts of protecting the general welfare, there can be no absolute tests of moral authority, only of legitimate authority. Power rests in the consent of the governed, which is the centerpiece of legitimate authority.

CHAPTER SIX

Principled Courageous Leadership: The Lost Core of American Politics

STANLEY A. RENSHON

PROFESSOR OF POLITICAL SCIENCE
CITY UNIVERSITY OF NEW YORK

IT IS THE HOLY GRAIL of American politics. The Archimedean, point at which North, South, East, and West; men and women; urban and suburban; left and right; and race and ethnicity are in harmonious political balance. It is the fulfillment of the modern alchemist's dream of transmutation—of views into votes, and political conflicts into public consensus. It is the political center, which is increasingly difficult to discern, much less to lead from, in contemporary American politics.

Why? Because in recent decades the very fabric of American political and national identity has been challenged by an assertive expansion of individual and group rights, acerbic debates regarding the legitimacy and limits of these claims, and a preference on the part of national political leaders to finesse rather than engage these controversies. Freed by the end of the cold war from a need to focus on external enemies, the country appears at a crossroads, if not a dead end.

Race relations have in many ways improved, yet paradoxically worsened. The past decade has brought unprecedented levels of immigration and with it rising levels of public concern, coupled with some very profound questions about what it means to be, or become an American. Is assimilation still possible? Is it desirable? Immigrants are idealized by some, even as high levels of immigration are greeted with suspicion and apprehension by many others. Definitions of the family and relations between men and women, at home and in the work place, have dramatically changed, but a question remains as to whether they have improved. There are real differences and practical consequences involved in such divisive policy issues such as affirmative action, abortion rights, immigration and assimilation, English as the primary language, and homosexual marriage, to name a few.

Behind these questions lies a deeper cultural and political conflict, "a struggle to define America."[1] What is fair? How are we to define opportunity, and how much should merit count? What does and should it mean to be an American? Where, exactly, is the "political center" in these issues?

These questions have provoked enormous, but paradoxical political conflict. The paradox is simply this: In many major polls of contentious issues—bi-lingual education, affirmative action, abortion, and so on—the evidence is that there is a clear, decisive, and reliable political center on each and all of these issues.[2] One might almost say that the more political agreement there is among ordinary Americans the more savage the battles become. Why? The answer is suggested in the following notation:

Displacement of political politics ↔ Leaderless politics ↔ Reluctant citizens

As this schematic makes clear, I place leaderless politics at the core of our difficulties, and therefore at the possible center of our political and cultural redemption.

CULTURAL CONFLICT AND THE DISPLACEMENT OF POLITICAL POLITICS

As obvious as it sounds in retrospect, Hunter's important insight was that the "culture wars" in politics were basically cultural, not political.[3] Yet, he failed to see the extent to which "cultural politics" had become fused with traditional forms of American political and procedural conflict to create something quite new: core conflict which is both primal and boundaryless.

It is primal because the elements that form the foundation of American identity and culture are at issue. Only the Civil War tested our ability to share a common future without a common national and regional culture. The answer, over which the war was fought, was that we could not.

Now, another primal conflict is unfolding, but one which, unlike the Civil War, is boundaryless. It does not pit commerce against agriculture, urban against rural, or North against South. Rather, it is fought between people of different racial, cultural, and ethnic heritages, and between those who view themselves as culturally disadvantaged against those whom they see as privileged. Unlike the first civil war, it's primary focus is not one section of the country against another, but rather it is a war being fought in every section of the country. Consequently, unlike the first civil war the antagonists can not take the institutions in their part of the country—their family, religious, social, cultural, or political values and institutions—for granted. These are precisely the places where the wars are being fought.

LEADERLESS POLITICS

The rise of leaders anxious for office and lacking either strong principled convictions or the courage of them, leads to a mismatch between ambitions and performance. We therefore elect "leaders," but receive little leadership. As a result, it is the public's hopes and emotional connections with their government that are squandered. I take up the question of leadership, and especially presidential leadership, more directly below.

RELUCTANT CITIZENS

Wolfe's survey found that America seems to have added a new eleventh commandment to the original ten: "Thou Shall Not Judge." Americans, he found, are loath to express a preference for any point of view, and certainly not willing to "pass judgment" on anyone else's behavior. The consequences of this are profound and little examined, the reasons for it even less so.

Briefly, I locate the reasons for this both in inner and public psychology. Adaptability, psychological and "moral," has become a key component of American character. Reisman[4] was right, but failed to anticipate the ways in which other directed and narcissistic characters would merge to create a new American character type for the last decades of the twentieth century. A parallel development is the rise of therapeutic politics—a politics of feeling—which threaten to displace America's traditional concern with pragmatism—the politics of adjusting self-interests. Finally, both of these developments are made more potent by the triumph, among some, of self-righteous ambition and the politics of "lying for justice."

PRESIDENTS AND THE POLITICAL CENTER:
THE POLITICS OF AVOIDANCE

The two basic elements of American public life noted above, the displacement of political politics and a reluctant citizenry, are the essence and the central dilemma of presidential leadership in contemporary American life. It is an axiom of American politics that presidents must appeal to the center, however they govern. Yet, given that America remains a country of basic disagreements, how is that possible?

Have candidates and presidents simply been unable to discern the direction or contours of the political center? Do they, as a group, lack the intelligence, political insight, or judgment to find it? Some might find this a tempting explanation, but it makes no sense for two basic reasons. First, if one equates long-standing majority views on such contentious issues as abortion, immigration, and affirmative action with the political center, it is quite clear what the majority of Americans think, and have thought over a long period of time. It does not take a political genius, good judgment, or keen insight to discern these basic facts. Second, most modern presidents have been generally intelligent—some like Clinton exceedingly so—and would not have gained the presidency without a good appreciation of the country's politics.

The answer lies elsewhere. Leaders are torn between their ambitions, the escalating public demands to offer "solutions" to every problem, and the limits of their competence and the public's tolerance for difficult truths.

What is the relationship of leadership to the political center and of presidential principles? Simply this: In order for political leaders to have the courage of their convictions, they must first have both.

Yet evidence for their twin existence has been rare in both political parties. Presidents and candidates have tried to negotiate these treacherous currents for a decade, primarily by trying to finesse rather than engage them. Michael Dukakis famously suggested in 1988 that his presidential campaign was about competence, not ideology, and was soundly trounced by the most publicly ideological president of the decade. George Bush lacked a discernible domestic political or policy center and failed to get a second term. Bill Clinton ran and won the presidency as a "New Democrat," governed as an old one—and won reelection by declaring "the era of big government is over," even while copiously adding new programs to it.

Consider the Clinton administration's initiative on race—born at the intersection of presidential ambition and interest group activism, and beset by controversy from its inception. Some questioned whether such a discussion was needed. Some thought it had already been going on for decades, in many political, legal, and cultural forums.

However, early on, there were even more basic questions. The president's initiative on race was entitled "One America" and presumably was meant to address diversity issues for all Americans. However, it soon became clear that the president and the chair of the initiative had other things in mind. The chair, Professor Franklin, created a stir when he said he had nothing to learn from opponents. And, while at least one board member (Ms. Oh) expressed the hope that the initiative would deal with all minorities, the chair had other ideas. Thus from its inception the initiative on race was cast primarily as an initiative on relations between African Americans and "white" Americans. This was a direct result of the lobbying of Jesse Jackson and like-minded advocates who had urged a presidential commission to address what they saw as the continuing, harrowing plight of African Americans in this country.

Not surprising, other ethnic and racial groups felt they were being excluded. And even those who supported the proposal questioned whether public, televised forums with hand-picked participants were the best, or most useful, venue for conducting such discussions. Early initiative events were marked by platitudes and the avoidance of anything that might give offense. Bland, but carefully chosen personal narratives meant to highlight experiences that might lead to a consensus about what "needs to be done" predominated. An adolescent minority youth related an experience of taking his mother's check to the bank and being asked for identification. This, he submitted, was an example of the special burdens placed on those like himself. No one, including the president who served as moderator, pointed out that trying to cash a check made out to someone else at a bank where you are not personally known might lead to questions for anyone.

President Clinton's legitimacy as the national leader of a frank dialogue was further compromised by the almost dizzying succession of his positions on the Taxman affirmative action case, settled by affirmation action advocates before the Supreme Court could render its decision. He holds the unique and—from the perspective of principle and candor—dubious distinction of heading the only administration ever to submit three distinct briefs to the Supreme Court, each taking a decidedly different position.[5] President Clinton's multiple, conflicting, and seemingly strategic positions in this case make it hard to know just which conviction he has the courage of; but at least in this case there are three different ones to chose from among.

As much as Mr. Clinton may personify some of the problems that affect our current inability to make progress on the issues that divide us, however, he is by no means alone. Indeed, for some national leaders, no expressed position seems to be the most politically comfortably one. Consider in this respect former Senator Robert Dole's response to a question asked of him during the third national presidential debate with his rival.[6]

He was asked by a woman, a minister with the Universal Fellowship of Metropolitan Community Churches, to explain his reference to being against "special rights," in this case for homosexuals. It was clear from the thrust and tone of the question that the woman supported such rights, but regardless of her personal position, it was a fair and reasonable question.

> **Q:** President Clinton, perhaps you can help me with something tonight. I've heard Mr. Dole say several times, "all of us together." And when he was asked if he would support equal rights in employment for gay and lesbian people, you said you favored that, and he said that he did not believe in special rights. And I thought the question was equal rights for all people, and I don't understand why people are using the term "special rights" when the question is equal rights. Can you help me in understanding that?

> PRESIDENT CLINTON: I want to answer your question, but first let me say one other thing . . . [*the president goes on to discuss school prayer, and declines to characterize Mr. Dole's statement because,* I'd mischaracterize it and try to make you happy]. Under our constitution, if you show up tomorrow, and obey the law, and you work hard, and you do what you are supposed to do, you're entitled to equal treatment.

> MR. LEHER: Senator Dole?

> SENATOR DOLE: Well, I hope I made my answer clear. I said I'm opposed to discrimination. You know we've suffered discrimination in the disability community. There are 43 million of us. And I can recall cases where people would cross the street rather than meet someone in a wheelchair. So, we want to end discrimination. I think that answers itself. No discrimination in America.

We've made it clear. And I would just say that it seems to me that's the way it ought to be. We shouldn't discriminate—race, color, whatever, lifestyle, disability. This is America, and we're all proud of it. But we're not there yet. What we need is good strong leadership going into the next century. [*Mr. Dole then goes on to raise a foreign policy issue with his remaining time.*]

That question provided a perfect opportunity for Senator Dole to educate the public and specify both where he and the President agreed (being against discrimination), and where they didn't (special rights), and why. He might have noted that he worried that some advocates and their allies might make use of these laws in ways which most Americans would not support, for example using the idea of hostile climate to require teaching about gay life style in public schools to small children. That worry would not have been farfetched. In New York City public schools a rancorous debate broke out over plans to teach primary school children about homosexual life styles, and present them as one of a number of equally appropriate family life style choices. And more recently, the Provincetown School Board voted to require teaching pre-schoolers about homosexual life styles.[7]

Or, he might have pointed out that since laws baring discrimination on the basis of sex were already on the federal statute books, he opposed placing additional and unnecessary ones on them. He might have said that he would support the law if it specifically included the idea that the law was a two-way street, that gays and lesbians who in positions of authority misused their positions with heterosexual men and women would be equally subject to the law, the position taken by the Supreme Court in a recent decision.

I don't really know what Mr. Dole would have said, but the point is that neither does anyone else who followed the debate. By either being unclear about the nature of his opposition, or reluctant or unable to express it, he deprived the public of the opportunity to have something to think about.

PRESIDENTIAL CHARACTER AND THE SEARCH FOR THE PRINCIPLED POLITICAL CENTER

Why has it been so difficult for presidents and candidates to find and to lead from, the political center? In part because of the mismatch between presidential ambitions and ideals on the one hand, and the contour of American politics on the other.

Traditionally, presidents (and the public) have defined leadership as having those seeking office articulate their own views and then mobilize others to accept and implement them. This may be appropriate in periods of public consensus or where the implications of alternative views have been openly and honestly debated. But neither of these is the case for the country's present basic disagreements concerning diversity, inclusion, and our identities as individuals and Americans.

Leadership in times of deep national divisions requires leaders of a particular kind: those who have both courage and convictions; who are not afraid to raise and honestly answer difficult political questions, and make these honest answers the basis of their leadership. To locate such leadership, one must look first to the president's interior psychology, his character, and more particularly, the extent to which his principled ideals have developed and provided boundaries and purpose for the exercise of his ambition.

Leadership cannot be divorced from the person exercising it. It makes use of, and often amplifies, a president's character—his ambitions, ideals, ways of dealing with others, and of course his political skills. A president who discerns the true nature of political center debates and has principled positions on them, must still find political means to articulate and consolidate these views among the public.

Polling and Pandering: The End of the Presidency's Moral Authority?

ROBERT Y. SHAPIRO

PROFESSOR OF POLITICAL SCIENCE
COLUMBIA UNIVERSITY

LAWRENCE R. JACOBS

PROFESSOR OF POLITICAL SCIENCE
UNIVERSITY OF MINNESOTA

Clearly, they [American presidents] engage in moral—and explicitly religious—activity. Literally they preach, reminding the American people of religious and moral principles and urging them to conduct themselves in accord with these principles. They lead prayers, quote from the Bible, and make theological statements about the Deity and His desires for the nation . . . the public perceives Presidents as altruistic and benevolent. They are the moral leaders and high priests of the American society.

BARBARA HINCKLEY, *The Symbolic Presidency*

THE PROLIFERATION AND VISIBILITY of public opinion polling during the Clinton administration, at century's end, have led many critics of American politics to fear that poll-taking—or focus groups and the like—has permanently replaced political leadership. Politicians and presidents from here on will blow with the winds of public opinion, and pandering will come to dominate presidential politics. What then, we can ask, will this mean for the moral authority of the American presidency? Will the moral leadership that Barbara Hinckley described end?

We think not. Neither moral leadership nor prospects for leadership in general will end with the rise of polling and other means to listen to public opinion. There are three reasons for this. First and foremost, presidents' moral leadership and authority come from what presidents say and do. The fact that Bill Clinton could claim little moral authority as Congress impeached him had little to do with his conducting and responding to polls. The public saw his sexual misconduct and deceit for what it was: immoral but not warranting his removal from office. That his use of polls may have led him to believe he could "get away with it" (e.g., his infamous comment to Dick Morris in January, 1998) does raise the question of whether polls invite immoral behavior on the false belief that public opinion can be fooled. The public, however, was not fooled regarding Clinton's morality, but applied a different standard regarding impeachment and conviction. But would voters have re-elected him if he had still been in his first term? Could he even get his party's nomination? We doubt it.

The second and third reasons require more discussion and historical detail. They have to do with the highly moral nature and content of American public opinion itself, and also with how presidents have actually used their polling and other information about public opinion that has attracted so much criticism. The remainder of this essay draws on much that has been written about presidents, polling, and public opinion, in addition to our own analysis.[1]

AMERICAN MORALITY AND PUBLIC OPINION

If future presidents simply responded to public opinion, the end result would surely be a presidency with considerable moral authority. This is not to say that we would all agree with the resulting moral leadership—majority versus minority opinion can disagree about what is good or bad, right or wrong—but the presidency would readily draw on public opinion to exert considerable moral force. Bill Clinton would have behaved differently in his personal life (or at least have been much more discreet), or he would have resigned from office.

The evidence for the morality and religiousness of the American public is overwhelming. Public opinion and other data have long shown that Americans are among the most religious people in the world, in terms of belief in a supreme being, memberships in religious organizations, and attendance at religious services. The fact that the Clinton scandal captured the nation's attention and that polls showed a sharp jump in the percentage responding that morality and values were most important speaks for itself. The public has a strong sense of morality that is readily primed and evoked. Beyond their religiousness and the moral lens through which they view politics, Americans' opinions themselves have long reflected religious and moral values; indeed, some might still seem puritanical. While the extent to which these values have been translated into actual national policy has been more pragmatic than dogmatic, and while there are constitutional protections that prevent some of them from being rigidly imposed, these values are pervasive in American life and public discourse.

The moral force in public opinion can be found directly in Americans' attitudes related to religiousness and personal behavior. Large and stable majorities of the public continue to favor allowing prayer in public schools and have conservative values and attitudes regarding sex. Underlying public attitudes toward homosexuals is the widespread belief, still, that homosexuality is morally wrong. The public is largely supportive of allowing legal abortions, though underlying this, too, is disapproval of women having abortions except under compelling circumstances. The public supports having sex education in schools and making information about birth control widely available, but it is protective of the rights of parents to control the actions of their children in this regard. Most notably, polls show that less than 10 percent of the public favors the unrestricted availability of pornography.

This morality goes beyond sex, though in this regard the public is not consistently conservative in terms of liberal/conservative ideology. The public has long opposed legalizing drugs; even in the case of alcohol, 20 percent or so of the public has continued to favor prohibition. The public is reluctant to support euthanasia in a very broad, permissive sense, but in the end it supports allowing terminal patients to tell doctors to let them die without further heroic measures. In the case of crime and punishment, very substantial majorities of the public favor capital punishment for murder and feel that prison sentences for convicted criminals are not harsh enough. And in the same spirit of controlling immoral and dangerous behavior, the public has continued to support stronger gun control measures and regulations (though it opposes outlawing all guns). The same moral efforts to promote the public's safety can be found in the substantial support for a wide range of government regulations concerning specific problems having to do with the environment and pollution, and consumer products and the like, despite the public's suspicion of the heavy hand of government when asked about potentially excessive government intrusion in the abstract.

The moral force of public opinion also speaks to other kinds of government activism. Underlying public support for large-scale spending on Social Security, medical care, and assistance to the "deserving poor" and others in genuine need, is a moral concern and compassion to help others. While the public does not extend this kind of compassion to foreign aid in the abstract, it may do so in specific cases of humanitarian assistance; and also, in a different context, in how it reacts, when prompted, to foreign aggression (e.g., the public's response to Iraq's invasion of Kuwait and to Serbia's invasion and "ethnic cleansing" of Bosnia and Kosovo).

Thus, if presidents simply echoed these voices, moral soundings would loudly be heard. This would not necessarily guarantee the best government and public policies, nor serve presidents' other concerns. But we would not blame a president who is responsive to public opinion for any lack of moral fervor.

POLITICIANS DON'T PANDER

Presidents, however, have not mechanically responded to public opinion, even as the White House has increased its attention and institutional capacity to track and analyze public opinion. At the same time, presidents have continued to offer moral and religious leadership. Barbara Hinckley's analysis in *The Symbolic Presidency* shows how presidents from Truman through Reagan persistently emphasized moral value and religious references in their public addresses to the nation. This emphasis continued even as Presidents and their parties increasingly conducted private polls and extensive public opinion research. While there was no break over time in the scope of these presidents' exertion of moral authority, we need to ask whether the content of what presidents said and did changed. That is, did presidents become more likely to respond to, rather than attempt to lead, public opinion? This is a more complicated question.

Based upon what we know from archival and other evidence

on how presidents used polling and related information, the time at which they were most likely to respond to public opinion was near their own (re)election. At other times they were interested in information and insight into how to gain public support for what they wanted to do for other reasons—stemming from partisan or ideological influences or their own programmatic or other interests or objectives.

Our best synthesis so far of the history of this begins with John F. Kennedy (although a preview of this came with Franklin Roosevelt), after which polling and public opinion analysis became routinized into the institutional functioning of the presidency. The initial driving force for this was electoral, as presidents once in office strove to be reelected. Presidents started to use their own pollsters and political consultants during their campaigns, with private polls being paid for by the political parties or other nongovernmental sources. In this history the most important evidence is the increasing number of polls that Johnson, Nixon and later Presidents conducted. Most notable were the figures for Reagan and, of course, Clinton during their two terms in office, especially during the governing period (not just during election campaigns) which show the striking continuity and high level of this polling. Most important, beginning with Carter (as presidents' pollsters became publicly known figures) the scope of the sharing and deliberation over public opinion information within the administration expanded so that the White House became increasingly better positioned than in the past not only to respond to, but also to lead—or manipulate—public opinion.

While we can point to cases of presidential and congressional responsiveness to public opinion during presidential election years (e.g., in 1996, the minimum wage increase, modest health care reform, and, arguably, welfare reform), presidents and congressional leaders apparently see ample time between elections to leave public opinion in the lurch while pursuing their own agenda (e.g., Johnson's War on Poverty and the Vietnam War after his reelection; Reagan's efforts to continue support to the "Contra" rebel "freedom fighters" in Nicaragua; Clinton's decision to invade Haiti and some of his actions regarding intervention in Bosnia; the House and Senate Republican leadership's moral fervor in attempting to convict Clinton on articles of impeachment). Jimmy Carter, as the first president to enter office publicly taking his pollster, Patrick Caddell, with him, became known to political scientists as the "trustee" president, acting in the best interests of the people, with moral aplomb, without taking direct instructions from them through polls, as their "delegate."

Understanding how polls can be used by presidents to respond directly to public opinion requires little explanation, but how they are used to provide guidance in how to lead public opinion is complicated and beyond our space limitations here. In short, presidents can use polls to determine how to explain and present already determined proposals and policies to the public. They, their advisers, and especially their polling and other political consultants have become increasingly sophisticated at doing this. Their methods have gone beyond polls and regular focus groups to include, in the case of the Reagan White House (guided by pollster Richard Wirthlin) having small groups of 50 adults regularly assemble to view Reagan's speeches and to use hand-held electronic devices to help pinpoint the most effective language or presentations—message, style, and delivery—for the president. This "pulse line" analysis was conducted, for instance, on the president's foreign policy speeches related to peace and national security in 1986, and the Venice Summit in June, 1987.

CONCLUSION

This, in brief, is our case for expecting the continued moral authority of America's public presidency. As presidents continue to poll and monitor public opinion, using the best methods and expertise, neither their prospects for moral leadership, nor leadership in general, will automatically suffer; they might even benefit. The fact that presidents and their advisors watch public opinion as carefully as they can, does not mean that they will comply with it. And even if they did, presidents would exert moral authority by reflecting the public's own.

CHAPTER EIGHT

A Gender Analysis of the Moral Legitimacy of the Presidency

JEAN REITH SCHROEDEL[1]

ASSOCIATE PROFESSOR OF POLITICS AND POLICY
CLAREMONT GRADUATE UNIVERSITY

CONSERVATIVES ARE APPALLED that feminists differentiated between Clinton, the man whose moral failings (particularly with respect to women) are patently obvious, and Clinton, the president they supported throughout the impeachment. To many conservatives it is rank hypocrisy to separate the two. It is, however, a distinction that the American public, according to the polls, also has made. One public opinion poll showed that only 39% of respondents approved of Clinton's personal behavior but that 62% approved of his job performance.[2] Moreover, many polls show women as more disapproving of Clinton's private behavior but more approving of his job performance than men. The seemingly paradoxical finding—that women continue to support a president whose personal behavior toward women is abhorrent—is explicable when a gender analysis is employed.[3]

A gender analysis frames the question of presidential morality more broadly than is currently being put forth. The moral legitimacy of a president is primarily a function of the representative character of his administration rather than his private sexual conduct. During his campaign, Clinton promised to have an administration that "looks like America," and he fulfilled that pledge with respect to women. Given that women comprise a numerical majority of the population and have never comprised more than an extremely small percentage of presidential appointments, it is fair to claim that in the executive branch, women have been the most under-represented group in American society.[4] At a very fundamental level the legitimacy of our system of government has been undermined—not by Clinton and Lewinsky—but rather by earlier administrations that systematically excluded women.

The women's movement of the late 1960s and 1970s can claim credit for raising the issue of women's under-representation in politics. Although the primary focus has been on women's representation in electoral office, the executive branch has come under heightened scrutiny in the past decade.[5] Although there has been a tendency to focus on the symbolic aspects of representation more than the substantive ones, both matter. On a symbolic level, appointment "firsts" and other measures of administrative diversity provide role models and tangible evidence of the increased legitimacy of the political system. On a substantive level, these appointees often bring different perspectives to the policy process.

There has been greater acceptance of women being appointed to positions that are viewed as extensions of their "natural" caregiver roles (e.g., health and human services) than in traditional male roles, such as in the military and foreign policy.[6] According to Cronin,[7] the State, Treasury, Defense, and Justice Departments comprise the most prestigious and powerful "inner" cabinet while all other departments are designated as the "outer" cabinet. White House staff positions also have been given the "inner" and "outer" label, with female staffers concentrated in the latter category.[8]

The Clinton transition team made diversity a major consideration in appointments. One of the most important conduits for women to influence the process was through the Coalition for Women's Appointments, which has compiled lists of potential female appointees for more than twenty years. Initially women's groups and the media focused on the question of whether the new administration would shatter the Bush record of three female cabinet appointees. When feminists criticized him for not breaking this record, Clinton responded by labeling them "bean counters who were more interested in quotas than competence."[9]

Both in terms of the numbers of women and the types of appointments, the Clinton administration represents a dramatic departure. There are a significantly higher proportion of women in high-level posts in this administration than in any previous one. Women comprise 30.5% of top appointees of the Clinton administration, as opposed to 21.4% and 13.2% in the Bush and Reagan administrations.[10] But there are substantial differences across departments. In the first year of the Clinton administration, only 22% of State Department appointees and 18.5% of Defense Department appointees were women.[11]

Clinton was the first president to appoint women to "inner" cabinet positions—Janet Reno as Attorney General and Madeleine Albright as Secretary of State. He also appointed more women to defense and foreign policy positions that required Senate confirmation than did any of his predecessors. Roughly twice as many women are serving as ambassadors to major countries.[12] He also set records in the appointment of women to White House staff positions. According to Tenpas,[13] 39% of the Clinton White House staff are women, as opposed to 25% and 18% in the Bush and Reagan administrations. Moreover, the women serving in the Clinton White House are far more likely to be in mid-level and senior-level policy positions; they also have made some inroads into traditionally male policy domains, such as foreign affairs, defense and economic policymaking.

Clinton also created new institutional channels, such as the White House Office for Women's Initiatives and Outreach, and the President's Interagency Council on Women, for communicating women's policy concerns to senior officials.[14] Although the administration has pushed only a few explicitly feminist issues, many of their proposals are ones that women support and disproportionately affect them. The Family and Medical Leave Act, the very first act signed into law by President Clinton in 1993, is a good example of this type of initiative. The law's provision apply equally to both men and women, but the primary beneficiaries of the measure are women because they are more likely to fulfill caretaker roles. After the failure of Clinton's comprehensive health care plan, the administration shifted to pushing incremental health care reforms; but again the emphasis is on ones that disproportionately impact women—proposals to provide health care for uninsured children, fund research on breast cancer, require insurers to cover minimum hospital stays following child birth, and develop programs to combat osteoporosis.

The administration also has pushed a number of explicitly feminist policies, some of which required statutory enactment and others which could be done by administrative fiat. Probably the highest profile feminist initiative passed into law during the Clinton years was the 1994 Violence Against Women Act. Others have dealt with reproductive rights, most notably ensuring access to abortion. Shortly after taking office in 1993, Clinton revoked the "gag rule" which prevented any clinic or medical practitioner receiving government funds from providing information about abortion unless the woman's health was threatened by carrying the pregnancy to term. Early on Clinton issued an executive order instructing the Food and Drug Administration to re-evaluate its ban on mifepristone[15] (also known as RU 486) and then in 1996 after reviewing medical trials involving more than 2,000 women, the FDA labeled mifepristone "approvable," which means that the drug is on track to reach the American market in 2000. The administration also strongly supported the 1994 Freedom of Access to Clinic Entrances Act, which makes it a federal crime to damage abortion clinics or interfere with anyone obtaining or providing such services.

One unrecognized and very important long-term impact of Clinton's appointment of women throughout the executive branch is that it will be difficult for future presidents to argue that they cannot find qualified women nominees. By appointing substantial numbers of women to mid-level policy positions, Clinton has made sure there will be women with the requisite experience and credentials to fill high-level appointments in the twenty-first century. This "pipeline effect" may very well be Clinton's most important legacy.

FINAL THOUGHTS

Given his commitment to the inclusion of women in positions of political power and support for policies designed to improve their lives, it is completely understandable that women reciprocated by supporting Clinton throughout the impeachment proceedings. Not only are women more likely to be Democratic party identifiers and therefore oppose efforts to drive a president from their party out of office, they recognize that Clinton is the first president to give them a "seat at the table." Perhaps the polls would be different if the Republicans, who orchestrated the impeachment drive, had an equally strong record on women's issues and appointments of women to policy positions. But they have not. Many women believe they cannot afford to allow their outrage at Clinton's private actions to outweigh their vision of the public good, a vision that is far more gender-inclusive than that put forth by the president's political opponents. If one limits the definition of morality to sexual conduct—as many conservatives have—then Clinton, like many of his predecessors, has fallen short of the standard expected of a national leader. However, if one considers the moral legitimacy of the presidency as a representative body, then Clinton has set a high standard that others would do well to emulate.

How "Bully" is the Pulpit? Moral Authority of the American Presidents in the Twenty-First Century

FRANK KESSLER

PROFESSOR OF POLITICAL SCIENCE
MISSOURI WESTERN COLLEGE

> *If Darwin and his followers are right, . . . the moral sense must have had adaptive value; if it did not, natural selection would have worked against people who had such useless traits as sympathy, self-control, or a desire for fairness and in favor of those with the opposite traits . . . (ruthless predation, or a preference for immediate gratification, or a disinclination to share).*
>
> JAMES Q. WILSON, *The Moral Sense*

ONE HUNDRED YEARS AGO (January 18, 1899), as Congress was chartering the National Institute of Social Sciences, which commissioned this book, Theodore Roosevelt enthused that the American presidency was indeed a "bully pulpit" from which to inspire the best instincts in the American people.[1] This chapter will examine the authority that the presidents have to mount that pulpit and give moral leadership and direction to the citizens of the republic. It will also consider the willingness of the electorate in a democracy to follow presidential leadership. In addition, it will examine the difficulties of moral leadership in a diverse nation seemingly averse to having someone "impose morality on someone else." "In today's live and let live culture, the morality of actions too often tends to be judged as a matter of taste, much in the way one has tastes in art, literature, music or the like." This fluidity in moral values could make leadership based on moral authority difficult to exercise. Finally, this essay will provide some prescriptions for successfully mounting that pulpit to appeal to the "better angels of our nature."[2]

Despite the credibility problems which President William Jefferson Clinton encountered as a result of both the Lewinsky scandal and his subsequent impeachment trial, he continued to focus on values in a process some called seeking a "politics of meaning."[3] His decision to involve U.S. forces in a "NATO" operation in Serbia to protect the Kosovar Albanians from possible genocide was also justified as being what Americans ought to do in situations in which we were able to do it.[4] Like Jimmy Carter, his immediate Democratic predecessor in the Oval Office, who campaigned on the promise to make the government as honest and decent as its people,[5] Clinton appealed to the altruism of the citizenry to gain support for his actions. He seemed also to be seeking a sort of personal vindication for the history books, lest future generations be tempted to judge him on the fact of his impeachment first rather than on his list of successes. In a book titled *The Politics Presidents Make*, Professor Steven Skowronek notes that successful political leaders do not necessarily do more than other leaders; but they control the political definition of their actions, which are the terms in which their places in history are understood.[6] While much of the literature on the presidency addresses variations of Richard Neustadt's classic writings on Presidential power[7] and the ability to persuade, Skowronek argues convincingly that authority is really the key to presidential success. Authority involves the expectations that surround the exercise of power at any particular time. Authority comes from the legitimacy the past provides to the actions at hand. It is the past that lends justification for the new actions that are being taken. Presidential history is littered with the political carcasses of presidents who depended on their powers to get things done only to have that exercise of power undermine their authority to govern.[8]

In Michael Genovese and Thomas Cronin, *The Paradoxes of the American Presidency*, the authors contend that the presidency "serves our basic need for a visible and representative national symbol to which we can turn our hopes and our aspirations." In addition, they suggest that Americans place the president on a "high pedestal," even as the citizenry demands democratic responsiveness. Thus the president serves as both national hero and national scapegoat.[9]

Where does the president get the moral authority to preach to the American electorate? It is clear that the framers of the Constitution, in 1787, envisioned this role when they decided on a single executive elected by the public at large and thus not beholden to the whims of the legislative branch as British prime ministers had been.[10] The American single executive was not to be so powerful as to be able to proclaim, like French King Louis XIV, "l'etat c'est moi." The divine right of kings was jettisoned as being an illegitimate source of justification for the exercise of authority and leadership. Just governments, the Declaration of Independence notes, derive their authority from the "consent of the governed." Lest the president be tempted to abuse his center-stage role in the system, the Constitution discourages presidential abuse of that authority with its elaborate system of checks and balances, making sure too much authority was not put in one set of hands.

The moral authority of government, and, by inference, presidents, is reinforced by Judaeo-Christian tradition which encourages respect for the institutions and personages of government among the citizens of the properly ordered state. For example, in *Gaudium et Spes*, one of the documents of the Second Vatican Council (1965), the world's Catholic bishops declared that to avoid the chaos of everyone following his or her own opinion,

> there must be an authority to direct the energies of all citizens towards the common good . . . by acting above all as a moral force which appeals both to each one's freedom and sense of responsibility.[11]

Respected Vanderbilt analyst and chronicler of Presidential leadership, Erwin C. Hargrove, asserts that "Americans have been willing to empower presidents in times of national challenge, but the empowerment is tentative and temporary."[12] Edmund Burke, British philosopher whose thinking was much in evidence at the Philadelphia convention of 1787, argued that the representative must not simply amplify the views of the current electorate saying, "your representative owes you, not his industry only, but his judgment, and he betrays, instead of serving you, if he sacrifices it to your opinion."[13] This style of heroic presidential leadership suggests that presidents may more successfully lead the public in a responsible direction if they use rhetoric which plays upon the American public's fear of crisis or sense of idealism.[14]

Elected office holders quickly learn, often to their dismay, that voters habitually view government officials with a healthy dose of skepticism.[15] Presidents have been no exception in this regard, but they have the advantage of the fact that there is only *one* president. The centrality of the presidential office gives its occupants a voice no legislator representing a locality can simulate. Still, public support for presidential initiatives is not automatic. Presidents squander public good will via perceived incompetence, as Jimmy Carter learned in dealing with the American hostages in Iran,[16] or mendacity, as Richard Nixon learned from the Watergate cover-up.[17] Bill Clinton's experience with Monicagate suggests that mendacity, even under oath, can be overlooked if the economy is doing well. Moral authority may be compromised, though.[18]

Getting the consent of the governed early in United States history was easier than it is today, but has always been problematic at best. Surely the framers of our present Constitution, in 1787, could not have foreseen the electronic podium (or pulpit) that twentieth-century media affords to today's presidents via mass market television, multiband radio, 24-hour cable networks, computerized speech crafting, fax machines, mass mailings, the Internet, and the likes. The next century is likely, with burgeoning digital technology and miniaturized computer chips, to provide even more venues to spread a president's message to the public. Unfortunately, since the institutional presidency is peopled by persons of varying abilities, each may not be gifted to be—as president Ronald Reagan was dubbed—the Great Communicator.[19] However, the expanded marketplace of information and ideas which presidents can use to preach their values, also presents a number of windows of opportunity for competitors who are likely to have other ideas about what is righteous and efficacious. In the twentieth century, not all moral compasses have pointed to a common magnetic North; and that situation is unlikely to change as we enter the twenty-first century.

MORALITY: IS EVERYTHING PERMITTED, IS ANYTHING PREFERABLE?

As the dawn of the new century approaches, the debate over whether God is dead seems to have been supplanted by questions about whether God is relevant and whether one set of moral codes is hard-wired into humans. In our era of tolerance for diversity and cultural relativism, the issue has been extrapolated into whether one set of moral precepts has any more validity than another. In one of my political science classes, I asked the students to respond to whether they agreed or disagreed with a comment in one of their fellow student's research papers to the effect that, "in a free society, there are no rights and wrongs, only choices." To my surprise, two thirds or more of the 90+ students agreed. In seeking to be "open-minded" and "nonjudgmental," they were unwilling to imagine social restrictions on others, and by extension, responsibility for others.

While recent polls have indicated that most Americans call themselves religious and a large percentage attend church services at least monthly, the guardians of the First Amendment in the media, and the advocates of a strict separation of church and state, seem quick to denounce moral pronouncements by religious leaders they consider out of their perceived "mainstream" as reactionary, hypocritical or, at best, judgmental.[20] Media mogul and self-styled moral commentator, Ted Turner, in response to expressions of moral outrage about the Clinton-Lewinsky affair, declared several of the Ten Commandments to be out of date. Likewise, he took Pope John Paul II to task for his views on human sexuality and reproduction.[21] Such philosophizing—commonly more subtle than Turner's tirade—by the media leaders and other self-styled guardians of the culture, has helped lead to a denial of any broad range of accepted moral principles and norms. Media reports remind us that students are mowing down their classmates with automatic rifles, often for the "joy of it" and then taking their own lives. Mere differences in skin color, or ethnic heritage, or religious preferences have resulted in rioting, killing, arson, and almost unfathomable mayhem. Is it possible to imagine Americans living together in peace based upon a common sense of moral (rights and wrongs) principles? Is there any common set of applicable moral precepts which can be promulgated to bring harmony out of the cultural and philosophical cacophony of "values neutral" thinking abroad in the land today?[22]

In light of so many graphic images of human depravity being reported in the press, it would be tempting to believe that Thomas Hobbes was right, and what is needed is a Leviathan state, armed to the teeth to keep order so that the selfish and aggressive instincts of the human animal could be kept at bay. James Q. Wilson reminds the despairing reader in his book *The Moral Sense,* such savage events are news, precisely because, thankfully, they are anything but everyday occurrences.[23] There is clearly a more hopeful perspective from which presidents can take heart as they seek to invigorate the more social and gentle side of human nature.

Aristotle saw human beings as naturally social beings, while Thomas Aquinas, who sought to marry Aristotelian thinking with Christianity, contended that people are both social and familial. The moral law, to Aquinas, is an innately perceived expression of this tendency to think and act with social consequences for others in mind. Today's philosophers and worshippers of human individuality tend to gainsay these more traditional notions. James Q. Wilson went so far as to say of twentieth-century thinkers,

> Modern philosophy, with some exceptions, represents a fundamental break with tradition. For the last century . . . few of the great philosophical theories of human behavior have accorded much weight to the possibility that men and women are naturally endowed with anything remotely resembling a moral sense.[24]

There is, fortunately, a certain disconnect between the popular perceptions among the voters (college students notwithstanding) in the area of rights and wrongs (morality) and expressions of philosophers on these subjects. Ronald Reagan, for example, appreciated that there was a need, within the public, for the president to reaffirm the rectitude of our causes and values and celebrate them on every possible occasion.[25] Reagan seemed to sense that nineteenth-century rhetorical style could still resonate well into the twentieth century. Woodrow Wilson, as an historian writing about Abraham Lincoln, affirmed the view that the president gained his moral stature from his symbiotic relationship with the people. "A nation is led," Wilson wrote

> by a man who . . . speaks . . . a new principle for a new age . . . in whose ears the voices of the nation do not sound like the accidental or discordant voices from the mob, but concurrent and concordant, like the united voices of a chorus . . . whose many meanings unite in a single meaning and reveal to him a single vision . . . so he can speak what no man else knows, the common meaning of the common voice.[26]

Wilson's words about Lincoln still seem to fit in well a century-and-a-half later, but successful leaders must be able to identify the common language which ties the chorus together. Presidents who would succeed in using the inherent moral authority in the office, must keep the following principles in mind. First, they must take advantage of existing long-standing constitutional and moral principles as they shape the rhetoric of their communications with the public. Next, they must demonstrate—even in their personal lives—their commitment to principle, especially those principles that they are enunciating. Talking about the value of public education while sending one's children to private schools would hardly ennoble the call for enhancing free public education. Integrity, real or perceived, will be the bedrock of a president's moral authority to bring about needed changes based on traditional principles. Finally, to retain moral authority, presidents must retain credibility by recognizing the need to combine lofty purpose with understanding of concrete, down-to-earth realities. In other words, presidents in the future must be willing to present bold initiatives based in long standing principles of freedom and equality and the like, but must be careful not to give into the campaign temptation to promise more than they can produce.

A president's moral authority in the twenty-first century, as in centuries past, will depend upon his or her ability to demonstrate integrity, high-minded purpose, political savvy, and a commitment to restore and retain the public trust. Erwin Hargrove has cogently noted that the greatest potential resource for presidents, as they seek to lead a fragmented institutional world, is drawn on the biblical prophetic rhetoric and tradition that is part of the American political culture in order to connect their messages to the wellspring of American idealism.[27] The bully pulpit is still very much intact for those with the integrity, vision, and communication capacity to mount it with confidence and trust in the ultimate good will and good sense of the historic American political culture and the American people.

CHAPTER TEN

When Governments Are Good

BETTY GLAD

OLIN D. JOHNSTON PROFESSOR OF
GOVERNMENT AND INTERNATIONAL STUDIES
UNIVERSITY OF SOUTH CAROLINA

THE MORAL AUTHORITY of a government is rooted in its ability to meet the demands for justice and security of its people. This capacity, as Aristotle has noted, is dependent upon the existence of a constitution that is adapted to the social structures and values of its people, and the presence of statesmen at the helm who are both prudent and committed to the common good.[1] The United States has been fortunate in that we live in a mixed regime with a relatively large middle class—a constitutional form, Aristotle noted, most likely to be just and stable over the long run. Moreover, as I shall argue in this essay, at critical points in our history, we have been guided by statesmen who have helped us navigate safely through difficult situations. Without the wisdom and the restraint with which Presidents Dwight David Eisenhower and John Kennedy reacted to two major foreign policy crises, the United States could have stumbled into war with the USSR.

At the time of the Hungarian uprising in the fall of 1956, Eisenhower took the issue of the U.S. response off the National Security Council (NSC) agenda.[2] His decision, after discussing the situation with his brother and confidante, Milton, was not to intervene militarily. The President also rejected proposals to give less visible military support to the rebels in Hungary, refusing the CIA permission to air-drop supplies to the anti-Soviet forces.[3] When the Soviet Union entered Hungary to put down the rebellion, the President did back political and moral condemnations of the Soviet actions in the United Nations and other forums. But he never took these actions to such lengths that there would be an irrevocable break with that nation.

In making these decisions the president showed a nuanced appreciation of the particulars of the case at hand, an ability to put himself in the shoes of his adversary, and a concern for broader political values. There was little he could do to prevent the USSR from reincorporating Hungary into its empire, as Ann Whitman suggests in her diary entry of November 15.[4] Certainly Hungary was relatively inaccessible to any Western force, as Eisenhower noted in his discussion with his confidante, his brother Milton. Austria was a neutral country; Yugoslavia would not provide access to noncommunist forces; and the difficulties in going through Czechoslovakia would be just as great, maybe even greater.[5] Moreover, the Russians saw themselves as having a vital interest in the matter, as noted in a meeting with top advisers in Eisenhower's office on Monday, November 5. The Soviets, he noted, are concerned about losing hold over their satellite and might start a world war. "Those boys are both furious and scared. Just as with Hitler, that makes for the most dangerous possible state of mind."[6]

Eisenhower's ultimate policy choices, however, cannot be understood fully without a closer look at his deeper values. As his management of the D Day landing indicated, he was certainly not a pacifist, nor adverse to taking military risks when the circumstances so required.[7] But war, as he noted in his memoirs, is a very clumsy political instrument. That process "has produced notable victories and notable men, but in temporarily settling international quarrels, it has not guaranteed peace with right and justice. War is stupid, cruel, and costly."[8]

Moreover, he was a man who did not abstract himself from the fact that the premature death of anyone is a real tragedy. This is evident in the conversation he had with Walter Cronkite, twenty years after the D Day landings. As he looked upon those rows of crosses on Normandy Beach, he noted that on the very day the American, British, and other Allies stormed those beaches, his son graduated from West Point. Many thousands of these men died for the ideal of preserving freedom. But their deaths were still personal tragedies.

> Now, my own son has been very fortunate. He has had a very full life since then. But these young boys, many of them, whose graves we have been looking at, contemplating their sacrifices— they were cut off in their prime. They had families who grieved for them. But they never had the great experience of going through life like my son.[9]

In his decision in 1956 not to risk war over Hungary, Eisenhower also showed a certain courage and political finesse in dealing with potential domestic opponents of his policies. His choice required a reversal of the Republican policy of rolling back Soviet power in Eastern Europe, and was very disappointing to several key foreign policy decisionmakers in or close to his administration. The plans people in the CIA were very upset at this policy reversal. "This [support for the Hungarian uprising] was exactly the end for which the Agency's paramilitary capability was designed . . .," as William Colby, then a junior CIA officer, later noted.[10] Clare Booth Luce, Ambassador to Italy and the wife of the publisher of *Time* and *Life*, on November 19, 1956, met with the president to express her extreme concern over developments in Europe, suggesting the need for radical action.[11] C.D. Jackson, Henry Luce's associate and head of psychological warfare up to 1955, peppered administration officials with exhortations to keep the rollback orientation alive.[12] Indeed, the Committee for a Free Europe, a private group close to the government and led by Jackson and other former administration officials, had developed a full-scale plan envisaging the incorporation of liberated countries in Eastern Europe into a United Europe.[13]

The president's procedural choices, however, served to minimize the crystallization of these concerns within his administration. In taking the issue off the agenda of the NSC, the Joint Chiefs and other more hawkish members of the administration were not in a position to consolidate support for positions that Eisenhower would have to oppose.[14] Pressures within the United Nations to intervene in the affair actively were minimized, also, by the failure of the United States during the first week of the crisis to transfer the discussions of the matter in the United Nations from the Security Council, where the Russians had the veto, to the General Assembly, where a two-thirds vote could have put the United States in an awkward position. Eisenhower did not want to intervene in the affair, but it would have been difficult for the United States to oppose any proposals to provide direct military aide to the Hungarian freedom fighters at a time when it was not clear what the Soviet Union would do. But shortly after word of the Soviet attack reached New York on November 4, Ambassador Lodge brought a resolution before the Security Council calling for the withdrawal of all Soviet forces from Hungarian territory. When the measure was vetoed by the Soviet Union, it was moved to the General Assembly, where it passed the same day, by a vote of 50 to 9, with India, Indonesia, and certain representatives from other Asia or Arab nations abstaining.[15]

The president, in short, managed this crisis with prudence. He had the military knowledge and command experience that gave him the confidence to assess, on his own, what he would and could do in high risk situations, such as that presented in the fall of 1956. Where men less expert and less self-confident might have felt compelled to ask for the recommendation of the Joint Chiefs of Staff and the operations people in the CIA, he was able to anticipate that their advice would only complicate his decision making.[16] Moreover, he had the self-control and the political skill that enabled him to choose and stick to the peace-making option and to do it in a way that minimized the articulation of opposing positions within his own administration and the United Nations.

During the Cuban missile crisis, John Kennedy showed similar qualities of prudence. The situation, however, differed somewhat from the Hungarian uprising and called for different responses. The Soviet Union, whatever the complexity of its motives, by putting offensive missiles in Cuba was challenging the United States in its own traditional sphere of influence. In these circumstances John Kennedy knew that he had to apply some sort of pressure to the Soviet Union to bring about a reversal of that deployment. But he opted for a naval blockade as the least risky military option at his disposal. Moreover, at the end of the second week, when faced with a possible prolongation or possible escalation of the crisis, he provided a face-saving out for Khrushchev. Not only did he make a public commitment not to invade Cuba, he also agreed, secretly, to withdraw American missiles in Turkey in exchange for the Soviet withdrawal of their offensive missiles in Cuba.

In making these compromises, Kennedy showed the same kind of empathy for his adversary that Eisenhower had shown in 1956. As the transcript of the October 27 meeting of the Executive Committee of the National Security Council (EXComm) shows, John Kennedy pushed the point, more than any of his advisors, that the Soviet Union might insist on some sort of symmetrical trade as a condition of backing down.[17] He clearly understood the shame and humiliation Khrushchev might be feeling and the difficulties he would have had in making clearly unilateral concessions.

One can contrast Kennedy's capacity for empathy and a realistic concern about what the other side might do with Maxwell Taylor's disregard of such considerations. Some years after the Cuban missile crisis, Taylor reported that during the crisis he had experienced no fear of Soviet retaliation should the air strike have been carried out. If Khrushchev were rational, Taylor argued, Khrushchev would have looked up the escalation ladder and have seen that he had to back down. If he had not done so, his colleagues would "look after him."[18]

In making these decisions, moreover, Kennedy also showed political skill in navigating the issue through some difficult domestic waters.[19] Unlike Eisenhower, he sought the advice of his foreign advisers via the ExComm meetings that met throughout the two weeks of the crisis. Initially, these meetings were useful to him in flushing out the pros and cons of particular policy alternatives. Also, the free-ranging discussions, by allowing the members of the committee to ventilate their various views, would have them more likely to accept his ultimate policy choices. But over time, positions were articulated in that body that the president had to reject. Thus Kennedy vetoed the proposals of the Joint Chiefs of Staff, Paul Nitze, and others that the United States go beyond a quarantine to undertake a massive air strike against Cuba. The President even had to resist suggestions on October 27, the final and most difficult day of the crisis, that the United States should at least undertake one or more retaliatory air strikes for the shooting down of its United States U2 plane over Cuba. Moreover, his final pledge that the United States would not invade Cuba clearly distressed the Joint Chiefs—as well as John McCone, the head of the CIA. In his most controversial choice, however, the president employed techniques similar to those used by Eisenhower. The initial exploration of a possible missile trade was made in a small group of trusted advisers. The final offer was made without the ExComm even knowing about it and the deal was kept secret for some time thereafter.

There has been some debate about how close the United States was to a war with the USSR in either of these episodes. Those who suggest that war was not very likely overlook the impact of the choices Eisenhower and Kennedy made in reducing those risks. Hungary never ripened to a full-blown crisis the way that Cuba did for two reasons: The Soviet Union was operating within its own sphere of influence at the time, and Eisenhower did not take public positions from which the United States could not back down.

The confrontation during the Cuban missile crisis was much more dangerous. The Soviet Union and then the United States undertook major competing commitments, and one of them would have to back down if escalatory responses were not to occur and the crisis possibly spin out of control. Certainly, at the high point of the Cuban missile crisis, Kennedy had to face the ominous possibility that the Soviet Union had no intention of backing down on deployment of offensive missiles in Cuba. On October 27, the FBI reported that Soviets were burning papers in some of their embassies in likely preparation for war. American surveillance aircraft were fired upon in their flights over Cuba and a U2 plane was shot down by a SAM missile. Llewellen Thompson, the United States ambassador to the Soviet Union, interpreted the order to shoot down the U2 as a conscious decision made in Moscow to up the ante in its confrontation with the United States.[20] Kennedy would later recall that he thought the chances of war were one out of three. Those who say he overestimated that possibility overlook the extent to which his policies, based on those considerations of a real likelihood of war, made that war less likely.

As the foregoing suggests, the United States has been fortunate, not only in its form of government, but in the prudence exercised by at least two of its statesmen at critical points in its history. Both Eisenhower and Kennedy brought to the two crises discussed here, a knowledge of the relevant details, an awareness of the values that were at stake, the empathic judgment that enabled them to project themselves into the position of others, and the political savvy in the adoption of procedures that minimized opposition to their policy choices within their own camps. In serving the American people well, then, they contributed to their government as a source of moral authority.

CHAPTER ELEVEN

Eisenhower and the Moral Authority of Government

TRAVIS BEAL JACOBS

FLETCHER D. PROCTOR PROFESSOR OF HISTORY
MIDDLEBURY COLLEGE

GENERAL DWIGHT DAVID EISENHOWER, the conqueror of Nazi Germany and America's most popular WWII hero, accepted the presidency of Columbia University in 1947, and this forum in New York City provided him with an excellent opportunity to express his fervent belief in democratic citizenship. For him, herein lay the moral authority of government. Eisenhower's thoughts had evolved during the war, and he articulated them in a series of speeches as president of Columbia, before he was elected president of the United States. No other prominent public figure in mid-century America expressed such a passionate commitment to citizenship in a liberal democratic society, and Eisenhower did so more than any president of the United States since Woodrow Wilson, also a university president.

Historians and biographers have minimized or neglected the importance of these themes for Eisenhower. His World War II responsibilities as Commander of Allied Forces in Europe had contributed to the development of his passionate concern and given it focus. Throughout, GIs asked him, "General, what are we fighting for, anyway?" and he wrestled with the question. Shortly before the invasion of North Africa in 1942, he had emphasized that every GI must realize that, "His right to speak his own mind, to engage in any profession of his own choosing, to belong to any religious denomination, to live in any locality where he can support himself and his family, and to be sure of fair treatment when he might be accused of any crime—all of these would disappear if the Nazis win this war." During the war he came to understand that "we had seriously neglected the full education and preparation of our young people to be vigorous and productive members of society."[1]

The presidency of Columbia University offered Eisenhower, a colleague recalled, "a tremendous opportunity to get across to the youth of America what it all meant." It was his first civilian position; earlier, his interest in the training of youth had tempted him to accept an offer to head the Boy Scouts of America. He officially assumed his Columbia responsibilities four years and a day after D Day, and a reporter emphasized that his task "is again to lead young people to important objectives, [and] is but the peacetime extension of the job he began in Europe." As Columbia's Pulitzer Prize-winning historian, Allan Nevins, noted, "it is not strange that with this interest in youth and its training, General Eisenhower should have chosen education for the second part of his career." Eisenhower would recall that he had a chance at Columbia "to advance education in citizenship, to promote faith in the American way of life among its youth who will be the leaders of America in the near future."[2]

Shortly after his arrival on Morningside Heights he spoke at the Jewish Theological Seminary's 62nd Opening Convocation. Referring to the wartime's Axis dictators, he declared: "We believe that because men have each been born with a soul, they have inalienable rights and none can take them away . . . That belief came from the ancient Jewish leaders. They taught and gave their lives in this belief. . . . The true purpose of an educational institution," he asserted, "is to make certain that each of us is equipped to be a citizen in a democracy, and to perform his duties voluntarily."[3]

Eisenhower used his installation address at Columbia in October, 1948, to launch his crusade for democratic citizenship. Twenty thousand people, including dignitaries from the world's oldest universities, attended the colorful academic pageant. "The soldier who becomes an educator," he began, "finds himself . . . engaged in a new phase of his fundamental life purpose—the protection and the perpetuation of basic human freedoms." He continued, "Every institution built by free men, including great universities, must be first of all concerned with the preservation and further development of human freedom. . . . From the school at the crossroads to a university as great as Columbia, general education for citizenship must be the common and first purpose. The University," he specifically concluded, "will forever be bound by its loyalty to truth and the basic concepts of democratic freedom. From Columbia will come scholars, statesmen, skilled professionals, and great leaders in every area, but Columbia shall count it failure, whatever their success, if they are not all their lives a leaven of better citizenship."[4]

Eisenhower's emphasis on "those fundamentals that make our society free," received praise that evening from CBS's Edward R. Murrow, who reported that "those who believe in academic freedom have this day secured a very powerful ally." It was, one New York newspaper added, "a brilliant inaugural address before one of the greatest assemblages of world educators." Supreme Court Justice Felix Frankfurter wrote to the General: "how can I avoid applauding when the head of a great university proposes to save this democracy through candid and truthful education."[5]

Eisenhower's speeches as Columbia's president, and the themes he emphasized, would receive widespread media attention; and this publicity became even more extensive after the 1948 election, when he was increasingly seen as a potential candidate for the presidency. He had viewed his task at Columbia as educating better citizens. "I accepted . . . in the belief I could do more than anywhere else to further the cause to which I am devoted, the reawakening of intense interest in the basis of the American system." His title for a major speech was "The Individual's Responsibility for Government." For Eisenhower "the one underlying principle . . . binding on every American" was "that every citizen is required to do his duty for country no matter what it may be."[6]

On Lincoln's Birthday, 1949, his comments to secondary school student leaders at Columbia College's First Forum on Democracy prompted a history professor to conclude, "I was listening to the best extemporaneous speaker I had ever heard."[7] It is not surprising that Eisenhower, with these interests, was far more at home with undergraduates and the training of students by Columbia's Teachers College. He came to realize that the majority of the university's faculty emphasized the goals of scholarship and the pursuit of knowledge and had little interest in "general education for citizenship." Eisenhower, consequently, increasingly focused his efforts on promoting new vehicles for his crusade at Columbia.

He specifically articulated his vision for Columbia in the inaugural Gabriel Silver Lecture on Peace in 1950, and the speech received front-page newspaper coverage. The University's purpose in furthering "the cause of peace" "can be epitomized in one phrase—the good of humanity." He proposed a Chair for

Peace "to study war as a tragic social phenomenon. . . . the most malignant cancer of the world body—war," and this would lead to the creation of the Institute of War and Peace. He declared that the emerging Conservation of Human Resources Project "will be of immeasurable benefit to all the world in furthering the dignity of man as human being," and the project would produce a series of significant publications. He proposed, in what would become the American Assembly, "to conduct an exhaustive study into the ways and means of applying to every man's good, in today's intricate economy, *all* the resources of America, in such way as to maintain and enlarge every freedom that the individual has enjoyed under our system." These projects, he concluded, would help Columbia "a little better to fulfill its purpose—the peace, freedom and good of America, and, therefore, of humanity."[8] He knew that these programs would take time, effort, and money, and he was ready to accept the challenge; meanwhile, he saw a law grant from the Carnegie Corporation for the Citizenship Education Program at Teachers College as an important step for his commitment to democratic citizenship.

During 1950 he devoted more and more of his time to his assembly proposal, his "vision of a great cultural center where business, professional, and governmental leaders could meet from time to time to discuss and reach conclusions concerning problems of a social and political nature." Democratic citizenship, and one's duty as an individual, would be at work at these conferences. He had seen, moreover, on the Columbia faculty "an immense pool of talent, scholarly and humane in its comprehension of human needs and aspirations, above the bias of sect and party." Columbia, he believed, was "ideally suited to pioneer methods by which our educational institutions may be useful to our country." He stated: "The failure of most of us to remember that the basic values of democracy were won only through sacrifice and to recognize the *dangers of indifference and ignorance*," and he emphasized "that democracy could be destroyed by creeping paralysis within."[9]

The outbreak of the Korean War in June, 1950, made it "even more important . . . that a greater effort be made to study these problems, and he asserted that the American Assembly concept "is action, not just words."[10] He appealed to his friends for funds for his "convocation" project, and he energetically traveled throughout the country during the academic year to raise money.

Eisenhower's conviction, determination, and enthusiasm produced results, and he announced the American Assembly—his "most important step" at Columbia—in October, 1950, just before President Truman asked him to return to active duty as Commander of NATO forces in Europe. The intervention by the Chinese Communists in the Korean War that fall and the disastrous American casualties, made it for him "more imperative than ever before to push the plan"; "the Korean debacle," indeed, showed "the additional problems it posed upon us as citizens." The first American Assembly conference would be held the following spring and was, according to a prominent participant, a "1951 version of the old-fashioned town meeting."[11] Eisenhower saw the Assembly as democratic citizenship in action, and it has had a long and successful history.

Eisenhower's active period at Columbia came to an end when he accepted the NATO assignment and took a leave of absence in early 1951. The American Assembly and the Conservation of Human Resources were established; however, his emphasis on "general education for citizenship" and his traveling and fundraising for the American Assembly, as well as his association with wealthy businessmen, led to a growing estrangement with the University community. While he was seen as having been away too much and his speeches and fundraising, in the highly charged political atmosphere of postwar America, had sounded increasingly conservative to the academic community, he saw his proposals as enhancing Columbia's role in society.

General Eisenhower returned to the United States in June, 1952, to seek the Republican Party nomination for president. His valuable support from "Citizens for Eisenhower," a group of prominent friends he had met in New York, and from influential supporters of the American Assembly throughout the country contributed, as did his enormous popularity, to his success at the Republican Convention and his election. The Columbia experience had given him an opportunity to express his convictions and had helped to prepare him for the White House.

The demands and constraints he faced as President, from the Cold War and national security requirements to partisan politics, limited his opportunity to pursue goals similar to those he had at Columbia. Nonetheless, in the nuclear world of the 1950s, he quickly obtained an armistice in the Korean War, and he "waged peace" for eight years. Echoes from Columbia could be heard in proposals ranging from his Atoms-for-Peace Plan to his educational exchanges and people-to-people program. And in his "Farewell Address" in January, 1961—"The Military-Industrial Complex" speech—he emphasized the theme he long had considered essential for a democratic society, the need for "an alert and knowledgeable citizenry."[12]

CHAPTER TWELVE

The Authority of Presidents: Personal Morality and Political Effectiveness

DONALD L. ROBINSON

CHARLES N. CLARK PROFESSOR OF GOVERNMENT
SMITH COLLEGE

IS IT IMPORTANT for a political leader to be morally good?

This question has lately forced itself on our attention, owing to the travails (for him and for us all) attendant upon President Bill Clinton's tawdry affair with a White House intern and his months-long effort to hide it by lying. Despite his high approval rating throughout the crisis, reaching a loud crescendo as the impeachment trial came to a close, the affair sapped Clinton's ability to lead effectively. At the very least, the exposure of his flagrant breeches of conventional morality led to distractions that kept him from attending to public business and prevented him from gaining any traction for the program of his administration.

Several questions follow from this episode. What is the relation between personal morality and effectiveness as a political leader? Is personal goodness essential to effective leadership? Do immoral acts invariably undermine a political leader?

American culture provides a particular context for exploring these questions. In that context, we need not probe moral questions to their theoretical depths. We do not need to ask how we know whether certain acts are good, and others evil. For purposes of this analysis, we can accept the moral conventions of a given society, in this case, the American.

We do need to notice that American culture is diverse. Acts deemed immoral in North Carolina—homosexual commitment, for example—are affirmed as positive acts of loyalty and welcome evidence of diversity in many New England communities. Sometimes cultural differences across America become occasions for harsh inter-regional and inter-group conflict. This was evident in the reaction to Clinton's behavior. Many feminists tended to adopt a forgiving attitude toward a leader who had been a champion of their causes, a stance that opened them to ridicule from the right. Meanwhile, the censorious attitude of the House Republican leadership seemed self-righteous from the perspective of prevailing public opinion.

Despite these important nuances, however, politicians in America do operate in the context of a moral consensus. It is broadly tolerant, but within limits that sometimes strike foreign observers (Europeans, for example) as almost puritanical. At any rate, American politicians have a pretty good sense of what the public will tolerate, even when their personal behavior steps over the limits.

Let us begin with an important distinction. At least since St. Augustine drew his famous distinction between the City of God and the City of Man, writers in the Western tradition have wrestled with the idea that those who govern operate according to moral standards that are somehow different from those that regulate other human behavior. Earthly cities are full of evil people. Those in political power must take this fact into account. In dealing with people in our private lives, we may choose to act benevolently, as if in anticipation of God's heavenly kingdom. We may be willing to sacrifice ourselves, to forgive readily, to speak with candor. We may turn the other cheek, share our wardrobe and larder, walk the extra mile. But the Head of State (a president, prime minister, or governor) cannot be so generous. The resources at her disposal do not belong to her personally. The consequences of generous behavior that is abused by the recipient must be borne by everyone. So she must be cunning and calculating, and often she must be hard.

Machiavelli was a tutor to those in power. He taught that princes might find it useful to *seem* good, but they must remember that the end of "saving the state" not only justified, it often required, means not sanctioned by conventional morality. Max Weber took a similar line, arguing that those who adopt "politics as a vocation" must avoid sentimentality. They must calculate the likely consequences of their acts, for they are responsible for outcomes in an uncertain and often hostile environment. To act in accordance with the beatitudes of Jesus in matters of state was not virtuous, but self-indulgent and irresponsible.

Reinhold Niebuhr was the great American thinker in this tradition of realism. [In writing these words, I am reminded of Nie-

buhr's reminder that realism is not a philosophy; it is a boast.]
Moral men exist in an immoral society. In arguing that isolationist America must confront the evils of German fascism (and later
Soviet Communism), Niebuhr insisted that our leaders must be
no less cunning and crafty than the "children of darkness," lest
they permit great suffering.

To lump St. Augustine with Machiavelli, Weber with Niebuhr,
ignores crucial differences in their teachings. Niebuhr, for example, wrote scathingly of the "easy conscience of modern man." He
would have been critical of behavior that a Machiavellian sensibility might easily condone. Nevertheless, there is a common thread
in their teaching. Realists teach that governing involves a moral
calculus different from that of other human behavior.

Even from the perspective of the Augustinian tradition, however, retaining the popular mandate in American politics
requires respect for moral values, particularly the rule of law and
the constitutional tradition of human rights. Perhaps this is the
American version of Machiavelli's injunction that a leader must
be careful to *seem* good. An American president cannot survive if
he seems contemptuous of values rooted in the Western ethical
tradition. Theodore White's book, *Breach of Faith* (New York: Atheneum, 1975), traces the collapse of Richard Nixon's presidency
to his lack of respect for the rule of law and for those with whom
he shared power in the American system. In this connection, one
recalls attorney Joseph Welch's scathing dismissal of Senator Joe
McCarthy: "Sir, have you no decency?" Also, the price paid by
Lyndon Johnson, when his administration bogged down under a
"credibility gap" for repeatedly lying about the war in Vietnam.

In a democracy, no leader can ignore the claims of conventional morality. To govern, a person must first get elected. In
office, his opportunities and power are affected by people's
assessment of his character. Richard Neustadt identified and distinguished two layers of opinion with which a president must contend. Government insiders—politicans in the Cabinet and on
Capitol Hill, bureaucrats, journalists, lobbyists and others—make
and daily remake, an estimate of his abilities. At the same time,
the wider public is assessing his performance, relying partly on
the media, but reacting independently of that, too, as shown by
insiders' astonishment at public reaction to Clinton's affair.
These two responses interact, and they form the basis of a president's power—which thus varies, from day to day.

To understand the relationship between effectiveness and morality, it may be useful to offer a rough sorting of recent presidents (since mid-century, beginning with Truman) along a spectrum from highly effective to relatively ineffective. Such a sorting is subjective and rough but not impossible. It would go something like this:

Highly effective ————————————— Relatively ineffective
   Truman
        Eisenhower
               Kennedy
       Johnson
               Nixon
                           Ford
                           Carter
 Reagan
             Bush
             Clinton

The *presidents* are men who had reputations for personal probity. No person is perfect, and certainly few persons in high office, carefully scrutinized as they are, emerge with unblemished records of personal behavior. But the five men here identified as notably good men did win reputations for honesty and decency.

Note that the names in italics range across the spectrum of effectiveness. Harry Truman's achievements have been burnished by sympathetic biographers over time, but they do seem solid and substantial in retrospect. One can quarrel about Dwight Eisenhower and George Bush. The reputation of the latter, particularly, has not settled. But they probably belong somewhere in the middle of this spectrum. As for Gerald Ford and Jimmy Carter, fate was cruel, but for Carter, especially, there was great frustration in high office.

The men whose names are in **bold** were undermined in office by reputations for personal immorality. Kennedy's presidency was spectacular, but unfulfilled. Reagan, for better or for worse (too early to tell), initiated a new order. In terms of personal behavior, Kennedy operated on a plane where conventional morality was pretty much irrelevant. Reagan seemed to be playing a part, and questions about his behavior behind the façade never penetrated very deeply.

Perhaps the two most interesting cases, from the standpoint

of the interaction of personal morality and public performance, are Nixon and Clinton. Both are regarded as extraordinarily able men, intelligent, experienced, determined, with a keen eye out for their places in history.

They have one additional factor in common: they governed at a time of divided government. American politicians must be adept at navigating our unique system of separated powers and divided politics. Not many of them can boast of great achievements, but most of them survive politically, and so has the system, so far. Nevertheless, it is undeniable that a division of partisan control does greatly complicate the task of governance.

Opposition Democrats controlled Congress throughout Nixon's time of office; and, after the congressional elections of 1994, Clinton faced Republican majorities in both houses for his six remaining years in office. These systemic facts contributed greatly to the difficulties of their tenure. In both cases, the presidents behaved badly, opening themselves and their governments to crippling attacks by partisan opponents. Divided government does not always lead to paralysis, as the achievements of Truman, Eisenhower, Reagan, and Bush demonstrate. Nevertheless, in the cases of Nixon and Clinton, behaving in ways offensive to conventional standards allowed their partisan enemies to cripple the federal government for extended periods in the process.

What is most striking about the graphic, however, is the apparent lack of correlation between personal goodness and political effectiveness. There are good men at both ends of the spectrum of effectiveness. And men whose personal behavior was most offensive to conventional standards end up in the middle of the spectrum of effectiveness. Johnson lied his way into the war in Vietnam and saw his government sink into a quagmire there, but he also helped to make historic inroads on the ancient problems of poverty, racial division, and environmental abuse. Nixon's presidency collapsed under the weight of egregious criminal offenses known collectively as Watergate, but he made a diplomatic breakthrough to China, encouraged innovation in domestic policy, and helped his party to secure a footing in the South, among other lasting achievements.

Clinton is the other case of a president whose moral offenses prevented a realization of potential greatness. Clinton's opportunities were checked by several factors. As Steven Skowronek has emphasized, a President's chance for innovative leadership is heavily conditioned by his place in "political time."

- If he approaches office when an old political order is collapsing (as Andrew Jackson, Abraham Lincoln, and Franklin Roosevelt did), he may have an opportunity to initiate a new order.
- If he governs at a time when an old political order is exhausted, but a new order is not yet ready to form (as Franklin Pierce and Calvin Coolidge did), he may experience impotence in office from which there is no escape.
- If, on the other hand, he comes to office when an established order is still resilient, winning most elections at other levels of the system, but divisions in the prevailing condition prevent a true representative of that order from winning the presidency (as Grover Cleveland, Woodrow Wilson, Eisenhower, and Nixon did), he may survive politically, despite his minority position, and even win re-election (as these four all did), but his time in office is likely to be difficult and frustrating.

Clearly these latter conditions prevailed when Clinton came to power. Clefts in the Reagan coalition had encouraged challenges to Bush's renomination (the man who dared critics to read his lips had raised taxes), but Democrats were in no position to reassemble the New Deal coalition (the bedrock of that grouping, the Deep South, was shattered forever), nor were they ready to put together a *new* formula for long-term governance. Reaganism was still regnant. Republicans controlled most state houses and state legislatures, and soon they would gain control of both houses of Congress.

In these politically parlous circumstances, Clinton came to power. He stumbled badly in assembling his cabinet and on gays in the military. Then he raised taxes, laying the foundation for long-term prosperity, but irritating many constituencies in the process. ("In American politics," as Robert Reischauer, head of the Congressional Budget Office at the time, observed, "no good deed goes unpunished.") And his major attempt at policy innovation, Hillary Rodham Clinton's health-care reform package, collapsed ignominiously. The result was a crushing defeat for Democrats in the Congressional elections of 1994, allowing Republicans to take control of Congress and setting the stage for a debilitating, bitterly partisan struggle over his Whitewater investment, Paula Jones, the White House Travel Office, the FBI files, Monica Lewinsky, Katherine Willey, and all the rest of it.

What are the lessons taught by the careers of Nixon and Clinton?

Conventional morality sets bounds on the behavior of American presidents. When they transgress these limits, as Nixon and Clinton did, leaders pay a high price in the loss of power at their disposal. Nixon, almost incredibly, even in retrospect, was forced to resign. Clinton has clung to office, but his party and his country would probably have been better served if he had resigned in disgrace during the summer of 1998. (In a parliamentary system, lying to his Cabinet, to the leaders of his party, and to the nation would almost certainly have required him to resign.) Clinton has apparently made good his boast to finish his term in office, but his opportunities for achievement have been severely diminished by his flagrant, contemptuous disregard for conventional morality.

Beyond the steep price paid for gross violations of conventional morality, what can we say of the relationship between personal morals and political achievement? Remarkably little. The qualities most important for a political leader seem to have little to do with conventional morality. (Permit me here, as a professor at a great college for women, to shift to feminine pronouns as I address future possibilities.) To achieve greatness, a president of the future must have a strategic vision, a sense of history, and keen awareness of the dangers and possibilities of her moment in political time. She must be firm in purpose, courageous and tenacious in the face of adversity. She will need great energy. Skill in the small arts of political dealing (what President Carter so conspicuously lacked) will be useful. She will need a certain detachment, an ability to rid herself, brutally if necessary, of troublesome cronies. (Personal loyalty is often a dangerous indulgence for a political leader.) She will also need prudence and magnanimity, Lincoln's great virtues—prudence, to tailor high goals to practical realities, and magnanimity, to be forgiving and generous-spirited toward defeated foes.

That she should also be a devoted spouse and faithful mother, not drink excessively, not use vulgar language, and not cheat—these virtues would be nice. But they will not determine her effectiveness in high office.

THE RULE OF LAW

Moral Authority and the Rule of Law

MOORHEAD KENNEDY

CHAIRMAN
MOORHEAD KENNEDY GROUP

FROM MORAL AUTHORITY exercised by a leader, we move to its exercise through the Rule of Law.

The essays in this section flow in a continuum, from the general to the particular. The opening essay sets the stage, the philosophic basis for the rule of law. The next three develop important questions suggested by the first. One discusses ways in which the term "rule of law" can be used (and abused) for a variety of ends, another the value of civil disobedience as a corrective to unjust laws. A third views with alarm the state of mutual trust upon which the rule of law depends. Two essays next explore the origin and meaning of the word "government." A final, very specific group of three essays discuss how the content of legislation and regulation is communicated to the citizenry, the moral authority of the Supreme Court, and how moral authority is exercised through one important body of legislation.

Dr. Judith A. Best, Distinguished Teaching Professor, SUNY Cortland, begins the opening essay with Alexander M. Bickel's assertion that law is "the value of values . . . the principal institution through which a society can assert its values." She observes that preserving the Union, to Abraham Lincoln, meant preserving the constitution and the laws. This, Lincoln urged, was akin to a "political religion," the shared idea about justice that constituted and animated a country.

The basis for the moral authority of government is therefore ruling for the good of the ruled, not the ruler. Hence, the rule of law must be based on consent, which becomes the source of its moral authority. But, moral authority must have a purpose, which is individual liberty.

To exercise moral authority effectively, it must be achieved. Moral governments must act to achieve moral purpose. Dr. Best moves on to the morality of legal process, which implies limits on what government—even if the majority may want it—can and cannot do. Hence, there is a higher law that cannot be altered by legislatures.

Law must also be a general rule, binding both the ruler and the ruled. Like cases must be decided alike. All citizens must be treated equally. Laws must also be freely obeyed. Therefore they must be understood and hence promulgated. Promulgation not only of laws, but also of administrative decisions, is a primary means by which citizens can hold government responsible for its actions.

Since citizens need to know the reason why they should obey the laws, explanation of the laws is the "ultimate test of leadership." Here she relates this section of these essays to the preceding one, and not only on the presidential level. "The laws," she says, "are no better than the men who make and enforce them. . . . The most distinguished mark" of George Washington's presidency "was his insistence that all in government, including himself, abide by the rule of law."

Dr. Best concludes that while we cannot always choose Washingtons and Lincolns to govern us, we should at least find the "decent, trustworthy, law-abiding" as our leaders. Hence, the people must be the guardians of those who are chosen to be their guardians. "Ultimately, the moral authority of the government rests on the character and vigilance of the people."

As Lincoln likened the rule of law to a political religion, so Michael Kahn, Esq., in his essay, "The Rule of Law at the Millennium," believes that the "dominant political theology of our time is a profound faith in and devotion to the moral and economic value of the rule of law." In contrast to the high moral principles set forth by Dr. Best, Kahn points out how the concept of the rule of law justifies less lofty objectives as well.

Mr. Kahn uses several examples, chief of which is the impeachment and Senate trial of President Clinton. He describes the episode as a "modern comic opera played to the tune of the rule of law. . . . a public which believed their Chief Magistrate a liar and a cheat . . . also believed that he should remain in office because his offenses . . . did not meet the legal test for removal."

According to Kahn, this has demonstrated an unshakable faith in the rule of law on the part of the American public.

In her essay, "Civil Disobedience, the Rule of Law, and the Moral Authority of Government," Dr. Marie D. Natoli, Professor of Political Science, Emmanuel College, Boston explores the role of civil disobedience. She defines the rule of law in terms of "its justness, which may itself be contradicted by a particular law." When other forms of redress are not effective, civil disobedience is not only compatible with the rule of law but necessary to it.

Dr. Natoli posits a list of criteria to determine when civil disobedience is justified. Like Dr. Best, she argues that a law is just only when it binds everyone, including those who have made it. Similarly, as Martin Luther King noted, "a law is unjust if it is inflicted on a minority that, as a result of being denied the right to vote, had no part in enacting (it)." And similarly with how it is applied.

Those who practice civil disobedience must be prepared to accept the penalty. She adds that "deviation from any of these conditions denies to the protestors the status of civil disobedient." Dr. Natoli assumes that enough citizens still care enough about the rule of law to risk the penalties of civil disobedience.

In his essay, "Constitutional Authority and Public Morality," Dr. Robert E. Denton, Jr., W. Thomas Rice Chair of Leadership Studies, Virginia Polytechnic Institute, expresses a different view. The moral authority of government derives from the collective beliefs, attitudes, and values of the citizens. The current climate is one of distrust and general public cynicism.

Dr. Denton allows a kind of "wary skepticism" on the part of citizens as a way of limiting government and preventing it from becoming too powerful. There is, however, a world of difference between that, and the intensification of public distrust in many basic American institutions.

Two essayists explore the sources of government and law. Foreshadowing the section of this book that deals with nongovernmental organizations, Dr. C. Lowell Harriss, Professor Emeritus of Economics, Columbia University, points out that, "Bishops govern. So do umpires and teachers and those who decree this year's clothing fashions." Authority thus comes from many sources, with voluntary adherence playing a role, and also a sense that the authority is proper, or "right."

Dr. Harriss explores sources of governmental authority. Respect for the ruler, even when the current holder of the presidency misbehaves, may reflect some visceral feeling about the divinity of kings. Authority has been gained through heredity, through victory on the field of battle, pomp and ceremony. Whatever its origins, government cannot be separated from the human beings running it. He believes that the "quality of personal character" on the part of the leader affects the willingness of the led to follow.

Dr. Francis Heller, Distinguished Professor Emeritus of Law and Political Science, University of Kansas, begins his essay, "The Concept of "Government: Historical and Comparative Observations," by pointing out how little agreement there is on what is "government." Like Dr. Harriss, he traces the varied sources of governmental authority. He concludes by urging a greater "recognition of differences about the concept of government."

A final group of essayists explore specific problem areas. Dr. Harold C. Relyea, a Specialist in American National Government with the Congressional Research Service of the Library of Congress, traces the history of "transparency and accountability" introduced by Dr. Best.

Dr. Relyea believes that promulgation is at the heart of accountability, and therefore of the moral authority of government. "Upon first convening in 1789, Congress enacted a series of laws providing for the printing and distribution of both statutes and treaties, the preservation of state papers, and the maintenance of official files in the new departments."

Dr. Relyea traces the antecedents of the present *Congressional Record* and the Superintendent of Public Documents. He observes how promulgation did not keep up with the increasing activity of government, resulting in the 1930s in the *Federal Register*, the *Code of Federal Regulations*, and the later Freedom of Information Act.

Samuel Leiter, Esq. and William Leiter, Professor of Political Science, California State University, in an essay subtitled "The Supreme Court and Affirmative Action," examine the moral quality of the Supreme Court's judicial review. Supreme Court review, they argue, have been "pockmarked by long periods of issue-avoidance; muffled cloudy opinions; sluggish advancing and retreating."

Affirmative action, the authors contend, has shown the Court to be at its morally least authoritative. They do present another side, quoting an historian of the Court. "The Court's greatest successes have been achieved when it has operated near the margins rather than at the center of political controversy, when it has nudged and gently tugged the nation, instead of trying to rule . . ."

In the essay that concludes this section, "Antitrust: A Codification of American Morality," Dr. Theodore P. Kovaleff, former Assistant Dean at Columbia University School of Law, gives specific examples from colonial days, through the Sherman and Clayton Acts, two World Wars, presidential changes, and today's era of deregulation. "The antitrust corpus," he points out, "is characterized by the embodiment of fair play, protection for the weaker and unprotected, and the goal of the welfare of the consumer." He thereby argues the case that in many ways, it is the best example of morality in the United States' legal system.

The Rule of Law

JUDITH A. BEST

DISTINGUISHED TEACHING PROFESSOR
STATE UNIVERSITY OF NEW YORK COLLEGE AT CORTLAND

> *The irreducible value though not the exclusive one, is the idea of law.*
> *Law is more than just another opinion, not because it embodies all*
> *the right values, or because the values it does embody tend from time*
> *to reflect those of a majority or plurality, but because it is the value of*
> *values. Law is the principal institution through which a society can*
> *assert its values.*
>
> ALEXANDER M. BICKEL
> "Notes on the Constitution"

THE RULE OF LAW directed toward individual liberty is the basis for the moral authority of the government of the United States. No one has ever understood this more clearly than Abraham Lincoln who used one word to describe the moral means and the moral end—UNION. It was he who pointed out that the wrong of slavery and the wrong of rebellion were in point of principle the same thing. If you will the end, a UNION dedicated to human liberty, you will the means, the rule of law—constitutional government. Wherever the rule of law ends, there tyranny begins.

The Civil War was not fought to free the slaves. It was fought to preserve the UNION. It was Lincoln's intention and it was his accomplishment to free *all* Americans, white and black, from the curse of slavery. It was Lincoln who argued that support for the Constitution and the rule of law should "become the *political religion* of the nation." It was Lincoln who declared that "the pillars of the temple of liberty" are formed from a reverence for the Constitution and the laws.[1]

Aristotle, the first political scientist, set down the bottom line on the moral authority of government: ruling, as it is properly done, is for the good of the ruled, not for the good of the rulers. Simply, the governors are the servants of the people. But what is the "good" of the ruled? Government is about giving rules and obeying then. Logic tells us that every rule and measure must be appropriate to the thing ruled and measured. Thus we measure speed in terms of time and distance, not in terms of volume or mass, and can say one man runs 100 yards in ten seconds and another in fifteen. Laws are rules for men, and thus the answer to the question must turn on the nature of man.

There have been many and varied definitions of the nature of man. The definition of the modern Western democracies, but most especially of the American government, is that men, as rational creatures, are born free, and equal in natural rights. There is no natural title to rule. The right to rule is not given to anyone, not to the virtuous, or the powerful, or the compassionate, or the pious, or even the wise. Nor has God sent his anointed minister to rule us here on earth. We are *born* free.

If men are rational creatures, they are self-governing, and the rule of law for man must be based on consent. This means that the old command idea—Do it because I say so—is *immoral* except for the immature (children), the patently defective (the insane), and the undeveloped (morons). The rule of law must be backed by reason, not merely by force. The consent of the people is *the source of law's moral authority.*

But mere consent can be dedicated to many different goals: to piety; to empire; to wealth; to safety; to glory; to virtue. Here again the American choice is based on a definition of man as a creature who is born free and independent. *The moral purpose of government*, as proclaimed in the Declaration of Independence, is individual liberty. Speaking of the immigrants who came after the founding period, Lincoln said, "it is the electric cord in that Declaration that links the hearts of patriotic and liberty-loving men together." He said the principle of the Declaration "is the father of all moral principle in them."[2] It is the core of our "political religion." It asserts our moral cultural horizon. To be viable, a country must have an internal unity; "a house divided against itself cannot stand." There can be no division on the moral aspiration of a people. Because he understood this, Lincoln said the nation could not indefinitely exist "half slave and half free."[3]

Again it was Lincoln who drew the connection between the Declaration and the Constitution in his first inaugural address. Having declared that, "the Union is much older than the Constitution," he points out that "in 1787, one of the declared objects for ordaining and establishing the Constitution, was 'to form a more perfect union'." Why was Lincoln categorically opposed to the repeal of the Missouri Compromise; categorically opposed to Stephen Douglas's proposal for popular sovereignty, the proposal to allow the inhabitants of a territory to decide for themselves if they would enter the Union as free or slave states? Because this would mean the repeal of the Declaration of Independence, of the matured goal that unites the people, and the abandonment of the Constitution created as the effective means to pursue and fulfill that goal. The connection between the Constitution and the Declaration is also stated in the last article, Article VII, which ends with the words: "Done in Convention by the Unanimous Consent of the States present the Seventeenth Day of September in the Year of our Lord one thousand seven hundred and eighty seven *and of the Independence of the United States of America the Twelfth.*" (emphasis added) The nation was founded in 1776, not in 1787. The Declaration states our principle of justice, the shared idea about justice that constitutes and animates a country. If you change this principle then you dissolve the UNION because the UNION is a moral association of men who, on that basis, constitute themselves a people.

Here Lincoln is clearly following Aristotle who, in the *Politics*, asks: what is it that animates a country, what is it that creates its identity? It cannot be the land because residence on the land does not make one a citizen, and because, if one looks at history, different countries have existed on the same land through time. Where are the Trojans now? Yet the land is still there. It cannot be any particular group of citizens; it cannot be the men themselves because the men who make up a country are always changing because of birth and death. Aristotle answers: what animates a country is its small "c" constitution, its shared principle of justice. This is the soul of a country, and if you change that fundamental moral principle, you have a fundamentally different country.

Alexander Hamilton Stephens, the vice president of the Confederate States, also knew, as Lincoln knew, that the principles of the Declaration are embodied in the Constitution, and he says it is precisely for that reason that the Southern states seceded.

> The prevailing ideas entertained by (Jefferson) and most of the leading statesmen of the time of the formation of the old Constitution, were that the enslavement of the African was in violation of the laws of nature; that it was wrong in principle, socially, mor-

ally, and politically. . . . These ideas, however, were fundamentally wrong. Our new government is founded upon exactly the opposite idea.[4]

Lincoln believed that our UNION was the last, best hope of the earth. Its principle was morally sound, but not yet achieved. It was an experiment still underway, an unfinished work. But he also understood that while good aspirations are necessary, they are not a sufficient base for moral authority. Moral governments must act to achieve their goals. It is not enough to mean well, governments must do well. There is something truly pathetic about meaning well without doing well. Objects of pity are not respected, and to have moral authority, governments must have respect. Good intentions do not create moral authority. Moral authority arises from achievement. People must be proud of their government; only the perverse take pride in failure.

As he saw them, the principles of the Declaration are more than a justification of a colonial rebellion, more than noble sentiments; they are a commitment to united action toward our common goal. They are a standard "constantly looked to, constantly labored for, and even though never perfectly attained, constantly approximated, and thereby constantly spreading and deepening its influence, and augmenting the happiness and value of life to all people of all colors, everywhere."[5]

In addition to a morality of source and of purpose, there is *a morality of legal process* for free men equal in natural rights. This means several things. First it means that government must be constitutional and thus limited. It means that there are some things that neither the government nor the majority have the authority to do. These things must be forbidden in a contract, a higher law that cannot be changed by ordinary Legislatures. It means the legal limitations on freedom should be the minimum needed for the protection of society and for the achievement of its fundamental declared moral principles—in our case, the protection of the natural rights of men.

Second, it means that since law is a general rule, it must apply to all, binding both the rulers and the ruled. No one, private citizen or governing official, may substitute his personal judgment for the law. The common sense base of this is found in two old truisms: a man will not make a rod to beat himself; and those who wear the shoes know where they pinch. If the law-givers must obey the laws, they will personally feel the rod, and personally know where the shoes pinch and thus will be less likely to oppress or impose excessive burdens on the people. But there is a more basic intuition of justice involved here, one that even young children recognize: like cases must be decided alike. Fundamental fairness in a free society means the law must not favor individuals or classes; it means equal treatment of all under law.

Third, the laws must be promulgated not only so that people can obey them, but more fundamentally so that they will freely obey them. The people's willing obedience arises from an understanding that the law is good in some way—that it is useful, advantageous to them collectively as well as individually. To really understand the rule of law for a free creature one must look at it from the perspective of good men and, not as Justice Holmes suggested, from the perspective of bad ones. The bad men, the men Lincoln calls "the lawless in spirit," care only for the sanction; all they want to know is: what is the punishment for disobedience and is it likely to be imposed? The good men, the men who, Lincoln says, "love tranquility, who desire to abide by the laws and enjoy their benefits," want to know the reasons for the law. Sometimes, the reasons are self-evident. If you ask people why they obey seat belt laws, or drunk driving laws, they will tell you such laws are beneficial to them and to others. If there were not such laws, they would demand them. Sometimes, the reasons are self-evident, and here we find the ultimate test of leadership in a free society. The leaders must provide convincing explanations or good men will not obey them.

But publishing the laws has another fundamental benefit, it allows us to test official governmental actions against declared rules. This is essential to prevent the arbitrary and oppressive uses of governmental authority. The government of free men must be limited by law, and this means that the governing officials must be held accountable for their violations of the laws. The referees must also be bound by the rules of the game. The rule of law is more important than any single law, and this means that the morality of legal process must be respected by the magistrates who enforce the laws. A free people have no king but the law.

Water does not rise higher than its source. In practice, the laws can be no better than the men who make them and enforce them. Thus the character of our chosen representatives matters. We must look for and choose as our leaders men who are courageous, moderate, prudent and just. And this must be the reality and not just the spin. This is not an impossible dream. We have had at least two presidents who fully fit the description: Washington and Lincoln. Washington, whose life work was to build a reputation for honesty, reliability, and integrity was the most trusted man of his time because of his demonstrated reluctance to accept power, his demonstrated willingness to relinquish power, and his dedication to the rule of law. As a field commander, his courage was legendary; as president, his prudence was remarkable—especially in keeping the country out of the European wars of the time, wars that would likely have destroyed a developing, infant nation. The most distinguished mark of his presidency was his insistence that all in government, including himself, abide by the rule of law.

Lincoln, the most reviled man of his time, willingly gave up honor and reputation in his lifetime for virtue. He was a man who was more concerned with doing good than with looking good. At times, he stood nearly alone but resolute in saving the UNION. He, too, was a man of enormous prudence, moral courage, and dedication to the rule of law—to the perpetuation of our political institutions. And no man has ever been clearer on the moral principle of the UNION than he was in his "Address at Sanitary Fair," Baltimore, in 1864:

> We all declare for liberty; but in using the same word we do not all mean the same thing. With some, the word liberty may mean for each man to do as he pleases with himself, and the product of his labor; while with others the same may mean for some men to do as they please with other men, and the product of other men's labor. Here are two, not only different but incompatible things, called by the same name—liberty. And it follows that each of the things is, by the respective parties, called by two different and incompatible names—liberty and tyranny.

It may be too much to expect that we can always choose such heroic men as our leaders, but it is not too much to expect that we can choose decent, trustworthy, law-abiding men—men we can be proud to claim as our leaders. To this end, a free people must be attentive and vigilant. Who is to guard the guardians? The answer is, we the people. Constantly aware that they are to guard the guardians, the people must not lapse into political apathy and live totally privatized lives. Aristotle pointed out that citizenship is an office; citizens participate in the offices of legislating (by voting) and judging (by serving on juries). But in a free society, their most important function is to guard the guardians.

If the people fail in this, their punishment will be to forfeit their citizenship and become subjects.

Ultimately, the moral authority of the government rests on the character and vigilance of the people. No constitution can save a corrupt, or foolish, or apathetic people from tyranny. As usual, Lincoln was right: "If destruction be our lot, we must ourselves be its author and finisher. As a nation of freemen, we must live through all time, or die by suicide."[6]

CHAPTER FOURTEEN

The Rule of Law at the Millennium

MICHAEL KAHN

SENIOR PARTNER
FOLGER, LEVIN & KAHN LLP

AS THE WORLD'S FIVE BILLION OR SO PEOPLE enter the new chronological era, it may be useful to take the temperature of the rule of law. Are we entering the new age with an exuberant laissez faire distaste for laws and the governments that make and enforce them? Or, is the spirit of the immediate future infused with an optimistic view of the role of government and law in our lives?

The burden of this essay is to argue that in the United States, and in the large global community, the dominant political theology of our time is a profound faith in and devotion to the moral and economic value of the rule of law. This thesis is best illustrated by discussing three sets of events which, on their face, would seem unlikely bedfellows: the impeachment of President Clinton, the NATO Alliance in Kosovo, and the emerging (or emerged) global economy. The subtext of each of these sets of events and circumstances is a devout fealty to the rule of law.

The impeachment and Senate trial of President Clinton was nothing if it was not a modern comic opera played to the tune of the rule of law. Every aspect of this year-long farce was justified in terms of legal imperatives. President Clinton's detractors, enemies, opponents and critics all proclaimed themselves to be motivated by an intense desire to preserve the rule of law. Each Republican initiative—Starr's Report, the House activities, the Senators' vote was inexorably compelled, we were told, by a desire to ensure that no man (and certainly not the perfidious Mr. Clinton) was ABOVE THE LAW! Each motion, speech, and brief tendered by the loyal (loyal that is to the rule of law) opposition wrapped itself in the cloak of preserving the moral integrity of the law for our children (always for the children, i.e., the future).

The Democrats ceded this high ground to no one. If believed, no Democrat gave one whit about the guilty (and embarrassed) Mr. Clinton. On the contrary, with nobility and held nose, the Democrats at every turn were defending the assault on the temple of our democracy—the Constitution, our sacred law. The Democrats ranted and raved that the impeachment and removal must be avoided to defeat mob rule and preserve the moral authority of our electoral law. The culmination of this effort was the brilliant performance of White House *lawyer* Charles Ruff, who at the glorious intersection of our three branches of government—a speech made to the Chief Justice on the Senate floor defending the president—made a brilliant *legal* case for saving his boss's skin.

When the dust settled, both sides measured their results in terms of the preservation of or damage to (depending upon which horse you backed) the rule of law. No one seemed to care whether we were better or worse off for the distasteful experience or whether or not it was a good idea for this particular person to remain president. The keystone was how the rule of law fared.

The public, for its part, seemed to internalize this measuring stick and voice its confidence in the result mandated by the law, the Constitution. Poll after poll revealed a public which believed their Chief Magistrate a liar and a cheat—but, also believed that he should remain in office because his offenses were not impeachable, i.e., did not meet the *legal test* for removal. The public's faith in the legitimacy of the standards for presidential removal set forth in our sacred law was unshakable from beginning to end.

Thus, it can be argued that the one overarching lesson of the impeachment event was that *everyone* involved—the public and their servants in each branch of government—shared a faith in the rule of law as the foundation of our society and as the paramount value in our lives.

It is precisely this shared vision of the moral authority of our laws that has motivated nineteen nations to join hands and launch airplanes in Kosovo. In Kosovo—as in the Kuwaiti affair—consensus is the name of the game. But, consensus over what? Consensus that Milosevic is a bad guy doing really bad things (like Saddam Hussein before him)? Bad things as measured by what? By our laws, of course, and their moral authority. It was pretty obvious that our collective guns were motivated by our thirsty gas tanks in 1991, but it is harder to make the argument that the billions of taxpayer dollars being spent in Kosovo are economically cost-benefit justified. Why are we doing this, rhetorically asks President Clinton, the leader of the alliance—because it is right. Why is it right? Because what the bad guys are doing is immoral and *illegal*!

The theme of the Kosovo war—echoing in the capitals of nineteen quite diverse countries—is that Milosevic's actions are an affront to and a threat to the rule of law. We are not putting our children's lives on the line in the ugliest European conflict since World War II to protect our territorial sovereignty or to defend an embattled ally or to preserve an economic interest. Instead, we—all of us—are doing it to make it clear, here and now, that the rule of law will be defended wherever it is being violated.

Such a proclamation (even if shaded by an ugly fear of refugees) is quite an expression of optimistic confidence in the importance and perseverance of the rule of law for our supposedly jaded and selfish European allies. The fact of the matter is that nineteen countries have—as Lenin would say—voted with their feet (money and young men and women) in favor of the rule of law as a guiding if not *the* guiding principle of international relations in the next century.

Having observed the rule and moral authority of law as a consensus value in operation of American governmental affairs and NATO foreign affairs, it is a logical progression to suggest that the dominant value in the new global economy is the rule of law. Thomas Friedman's new book, *The Lexus and the Olive Tree* (New York: Farrar Straus & Giroux, April 1999), enjoyably describes a new world order organized around a global economy. Friedman and many others wax eloquent about the global pervasiveness of multi-national corporations, the Internet, computers, and telecommunications. Global consciousness is breaking out in every sector of the world's society.

What is the glue that holds the global village together? The rule of law, of course. Why do CitiGroup and Ford and McDonald's and Coke want to do business almost everywhere? Because they are confident that in almost every place in the global village the playing field is made sufficiently level, and the rules are sufficiently fair, that they will be able to make money and safely bring that money home. In short, these mega-companies (and almost everyone else) have more confidence now than at any other time in human history that *rules* (i.e., law) govern human affairs with sufficient certainty and stability to allow everyone to rely upon them. It is the law and the law alone (certainly not our bombs) that protects and preserves the worldwide investment in the global community. The bedrock of the global economy is faith in the protection of the laws from arbitrary confiscation of assets or profits (or, God forbid—people). Moreover, the increased cross-national investments and mergers demonstrate the confidence of huge capital sources in the permanence of the global sanctity of the rule of law.

How will the Kosovo action or the global economy or the Clinton impeachment eventually turn out? No one knows. But, we do know that the legitimacy of these human activities—big and small, or of life, death, and money—were based on a firm, confident and optimistic belief in the moral authority of the rule of law as we enter the new millennium.

Civil Disobedience, the Rule of Law, and the Moral Authority of Government: Tension between Two Strains of American Thought?

MARIE D. NATOLI

PROFESSOR OF POLITICAL SCIENCE
EMMANUEL COLLEGE

> *If all mankind minus one were of one opinion, and only one person were of the contrary opinion, mankind would be no more justified in silencing that one person, than he, if he had the power, would be justified in silencing mankind.*
>
> J. S. MILL, *On Liberty*[1]

> *For justice exists only between men whose mutual relations are governed by law; and law exists for men between whom there is injustice. . . . This is why we do not allow a man to rule, but rational principle, because man behaves thus in his own interests and becomes a tyrant.*
>
> ARISTOTLE, *Nicomachean Ethics*[2]

> *Men of most renowned virtue have sometimes by transgressing most truly kept the law.*
>
> JOHN MILTON, *Tetrachordon*[3]

> *A fella ain't got a soul of his own, just a little piece of a big soul, the one big soul that belongs to everybody. . . . I'll be all around in the dark. I'll be everywhere. Wherever you can look. Wherever there's a fight, so hungry people can eat, I'll be there. Whenever a cop's beating up a guy, I'll be there. I'll be in the way guys get when they're hungry and they know supper's ready. When people are eating the stuff they raise and living in the houses they build, I'll be there.*
>
> TOM JOAD, *The Grapes of Wrath*[4]

As HE SAT IN HIS CELL, imprisoned for having defied the laws of his society, he was visited by friends who offered to bribe his guards and help him to escape. He refused; the law had been broken, he said, and he had to pay the consequences.[5]

As he sat in his cell, having defied the laws of his society, he was visited by a friend, who questioned what he was doing *in* there. He answered this question by a question, "What are you doing *out* there?"[6]

As he sat in his cell, having defied the laws of his society, he received extensive criticism from his colleagues. His response to them was patient, measured, reasonable.[7]

Socrates, Henry David Thoreau, and Martin Luther King, Jr., each in his own era, each with his own thoughts, sat in a jail cell—as have countless, often unknown, others throughout history—for having practiced civil disobedience in response to what each considered the wrongs of his/her society's laws. But since the American system is founded on the rule of law, civil disobedience presents a particular strain upon the American belief in the rule of law.

A tension seemingly exists between the two. The rule of law is what binds this society. Respect for the law and for lawmakers is what keeps societies stable. By contrast, civil disobedience, a concept thousands of years old and not uniquely American, nonetheless reflects the rugged individualism upon which America prides itself. Is there truly a tension or is there actually a *harmony* between the two, without which neither could exist? This question is the subject of this essay.

Opponents of civil disobedience argue that civil disobedience "flout[s] the law," is immoral because it is based on selfish interests, involves "taking the law into [one's] own hands," "undermines the respect for the law," is "self-defeating" because it alienates policy makers and public alike, cannot be justified in the face of "lawful channels," and "subverts" the democratic process.[8]

Supporters argue that the act is justifiable because it seeks not to overthrow the law, but to question its morality—"draw the attention of the community to the law in question"—so that the community may "consider the law's morality," providing the individuals with a method by which to follow their consciences; that civil disobedients are not condemning the entire social and legal order, but trying to purify it of immoral laws, thus leading to a better society; and that there is a higher law than man-made law.[9]

All those who advocate the purification of the *particular* law through civil disobedience look to the more *pervasive* rule of law, based upon a higher law, from which a government derives its moral authority to govern.

The rule of law refers not only to the actual laws of a society, but to the essence of a society's *justness*, which in itself may be contradicted by a particular law. Thoreau's observation that "we should be men first, and subjects afterward,"[10] underscores the role of the individual vis à vis a government and society. That role is not to blindly obey the law, but to pursue justice. Noted Thoreau, "the only obligation which I have a right to assume is to do at any time what I think right."[11]

It is this distinction which makes civil disobedience not only a force *compatible with* the rule of law, but *necessary to* it.

The Reverend Dr. Martin Luther King, Jr.'s "Letter from a Birmingham Jail"[12] provides one of the most eloquent statements regarding the role of civil disobedience in working within and maintaining the rule of law. Dr. King's actions were sparked almost a decade prior, by Mrs. Rosa Parks's refusal to give up her seat for a white passenger. Mrs. Parks consciously disobeyed Alabama law and served as a catalyst for civil rights movement. "That moment, which marked the resumption by black Americans of their struggle for civil rights and racial equality, made explicit a conflict between the obligations of law and of conscience— between the commands of law and the claims of justice."[13]

"Before this moment, law was thought of as the source of a rock firm stability for our social institutions. Now it serves as the stage for confrontation and change. This occurred just as the consensus that only certain forms of social change are acceptable has collapsed."[14]

Their actions have long roots in this country's history of rugged individualism, as evidenced by the dissenters during the Boston Tea Party—not an act of revolution, but of civil disobedience along with other acts of civil disobedience—such as "Susan B. Anthony['s] attempt to vote . . . [and those who] violate[d] the Fugitive Slave Act of 1850."[15] Consider the words of abolitionist Angeline Grinke:

> If a law commands me to *sin I will break it*; if it calls me to *suffer*, I will let it takes its course *unresistingly*. The doctrine of blind obedience and unqualified submission to any human power, . . . is

the doctrine of despotism, and ought to have no place 'mong Republicans and Christians.[16]

Noted one observer,

> It is significant that so many philosophical defenders of civil disobedience . . . have relied on a form of social contract theory. That tradition, especially in the Lockean form, has become a trademark of Anglo-American political thought. As a theory, contractarianism has the advantage of emphasizing *the values of individual consent and personal accountability.*[17] (emphasis added)

Civil disobedience might be best conceived as existing along a continuum with other degrees of reaction to governmental action. Thus:

general agreement	disagreement with a segment of the law/policy	complete disagreement with the laws/policies of a society
obedience	**civil disobedience**	**revolution**

Civil disobedience seeks to reform the law when it is out of harmony with the spirit of the laws of the land. The *spirit* of the laws of the land, civil disobedience would contend, is the spirit of the higher law. Since the rule of law is societally determined and subjectively determined, it, unlike the higher law, will vary. As one modern political theorist has pointed out, "The rule of law doctrine . . . appears to be not unlike the natural law of doctrine in that it provides for the critical evaluation of existing laws."[18] Noted another observer of natural versus man-made law, "Natural law theorists and legal positivists maintain that law is separable from morals, natural law theorists claim that any such difference is untenable."[19]

Civil disobedience is in harmony with the views of the natural law theorists, and "fills in the gap" by providing *external moral norms* by which *to evaluate man-made law.* Despite the natural law–legal positivist debate, "few legal thinkers would suggest today that a law must always be obeyed because it is the law."[20] The same author noted, "Ironically, it was the triumph of legal positivism that doomed total-obedience-to-law theories. Once we grant that power alone makes law, once we admit that that which should not be law can be made law, we must reserve the right to disobey."[21]

Advocates of civil disobedience would argue that "unlawful conduct" is necessary if a society is to purify the law. Of contemporary political activists, perhaps no one understood this need more than Martin Luther King, Jr. In a speech at the Holt Baptist Church in Montgomery, Alabama, King told his audience, "the great glory of American Democracy is the right to protest for right."[22]

In 1961 King "appeal[ed] to a higher authority . . . [but was] nevertheless profoundly aware of the important uses and authority of secular law."[23] Said King, "[E]ven though morality may not be legislated, behavior can be regulated . . . We need legislation and federal action to control behavior. It may be true that the law can't make a man love me, but it can keep him from lynching me, and I think that's pretty important also."[24]

Dr. King's Birmingham Jail letter delineates a *necessary* place for civil disobedience in the rule of law. Civil disobedience attempts to reform—to purify—*part* of the law rather than completely rebel against all of the law. The purification of the law through outright disobedience of the law reflects the selfless and highest respect for the law. But there are *boundaries* within which the purifying act of civil disobedience must remain in order to be within the rule of law:

- the individual must believe, in conscience, a law or policy to be unjust;
- there is the right, indeed, the *duty*, to disobey in order to draw the attention of the community to the injustice;
- the disobedience of *only* the law or policy the individual believes to be unjust;
- nonviolent disobedience; and
- acceptance of the consequences of having broken the law.

King's letter underscores the individual's relationship and obligation to other individuals and to society at large. "Injustice anywhere is a threat to justice everywhere,"[25] King wrote, and those who see the injustice have a moral imperative to respond. "We are caught in an escapable network of mutuality, tied in a single garment of destiny. Whatever affects one directly, affects all indirectly."[26]

King's life was devoted to his recognition that one must get involved in fighting injustices one sees in society. His life was also dedicated to the *means* by which the *individual*, guided by conscience, purifies the society of its injustices. "Nonviolent direct action," wrote King, "seeks to create such a crisis and foster such a tension that a community . . . is forced to confront the issue."[27]

King paralleled this tension to that which Socrates believed was necessary "in the mind so that individuals could rise from the bondage of myths and half-truths to the unfettered realm of creative analysis and objective appraisal."[28] In Plato's *Apology*, Socrates speaks to his judges, "If you put me to death, you will not easily find another, who, to use a rather absurd expression, attaches himself to the city as a gadfly to a horse."[29] King's Birmingham letter noted, "[W]e must see the need for *nonviolent gadflies* to create the kind of tension in society that will help men rise from the dark depths of prejudice and racism to the majestic heights of understanding and brotherhood."[30] (emphasis added).

The expectations of those who choose to live in a society is that laws will be obeyed, that the rule of law will prevail. Yet civil disobedience advocates disobeying laws. Contradiction? Tension? Neither. The difference lies between *just* laws and *unjust* laws. King's Birmingham letter provides a vital analysis of the distinction.

> There are two types of laws: just and unjust. I would be first to advocate obeying just laws. One has not only a legal but a moral responsibility to obey just laws. Conversely, one has a moral responsibility to disobey unjust laws. I would agree with St. Augustine that "an unjust law is no law at all."[31]

This difference between just and unjust laws, and the concept that "an unjust law is no law at all," are the keys to the reconciliation between civil disobedience and the rule of law. If an unjust law is no law at all, then the purification of the law to remove the unjust law reflects the ultimate respect for the law.

But who is to determine whether a law is just or unjust? King's Birmingham letter again provides guidelines.

> A just law is a man-made code that squares with the moral law or the law of God. An unjust law is a code that is out of harmony with the moral law. To put it in the terms of St. Thomas Aquinas: An unjust law is a human law that is not rooted in eternal law and natural law. Any law that uplifts human personality is just.[32]

Thus, the *effects* of a law may lead one, in conscience, to deem it unjust—and therefore necessary to disobey if one is to follow the precepts of civil disobedience.

Other factors will contribute to the individual's determination of whether a law is just or unjust. Who is *subject to* the law is another consideration.

> An unjust law is a code that a numerical or power majority compels a minority group to obey but does not make binding on itself. . . . [A] just law is a code that a majority compels a minority to follow and that it is willing to follow itself.[33]

Who created the law may affect this determination. Noted King, "A law is unjust if it is inflicted on a minority that, as a result of being denied the right to vote, had no part in enacting or devising the law."[34]

How the law is *applied* will also determine if it is just or unjust.

> Sometimes a law is just on its fact and unjust in its application. For instance, I have been arrested on a charge of parading without a permit. Now, there is nothing wrong in having an ordinance which requires a permit for a parade. But such an ordinance becomes unjust when it is used to maintain segregation and to deny citizens the First-Amendment privilege of peaceful assembly and protest.[35]

The two remaining requirements of civil disobedience—nonviolent disobedience and the acceptance of the consequences—are also addressed by King.

> In no sense do I advocate evading or defying the law. . . . That would lead to anarchy. One who breaks an unjust law must do so openly, lovingly, and with a willingness to accept the penalty.[36]

The essence of the civil disobedience–rule of law relationship as expressed by King is that "an individual who breaks a law that conscience tells him is unjust, and who willingly accepts the penalty of imprisonment in order to arouse the conscience of the community over its injustice, is in reality expressing the highest respect for the law."[37] Deviation from any of these conditions denies to the protestors the status of "civil disobedients."

Civil disobedients have come from all segments of society and span a long ideological gamut. Advocates of civil rights for black Americans, advocates for women's rights, advocates for gay and lesbian rights, protesters of the Vietnam War, opponents of nuclear power, reflect several generally considered on the left of the ideological gamut. But the political right has also engaged in civil disobedience, as Operation Rescue, the anti-abortion group, demonstrates.

Those who symbolically break a law felt to be morally objectionable must also act within the confines prescribed by true civil disobedience. Thus, those who protested the Vietnam War by burning their draft cards or refusing to pay a portion of their taxes, and who did so nonviolently, and were willing to accept the consequences, complied with the tenets of true civil disobedience. Those who objected to the war and expressed their objection by bombing buildings cannot be classified as civil disobedients.[38]

Similarly, those who believe that abortion is morally wrong and who picket abortion clinics peacefully and nonviolently and who break no other laws, are also complying with the tenets of true civil disobedience. But once there is interference with the rights of those choosing to utilize the services of the abortion clinics, or once there is violence of any kind, the status of civil disobedient no longer applies.

The purified law will be respectable. In its advocacy of purifying unjust laws, civil disobedience works toward increasing respect for the law. In doing so, it underscores the rule of law. Tension between civil disobedience and the rule of law? Perhaps Thomas Jefferson should have the final word. "A strict observance of the written laws," wrote Thomas Jefferson, author of the Declaration of Independence, a document essentially justifying civil disobedience, "is doubtless one of the high duties of a good citizen, but it is not the highest. The laws of necessity, of self preservation, of saving our country when in danger, are of a higher obligation. . . . To lose our country by a scrupulous adherence to written law would be to lose the law itself, with life, liberty, property and all those who are enjoying them with us; thus absurdly sacrificing the ends to the means."[39]

Constitutional Authority and Public Morality

ROBERT E. DENTON, JR.

W. THOMAS RICE
CHAIR OF LEADERSHIP STUDIES AND DIRECTOR
VIRGINIA TECH CORPS OF CADETS
CENTER FOR LEADER DEVELOPMENT
VIRGINIA POLYTECHNIC INSTITUTE

THE NOTION OF AUTHORITY is a central concept in social and political thought. There are many forms of authority: bureaucratic, technical, or professional, to name a few. But all forms of authority are based upon the structure of the social relationship between an individual and the State. Such a relationship may range from coercion, based upon force; to unreflecting obedience based upon habit; to enlightened deference, based upon a sense of values. The role of authority in government is upholding not only moral, ethical, and intellectual standards, but also in guaranteeing social and political freedom, and acting as a barrier to centralized, arbitrary, and despotic power. We use authority to protect our rights, to provide order and security, to manage conflict, and to distribute the benefits and burdens of society.

The authority of our government—its very structure, rules, and laws—originate from the Constitution. The *moral* authority of government originates from the collective beliefs, attitudes, and values of the citizens. Moral authority may be generally defined as the felt obligations and duties derived from shared community values, ideas, and ideals. From a democratic perspective, the very nature of authority—as defined as the ability to evoke purely voluntary compliance—must be moral in form and content. Otherwise, social violence, chaos, and coercion will be the norm. A social hierarchy is maintained by a willing acceptance of the social order, a unifying set of common values, and a world view which enshrines and legitimizes the established order. Moral authority rests on voluntary consent. Thus, democracy cannot exist without values. And political values are the distillation of principles from a systematic order of public beliefs.

As we approach the new millennium, what would a survey of our social and political landscape reveal? After twenty years in the field, I am alarmed, concerned, and even saddened by the political climate and attitudes reflected in our society today. There exists among the public a climate of change, a climate of distrust, and even a climate of fear. And on all levels of measurement, Americans participate less and are less concerned and interested in affairs of state.

For example, recent studies tell us that young people can no longer identify heroes. A quick review of major public opinion polls of 1999 reveal general public cynicism and distrust of government. Only 30 percent of Americans believe that the federal government represents their interests. Only 19 percent think that one can trust government to do what is right, down from 76 percent in 1964. Sixty-four percent of Americans think Congress cannot fix anything. In fact, according to the 1999 Citizen Alienation Index compiled by the Harris polling organization, 76 percent of Americans think people in Washington are out of touch with the rest of the country, 54 percent think people running the country do not care what happens to them, and 58 percent think people in power will try to take advantage of everyday citizens. Perhaps the most alarming statistic reported during this same time frame is that 74 percent of Americans think the American Dream of "equal opportunity, personal freedom, and social mobility" will be harder to achieve in the next 10 years.[1]

A report published in March, 1999, by the National Association of Secretaries of State, revealed that those between the ages of 18 and 24 want to help their communities by volunteering and raising their children well. They have very little interest in the political process and voting. The highest priorities of young people were having a close-knit family, developing job skills, and having a successful career. Alarmingly, the lowest-rated priorities were being a good American and being involved in democracy and voting.[2]

Perhaps such attitudes explain why in 1996, Americans conducted a presidential campaign that resulted in the lowest national turnout since 1924. Less than half of registered voters participated in the defining act of democracy. Even on election night, network ratings were the lowest ever recorded by Nielsen in an election year. Just 39 percent of homes with television viewed election night returns.

The 1998 midterm congressional elections reflect the same degree of low interest among Americans. The national turnout rate was just 36 percent of those registered, the lowest level since 1942.

It seems we are in a transition in America. "Anger" became the political watchword of the 1990s. Academic and civil leaders wrote about the absence of civility, the decline of intelligent dialogue, and rising decibels of hate speech. The unifying theme behind the social anger of the 1990s is *government*. Government suddenly became the scapegoat for all that we perceive wrong within our society.

Actually, voices of frustration were beginning to be heard in 1984. By 1988, Reagan capitalized on the emerging frustration of many Americans. Critics and academics labeled it as simply "the angry white male." However, the watershed elections of 1992 and 1994 revealed increasing waves of anger among all voters. Voters became more volatile, less patient, and simply more angry and frustrated than ever before.

After the cold war, the political climate became one of public distrust, cynicism, and even fear. According to public opinion polls, many Americans lost confidence in their government and trust in elected officials and politicians. Government and the political process were viewed as dominated by special interests rather than notions of the "common good" for all Americans. Citizens felt caught between the crossfire of self-interested politicians, special interest groups, and large corporations. In 1995, Francis Fukuyama wrote that Americans were experiencing a genuine "crisis of trust."[3]

The primary characteristic of our society in the nineteenth and early twentieth centuries was that of a social contract. We attempted to build a comfortable society based upon a covenant, contract or agreement for the mutual advantage of the members of society, of the citizens and the government. Essentially, free people govern by free agreement. The rise of contractual relationships results in the replacement of autocratic, repressive, and coercive governments by governments contractually elected, limited in power and contractually obligated to respect the rights and specified liberties of the citizens. By means of our Constitution, Bill of Rights, and common laws, the very values and prerogatives of society are promulgated and virtually guaranteed: freedom of religion, speech, press, and assembly, to name a few. Contractual government is democratic government, a "government of the people, by the people, and for the people."

Thus, at the heart of democracy is the notion of a contract. And at the heart of any contract is a notion of trust. There was a time in America when citizens understood the terms of their relationship with government and with each other that was based upon trust. The concept is very simple. I won't kill you, if you won't kill me. I'll help protect your property if you help protect mine. I'll help build your barn if you help build mine. If something happens to me, I know that as a member of the larger community, my children and family will be protected and taken care of. Our contract with each other was based on mutual respect, honesty, and responsibility.

Our contract with government was likewise based on trust. A government of the people, by the people, and for the people, meant that the common good would prevail. Government, in all its actions, would be fair, just, and operate in the interests of all citizens. For too many Americans, our "social contract" based on that has become null and void.

The conduct of civil affairs in America has always occurred under a cloud of public distrust, a wary skepticism that conveys meaning to every other part of the nation's life. James Madison, in "Federalist paper #51," recognized the tension between the need of a centralized government and a free people. He wrote "the interest of the man must be connected with the constitutional rights of the place. It may be a reflection on human nature that such devices should be necessary to control the abuses of government. But what is government itself but the greatest of all reflections on human nature? If men were angels, no government would be necessary. If angels were to govern men, neither external nor internal controls on government would be necessary. In framing a government which is to be administered by men over men, the great difficulty lies in this: you must first enable the government to control the governed; and in the next place oblige it to control itself. A dependence on the people is, no doubt, the primary control on the government . . ."[4] Individual integrity, responsibility, and accountability are the best check on government abuse.

The collective social values of the citizens become the conditions necessary for the existence of political authority. The gov-

ernment that encompasses and expresses our collective values
ensures the respect and voluntary compliance of all citizens.
Political authority rests on the assumption that it exists to promote the good of those who accept it, that the common good will
prevail, not the self-interests of those in authority or by the exercise of force.

Today there has been an intensification of public distrust
more than wary skepticism in many American institutions. There
seems to be an increasing disconnection between the nation and
its civic life. Paradoxically, while we have never had more access
to the processes and moments of the political process, we have
never felt less a part of the process.

The challenge is clear. As a nation, our greatest threat is internal, not external. We must stem the growing tide toward political
cynicism and despair. First, we must find common themes and
values that transcend our ever-deepening cultural differences. We
must all be able to identify, to articulate, and to appreciate the
core values of America. We need to reaffirm ourselves to our
national civic values—the principles embodied in the Declaration
of Independence, the Constitution, and the Bill of Rights—that
bring us together as a people. The ideals of freedom, equality,
democracy, and justice provide the basis for building community
and trust in America today. Second, civic responsibility, accountability, and initiative should once again become a keystone of
social life. Moral discipline means using social norms, rules, customs, and laws to develop moral reasoning, self-control, and a
generalized respect for others. Such an approach to social life
will help citizens recognize the values behind the laws, why laws
are needed, and increase the feeling of moral obligation to
respect government institutions. Democracy as government "of
the people, by the people, and for the people" shapes the form
and content of political action in America. Democracy makes
government accessible and accountable to ordinary citizens.
Finally, of course, we desperately need moral leadership in the
future, not defined by a specific set of standards or dogma, but
clearly recognized by the public as possessing the moral authority
of governing. In the early years of our nation, Alexis de Tocqueville observed, "America is great because it is good. If it ceases
to be good, it will cease to be great."

CHAPTER SEVENTEEN

The Moral Authority of Government

C. LOWELL HARRISS

PROFESSOR EMERITUS OF ECONOMICS
COLUMBIA UNIVERSITY

GOVERNMENT TAKES MANY FORMS. People exercise authority over others. Force of various degrees blends into voluntary acceptance of guidance. We tend to use the term "government" to apply to political agencies, the state. Coercion can be applied. Statutes, laws, enacted and enforced by human beings—notably legislators, governors, civil servants, the police, and judges—can force other human beings to do, or not do, something. The willingness to obey will depend upon the extent of belief that the lawmakers (or their predecessors) had proper, legitimate authority.

For most people, voluntary compliance with most directives of government presents no problem. Why does voluntary acceptance dominate? One explanation is a sense, rarely articulated, that the authority is "proper"—justified morally as right. The source has authority within the scope involved. Other types of governing can be noted.

Bishops govern. So do umpires and teachers and those who decree this year's clothing fashions. Their authority comes from different sources and has varying power, with a voluntary element predominating but some potential for using compulsion (imposing penalties, sanctions). Voluntary choice probably determines any person's belonging to the groups affected—in contrast to quite restricted choice as to our association with political government on a national level, and more locally. Though we are subject to the compulsion of government, we generally follow the rules of "the government"—less so with speed limits than with staying on the correct side of the road.

A sense that those exercising authority do so with some basis of morality must have a large, but unmeasurable influence. Civilization, the quality of life, the effectiveness of civil government— all these depend crucially upon voluntary obedience to law. The willingness of our neighbors to obey the law has an enormous influence upon the life of our family and ourselves. We take so much for granted!

Why do people respect the law? Not all do. The sources of respect, legitimacy, can be complex. The authority of government officials today rests to large extent upon the actions of humans in the past, e.g., those who framed our national and state constitutions. What has been written down under certain circumstances has authority. Their existence does not confirm that the moral foundations were originally solid or that, even if so, they would be best today. Their existence may well provide reason for retention—the desirability of continuity, the unknowability of the full results of any change, the respect for commitments made, assuming the persistence of conditions. Yet the potentials for improvement should not, it seems to me, be foreclosed by respect for the past. Reason must be man's best instrument.

What have been sources for the authority of government? At times, authority rested on someone's assertion of the divine right of kings. To some extent, perhaps, part of the respect for the ruler may have a tinge of ancient attitudes about the divinity of the king or queen. Who can know? But when we are told to respect the presidency, the office, even though the current holder inspires less than respect, one may wonder, "Just why?"

One may also sense a bit of deference to revelation—as with sacred texts. Not exactly the tablet from Mt. Sinai but respect as a source of authority, perhaps this sense could be cited as "moral" without a deeper look into justification. Probably there are elements to be found in this approach. There may be a basis for understanding without any need to appear to endorse justification.

Through history, rulers have often gained authority through heredity. The original basis of power was probably force of some sort, e.g., victory in combat. Whether or not the victor would be said to have had a better moral position—character—was secondary to the possession of power. And opportunities to question and challenge legitimacy were few. Perhaps over time the willingness of subjects to obey depended to some (slight?) extent upon a public's sense of the moral authority of the rulers. Also quite probable was the rarity of any serious questioning of alternatives as a basis for authority.

More relevant—probably significantly so—are pomp and ceremony—Nuremberg! The Fourth of July! State occasions! Emo-

tions are aroused. We are inspired to be loyal without truly rational grounding. Symbolism supports the ruler as he or she has
planned and staged theater. One feels good. (Nothing to be
ashamed of—except as it may dull critical capacity!) Such points
can help in trying to understand the complexities of authority of
government.

Government is human beings acting. Their actions today rest,
to varying extent, upon what other human beings did in the past
and the images carried over into the present. We personalize and
speak of "the state" or "the government" as an entity. These terms
are useful, but they are abstractions. They have no brain. Whatever is done, is done by human beings as individuals or groups.
Some groups are cohesive enough to be realistically thought of as
units while others are represented by one or a few leaders. And
always individuals and groups operate within an environment
that influences what can be done. A sense of right and wrong will
pervade feelings with influences beyond the clearly identifiable.

In a society such as ours "the people" have considerable
power to influence what government officials will do. Stability
dominates. But there is change. And a sense of right and wrong,
morality, will profoundly influence the authority accorded to
those persons who govern in their various ways—the local police
or the justices of the Supreme Court, or all of the many others
who constitute government. Some of us can remember when
there would have been great doubt about the authority of the
national government to tell states how to run elections or to prevent discrimination against women. Federal officials now have
authority that did not exist two generations ago because of
changes in public attitudes about race and gender.

Such rather fundamental change is a counterpart of some
changes that characterized the New Deal. The authority of the
national government—and of government generally—expanded
with a change in the sense of what is right and wrong. Today most
Americans could hardly imagine what was once considered to be
the proper range of governmental authority.

This expansion of the scope of permissible actions by government officials may seem rather remote from the more common
interpretations of "morality." But the implications deserve more
attention than I observe. My comments must be somewhat tentative. First, some observations about accepting the guidance of the
past are appropriate. What were the qualifications of those who

made the rules, defined the authority, we now observe? The quality of their character and the system of morality (right and wrong) they supported will be relevant. The value of legacies from the past must rest to some degree upon the value systems of the authors. Perhaps my concerns are too intangible to be helpful. Yet is there not reason to believe that the Founding Fathers were persons of exceptional integrity, persons who would be good examples for our children? If so, there must be a presumption of certain merit in their decisions about the acceptable authority of government. Yet one at once encounters another reality: we have much more information than they did and live under rather different conditions.

One difference is an enormous expansion of the role of government (politics, the civil service, and so on). Is there not reason for concern about the possible transfer of authority of "government" from the top to the men and women who carry on the specific elements of implementing laws—including the making of new regulations? The fact that someone can legitimately claim to be acting as a governmental official does not mean that he or she can claim to be operating with the moral authority of that entity, "the state." The potentials for abuse, subtle or overt, call for continuing oversight. The Senate hearings on the IRS revealed the failure of the Treasury Department over the years to develop reasonably effective protections against avoidable dereliction by persons acting as part of "the government."

Governmental definition and use of authority are by human beings, not that abstraction, "the State." And the quality of personal character of the president and others who seek to lead—mayors, governors, civil servants—must affect the willingness to follow. Intangibles that we associate with morality influence—as they should—our responses. Can we believe in the integrity of officials? Is there justifiable reason to doubt their veracity? What is the evidence of serious concern for the long run? Is there reason—or merely excuse—for rejecting requests that involve some sacrifice?

In short, what kind of human beings urge us to follow them? Do they justify granting them authority? To make and to execute laws? Some of us have seen evidence of distressingly wide departures from estimable standards of personal character.

Do persons who used the vulgarities recorded on the Nixon tapes disqualify themselves by lack of sensitivity to use authority responsibly? Perhaps I am unduly squeamish, but Americans do deserve better. There appeared not only a willingness to cut corners ethically, but a crude vulgarity of expression that reflects badly upon the personal qualities of some participants, including the president.

More recently, alas, confirmed reports tell of White House behavior that demeans the persons and must also discredit the office. I am reluctant to get more specific. Not necessary. What will follow as to the authority of the presidency? Perhaps a weaker rather than a stronger executive branch is preferable. Two closing comments indicate conflicting concerns.

Over time, this country has built what, as it were, is capital in the form of respect for the presidency—and other portions of government. Leaders could use this capital to try to get action. There is, at times, a "national interest." Though not always as articulated by a leader! At present, it seems to me, appeals to the "rightness" of a cause on the basis of a leader's assertion will encounter cynicism that may erode authority.

Finally, the power of persuasion will be used—and abused—in trying to establish authority. Skills of the highest nature are devoted to influencing attitudes toward government. Emotion gets emphasis as against reason. True, various aspects of the same issue can receive attention. Balance cannot be counted upon. Fascism in Europe gained force earlier this century as emotion was utilized to mobilize public attitudes. Manipulation can exploit a deteriorated sense of morality. Acceptance of slackening of standards can lead to an accumulation of worsening.

CHAPTER EIGHTEEN

The Concept of "Government": Historical and Comparative Observations

FRANCIS H. HELLER

PROFESSOR EMERITUS OF LAW AND POLITICAL SCIENCE
UNIVERSITY OF KANSAS

I. The Words We Use

Episode 1.

FOUR DECADES AGO, I was in the first of six years as a member of the local Planning and Zoning Commission. The item before us was a request from the largest financial institution in the state: In order to establish a branch facility in our town, it requested the rezoning of some property at the western edge of (but within) the city limits from agricultural to commercial use. Before the governing body could act on this request, our group had to review it and prepare a recommendation to the city commission. Everything had been according to applicable laws and regulations; now we were holding a public hearing on the matter. There was only one person who appeared in opposition, but he was one angry citizen. He owned the land adjoining the property in question but outside the city limits. If this change were to be approved, he argued with considerable agitation, he would have to move the horses he kept on his acreage and that would totally destroy the value of the property to him, both now and in the future.

Our commission had the practice of rotating the role of spokesperson in the hearing process. It was my turn to ask questions of the witness. He was a well-known physician. All of us also knew that he was the county chairperson of the Democratic Party. I confirmed that he considered his medical practice to be his principal occupation. Then, I inquired, was the keeping of horses recreational or commercial? He exploded—that was none of our business. One of my colleagues asked what financial loss he

feared as a result of the placement of a bank in his neighborhood, given that the area to the north of the property in question was already zoned to accommodate a neighborhood shopping center. His response was that it was obvious that changing
the neighborhood was an interference with his enjoyment of the
property he owned.

The discussion continued for a while, with the good doctor
getting more and more red in the face. Eventually it came to a
vote. We were unanimous that we should recommend to the city
commission that it should grant the change.

The doctor was outraged. "You are acting," he screamed, "like
you think you are the g——n government." Very calmly I said,
"But we are." He pointed his finger at me: "That's Communist
talk!"—and stormed out.

Episode 2.

It was near midnight when our group, as was our practice, ad-
journed for coffee in a restaurant across the street. Matt, the chairman, asked me why I had told the witness that we were
"government."

I replied with an experience I had in my first class at the University of Kansas.

I had decided to find out what the roughly one hundred students thought about when they enrolled in a course about "government." My interrogatory instructed the students to check
either of the columns headed "yes" or "no," depending on
whether the entity listed was, in their opinions "government."
The responses ranged from 100% "no" for the United Nations to
100% for the Congress of the United States, the governor of Kansas, and the state legislature. Intriguingly enough, only 80%
thought that either the president of the United States or the
United States Supreme Court were "government." In the discussion that followed, some of those who placed President Truman
and the Court (all of its judges by this time appointed by either
Franklin Roosevelt or Truman) in the negative column did so
because they considered them "politicians," not "government."
They divided almost evenly on whether the city commission was
"government" and only a minority placed the school board in the
"yes" column, let alone water district and bindweed control dis-

tricts. We agreed that most people we knew tended to think of Washington, D.C., when they talked about "government."

Episode 3.

I taught a course on the American Constitution at the University of Vienna. My lectures were subsequently published.[1] My editor was a very intelligent woman, with a doctorate in English literature from the University of London. She could not understand why we Americans insisted on referring to our government as "the administration," which her dictionary told her translated as "bureaucracy." We went to several other languages and found that the word "government" does not carry identical meanings in any two of them.

II. GOVERNMENT IN HISTORICAL PERSPECTIVE

Episode 4.

When Henry Morton Stanley embarked on his expedition to find the explorer Henry Livingston in Africa, he assured that, if he could locate the supreme king of the natives of central Africa, he would certainly learn where Dr. Livingston was to be found. Much to his surprise, there was no king above the many and varied tribes—but every tribe had a king of its own and they were frequently at war with each other. Neither he nor Dr. Livingston understood what the beginnings of this tribal kingship were.

We do not know when human groups became societies, and when these societies instituted government—if they ever did so conscious of what they were doing. All we can say with any degree of certainty is that, when human societies moved from being prehistoric, i.e., created intelligible records of their existence, some among them exercised authority over others who in turn accepted that domination. In some instances the evidence suggests that power may have followed on conquest; vanquished foes had to accept the victor's commands or even find themselves treated as slaves. Elsewhere there appears to have been a linkage between religion (the effort to find causation for events that human minds could not explain). When one tribe set out to subjugate another, there had to be a military leader. Sometime the need to gain access to food and water required a common effort, and with that leadership. But we cannot assert that any one or more of these causes provide the basis for a generalized statement about the beginning of government.

C. J. Friedrich, a native of Germany who joined the Harvard faculty in 1923, maintained that this argument about the beginnings are irrelevant. Government, he maintained, is not an institution until there are technicians (read "bureaucrats") whose task it is to maintain this institution. The methods of maintenance may vary: The Romans offered the populace *panem et circenses*—bread and games (in modern terms, food and fun). The dictatorships of the twentieth century resorted to the same basic categories: *"Arbeit macht frei"* (work makes you free) proclaimed signs leading into the horror-infested concentration camps; those not caught in that fearsome form of employment were promised *"Kraft durch Freude"* (strength through joy)—for all practical purposes compulsory recreation; and behind these (and other) aspects of "food and fun" there was the terror of the *Gestapo*—the secret state police—and the charismatic vision of a regime destined to last a thousand years.

Abuses of governmental power repeatedly have led to resistance and, as such actions succeeded, to limitations on the exercise of power. *Magna Carta*, often acclaimed as the foundation of English American restraints on governmental power, was initially a set of concessions which King John granted to restive nobles in his kingdom. It carried within it the basic notions that "government," whatever that meant, should observe limits on its power and exercise it according to set guidelines. It would be nearly four hundred years before Sir Edward Coke had the audacity to face King James I and assert that the king was "under the law," that government was not without limits.

Kings have since virtually disappeared and, where they still exist, they serve in conformance with a constitution, an instrument designed to limit government while (to varying degrees) it also aims to protect the rights of citizens. Is this "government"?

III. Comparative Views

Episode 5.

In 1988 a distinguished member of the law faculty of the University of Vienna spent the spring semester at our university, and he and I taught a class together. Early on he observed that he ought to observe a criminal trial in an American court. It was a short trial, and he was able to attend all of it. In the next meeting of our class, he expressed himself in highly critical language: How could people who knew so little about the law (i.e., jurors) pass judgment in a case at law? Why should the lawyers take over the case by the examination and cross-examination of witnesses? The judge was much better qualified than they were to interrogate witnesses and had the experience to weight the value of their statements. It just showed how inferior our system was to that in effect in the countries of continental Europe.

If history does not provide a clear cut understanding of "government," can we gain a clearer perception of the term if we look at the different ways in which it is practiced? In other words, can we understand "government" by looking at *governments*?

Political science courses taught with the suggesting word "comparative" in their titles do not *compare*; typically the text for American college classes has a section on the government of the United Kingdom, one on France, another on Germany. If the text was prepared before the days of Boris Yeltsin, there may be a section on the government of the Soviet Union. Occasionally, Japan or Italy or the Scandinavian countries are added. But they are devised to teach, descriptively, what some foreign governments or some foreign legal systems are like. But rarely is there any comparison.

John Henry Merryman, a former member of the Stanford University law faculty, illustrated the problem of comparison in these words:

> . . . [A] lawyer from a relatively undeveloped country in Central America may be convinced that his legal system is measurably superior to that of the United States or Canada. Unless he is a very sophisticated student of comparative law, he may be inclined to patronize a common lawyer. He will recognize our more advanced economic development, and he may envy our standard of living. But he will find compensatory comfort in thinking of our legal system as undeveloped and of common lawyers as relatively uncultured people.[2]

The Austrian professor who had been so critical of our legal systems has been dead for several years, but there are lawyers who were in that class who tell me that they were then (and are to this day) outraged by his derogatory statements. My response is always the same: To make comparisons, one must have standards, criteria for the judgments one intends to pass.

IV. The Obligations of Government

To ask what obligations "government" has requires that we first agree on the criteria to be used. When Louis XIV, more than three hundred years ago, asserted that "I am the State" he knew that this assertion of power was being accepted. When Adolf Hitler told the German people on the day after more than four hundred individuals had, on his personal order, been killed because "on that day I was the personification of the German people's sense of justice," he knew that even those who did not accept this assertion were too intimidated to contradict him. In a society based on the consent of the governed such assertions are unthinkable. Consent presupposes open discussion and frequently leads to compromises. That, in itself, means recognition of differences about the concept of government and about the role of government. Fisher Ames, a conservative member of Congress from Massachusetts, provided us with a guideline that is still appropriate:

> A dictatorship is like a merchantman which sails well, but will sometimes strike a rock, and go to the bottom; a democracy is a raft which will never sink, but then your feet are always in the water.[3]

CHAPTER NINETEEN

The Moral Authority of Government

HAROLD C. RELYEA

SENIOR RESEARCH LIBRARIAN
CONGRESSIONAL RESEARCH SERVICE

AT THE OUTSET of the American struggle for nationhood, the Declaration of Independence, consistent with eighteenth century suspicion of the State, reflected the Enlightenment assumption that neither society nor government is organic or natural to human existence. Earlier, the English philosopher John Locke, whose ideas were familiar to the Founding Fathers, proffered that individuals initially contract with each other to form society, and then collectively establish governmental arrangements to protect presocietal or "natural" rights, as well as to facilitate social affairs. This two-contract conception subsequently received expression in the preamble to the Constitution: "We the People of the United States . . . do ordain and establish this Constitution for the United States of America."

The transformation from British colonies to an independent, constitutional democracy resulted in a change not only in our form of government, but also in the character of our government. As Walter Lippmann once observed, governing was no longer the act of one person—the king. Substituted for the monarch was a corporate king, variously called "the nation, the people, the majority, public opinion, or the general will." With this shift, the power to act and to compel obedience was insufficiently centralized to be exercised by one will. Power became distributed and qualified so that its exertion was not by command, but by interaction. "The prime business of government, therefore, is not to direct the affairs of the community," Lippmann observed, "but to harmonize the direction which the community gives to its affairs."[1]

PRESCRIBING RIGHT BEHAVIOR

In many regards, the Constitution embodies the values of the society or community, setting standards of right behavior for both the governors and the governed. Concerning failure to conform to such standards, it prescribes, for example, for the impeachment of the president, vice president, and all civil officers of the United States. Allowance is made for each house of Congress to be the judge of the qualifications of its own members, assuming that such qualifications or standards of right behavior will be determined by each house as well.

The Constitution also allows further prescription of standards of right behavior through legislation, administrative instruments, and judicial pronouncements. Such prescriptions must be in conformity with the standards of the Constitution and, Lippmann has noted, serve "to harmonize the direction which the community gives to its affairs." Law "represents the most stable compromise among the interests which have made themselves heard."[2]

TRANSPARENCY AND ACCOUNTABILITY

Indeed, the need for societal or community interests to be heard during policymaking indicates that standards of right behavior pertain not only to the substance or content of law, but also to its formulation and administration. Important considerations in these regards are transparency and accountability. The Constitution, for example, specifies that each house of Congress "shall keep a Journal of its Proceedings, and from time to time publish the same, excepting such Parts as may in their Judgment require Secrecy."[3] The First Amendment guarantees the citizenry freedom to discuss public business (a privilege previously reserved for members of the legislature), freedom of the press (to assist the people in maintaining their watchful vigil over the State), and freedom "to petition the Government for a redress of grievances" (which may include presentations against State secrecy or for access to official records).

Moreover, with its system of checks and balances, the Constitution anticipates that each branch will be knowledgable of the activities and interests of the other two. In this regard, it provides that, when the president vetoes a bill, "he shall return it, with his Objections to that House in which it shall have originated, who shall enter the Objections at large on their Journal and proceed to reconsider it."[4] Concerning interbranch accountability, provision is made for the president to "require the Opinion, in writing, of the principal Officer in each of the executive Departments, upon any Subject relating to the Duties of their respective Offices."[5] The Constitution also indicates that the president "shall from time to time give to the Congress Information of the State of the Union, and recommend to their Consideration such Measures as he shall judge necessary and expedient."[6]

LEGISLATING TRANSPARENCY AND ACCOUNTABILITY

Upon first convening in 1789, Congress enacted a series of laws providing for the printing and distribution of both statutes and treaties,[7] the preservation of State papers,[8] and the maintenance of official files in the new departments.[9] The printing and distribution of both the Senate and House journals was authorized in 1813.[10] Beginning in 1824, Congress arranged for a contemporary summary of each chamber's floor proceedings to be published in the *Register of Debates*. In 1833, it switched to the weekly *Congressional Globe*, which sought to chronicle every step in the legislative process of the two houses, and then established a daily publication schedule for the *Globe* in 1865.[11] In March 1873, the *Congressional Record* succeeded the *Globe* as the official congressional gazette.[12]

Provision was initially made in 1846 for the routine printing of all congressional reports, special documents, and bills.[13] While these responsibilities were met for many years through the use of contract printers, such arrangements proved to be subject to considerable political abuse. Consequently, in 1860, Congress established the Government Printing Office to produce all of its literature and to serve, as well, the printing needs of the executive branch.[14] Additional aspects of government-wide printing and publication policy were set with the Printing Act of 1895, which is the source of much of the substance of the printing chapters of Title 44 of the United States Code.[15]

In addition to publishing the statutes and a variety of legislative literature (including executive branch materials, which were initially produced as Senate or House documents) and promoting newspaper reprinting of the laws and treaties, Congress also developed a depository library program to further facilitate public knowledge of government actions. In 1859, the Secretary of the Interior was statutorily tasked with distributing all books printed or purchased for the use of the federal government, except those for the particular use of Congress or executive branch entities.[16] In 1869, a subordinate officer—the Superintendent of Public Documents—was mandated to perform this responsibility.[17] Distributions were made throughout the country to certain libraries which were designated to be depositories for government documents. This arrangement had been begun in 1813 with regard to congressional materials,[18] and was extended in 1857 to include other federal literature.[19] The Printing Act of 1895 relocated the Superintendent of Public Documents to the Government Printing Office.[20]

In the relocation process, the superintendent was also given responsibility for managing the sale of documents and preparing periodic indices of Printing Office products. Until 1904, the sale stock available to the superintendent derived entirely from such materials as were provided for this purpose by the departments and agencies, or were returned from the depository libraries. The situation was altered when the superintendent was granted authority to reprint any departmental publication, with the consent of the pertinent secretary, for public sale.[21] Congress legislated comparable discretion to reproduce its documents in 1922.[22]

THE NEW ADMINISTRATIVE STATE

By 1922, however, the federal government had entered a new phase with the rise of the administrative state. Among the forces contributing to this development was the Progressive Movement, which sought greater government intervention into and regulation of various sectors of American society. An autonomous Department of Labor was established in 1913, along with the Federal Reserve. The Federal Trade Commission was created the following year. With United States entry into World War I, regulatory activities further expanded and the number of administrative agencies increased. In the postwar era, government expansion momentarily slowed, but began again with the onset of the Great Depression and the arrival of the New Deal.

As federal regulatory powers and administrative entities dramatically grew during this period, there was a concomitant increase in both the number and variety of controlling directives, regulations, and requirements. While one contemporary observer characterized the operative situation in 1920 as one of "confusion,"[23] another described the deteriorating conditions in 1934 as "chaos."[24] During the early days of the New Deal, administrative law pronouncements were in such disarray that, on one occasion, government attorneys appearing before the Supreme Court were embarrassed to find their case was based upon a nonexistent regulation,[25] and, on another, it was discovered that litigation was being pursued under a revoked executive order.[26]

To address the accountability problem, Congress statutorily authorized a new executive gazette—the *Federal Register*—in July 1935.[27] Produced each workday, it contains a variety of presidential directives and agency regulations. In 1937, Congress inaugurated the *Code of Federal Regulations*, organized in 50 titles paralleling those of the United States Code.[28] This cumulation of the instruments and authorities appearing in the *Federal Register* contains almost all operative agency regulations, and is updated annually.

The accountability arrangements established with the creation of the *Federal Register* and the *Code of Federal Regulations*, however, addressed only half the problem. Uniformity in the form and promulgation of agency regulations remained an issue. The Attorney General created a study committee to explore this matter, and it reported in 1941.[29] Although the events of World War II temporarily delayed consideration of the committee's recommendations, Congress and the executive subsequently cooperated in legislating the Administrative Procedure Act of 1946.[30] In addition to establishing a uniform procedure for the promulgation of agency regulations, the statute also directed the agencies to publish in the *Federal Register* "the established places at which, and methods whereby, the public may secure information or make submittals or requests."[31] However, broad discretionary allowances were made for protecting information, and a changing climate of opinion within the federal bureaucracy soon transformed this public information mandate into a basis for administrative secrecy.

Conditioned by recent wartime information restrictions, intimidated by zealous congressional investigators and other official and unofficial pursuers of allegedly disloyal Americans both within and outside of government, and threatened by various postwar reconversion efforts at reducing the executive work force, the federal bureaucracy was not eager to have its activities and operations disclosed to the public. Attempts by the press and others to gain access to agency records were increasingly stymied by a "need to know" policy, deriving from both the housekeeping statute and the Administrative Procedure Act. The first of these laws, dating to 1789, vested department heads with considerable latitude in regulating the custody, use, and preservation of the records and papers of their organizations, including setting limits on the public availability of these materials.[32] The Administrative Procedure Act indicated that matters of official record should be accessible to the public, but allowed restrictions to be applied "for good cause found" or "in the public interest." While such authorities did not foster the "need to know" policy, they did serve to justify it.

By the early 1950s, many sectors of American society, including legal and good government reformers, the press, and elements of Congress, found this situation intolerable. Subsequently, after a long congressional examination and a difficult legislative struggle, the public information section of the Administrative Procedure Act was replaced in 1966 by new law. The Freedom of Information Act established a presumptive right of public access to existing, unpublished agency records; specified nine categories of information that may be exempted from the rule of disclosure; and provided for court resolution of disputes over the availability of requested materials. Later amended on four occasions, most recently in 1996, with portions subjected to considerable judicial interpretation, the statute remains an effective tool for enabling public access to agency records.[33]

The Freedom of Information Act has also served as a model for securing accountability regarding other aspects of the administrative state. For example, the Privacy Act of 1974 set certain standards of fair information use, prohibited the collection of some kinds of personally identifiable information, and otherwise authorized American citizens to obtain access to many federal agency files on themselves.[34] Apart from the documentary realm, the Federal Advisory Committee Act of 1972 established a presumption that agency advisory committee meetings would be open to public scrutiny; specified conditions when the rule of openness may be modified; and provided for court resolution of disputes over the propriety of closing such meetings. The statute also set certain conditions regarding public notices of advisory committee meetings, and promoted balance in the selection of committee members.[35] Similarly, the Government in the Sunshine Act of 1976 established a presumption that the policymaking deliberations of collegially-headed federal agencies—such as boards, commissions, and councils—would be open to public observation, unless closed in accordance with specified exemptions. Public notice requirements for such meetings and court resolution of disputes over meeting closings were also prescribed.[36]

In no small measure, the moral authority of American national government rests upon the Constitution, which sets standards of right behavior for both the governors and the governed. Additional standards may be prescribed through statutory, administrative, and judicial law. The exercise of this authority has resulted in a long history of legislating standards of right behavior concerning the formulation and administration of laws—of guaranteeing transparency and accountability in the creation and implementation of law, with a view to realizing better informed and more knowledgeable participation in the policymaking process by societal or community interests. As Thomas Jefferson said over a century and a half ago: "I know no safe depository of the ultimate powers of the society but the people themselves; and if we think them not enlightened enough to exercise their control with a wholesome discretion, the remedy is not to take it from them, but to inform their discretion by education."[37]

CHAPTER TWENTY

The Supreme Court and Affirmative Action

SAMUEL LEITER

ATTORNEY, SALEM MASSACHUSETTS

WILLIAM LEITER

PROFESSOR OF POLITICAL SCIENCE
CALIFORNIA STATE UNIVERSITY AT LONG BEACH

OUR GOVERNMENT'S MORAL AUTHORITY is its power to define our rights and responsibilities. This power must be aligned with our constitutional guarantees, and it is for the Supreme Court—stationed at the pinnacle of our scheme of judicial review—to participate in defining these guarantees and their related principles of moral justice and political decency.[1]

Arguably, judicial review should stress vigorous, preemptively proactive efforts at producing a firm and unambiguous statutory and constitutional construction, and thus help generate solid moral guideposts. Where our constitutional guarantees have been subject to major disputes, however, Supreme Court review has been pockmarked by long periods of issue-avoidance; muffled, cloudy opinions; sluggish advancing and retreating.

So-called "legal realists" argue that the oft-muddied waters of judicial review reflect the Supreme Court's effort at continually adjusting to the necessities of the times, and that—consequently—such pragmatism is morally requisite. However, this view of judicial construction as involving the pragmatic shifting of legal sands would not satisfy those who hunger for a morality incorporating a clear and certain case law. People from this camp would doubtless conclude that in the area of affirmative action the Supreme Court has often and badly fumbled its responsibility to lead in the clear delineation of what is morally just and politically decent.

THE UPS AND DOWNS OF AFFIRMATIVE ACTION

Affirmative action has come to mean the use of race, national origin, and gender preferences to counter discrimination. Earlier efforts at advancing the rights of the oppressed included the Thirteenth, Fourteenth, and Fifteenth Amendments to the Constitution. While the Thirteenth Amendment abolished slavery in 1865, it was far from clear whether the framers intended to go beyond freedom from physical restraint and to incorporate the abolition of the badges of slavery. However, under the Fourteenth and Fifteenth Amendments and various congressional enactments in the 1860s and 70s, the freed slaves were declared full-fledged citizens with legal immunity from state interference. Initially, this bold initiative for racial equity in large measure failed, primarily on account of relentless southern resistance and lack of support by the Supreme Court. In the famous 1896 *Plessy v. Ferguson* case, the Court majority allowed that the purpose of the equal protection clause in the Fourteenth Amendment ". . . was undoubtedly to enforce the absolute equality of the two races before the law . . ." But it ruled nonetheless that ". . . in the nature of things it could not have been intended to abolish distinctions based on color, or to enforce social as distinguished from political equality."[2] Accordingly, the majority rejected an equal protection suit against a state law which required racially segregated "equal" railroad facilities. The effect of this abrasively immoral ruling was to legitimate the principle that racial segregation is not incompatible with equality. To be sure, the doctrine of "separate but equal" symbolized the moral gulf into which the cause of minority rights vanished until the aftermath of World War II.

In the mid-twentieth century school desegregation cases, "separate but equal" was put to the test and rejected. The legendary *Brown and Swann* decisions signified major changes in the government's moral calculus. First, the high court reversed itself. In *Brown v. The Board* (1954),[3] the Court held that racial segregation of *itself* deprives school children of their Fourteenth Amendment rights; and that "separate" educational facilities are unequal as a matter of law. Second, and some fourteen years after *Brown*, the Court finally ended a vexatious constitutional dispute grounded in *Brown's* ambiguity by determining that the equal protection of the laws required integration and not merely the end of state-imposed segregation.[4] Even later, in *Swann v. Charlotte-*

Mecklenburg (1971)[5] the Court held that race-conscious remedies, such as classroom integration and inter-district busing were appropriate, notwithstanding the attendant risk of collateral disadvantage for nonminorities. This ruling marked the birth of affirmative action, in concept, if not in name.

Was the aforementioned delay in post-*Brown* interpretation morally appropriate? The same issue arises in connection with the Court's slow-moving treatment of affirmative action in such other areas as employment, higher education, and voting.

The crusade for minority rights continued in the 1964 Civil Rights Act's omnibus ban of discrimination—the first in our history. Many hailed it as the entree to the Promised Land of universal equality. But plainly it was not if a strictly literal reading is employed. Facially, the Act contained sanctions only against *intentional* violations, and seemed to rule out any resort to remedial preferences. What about the spirit of the Act? Did Congress also intend to attack societal racism ("disparate impact") as well as intentional maltreatment of identifiable victims ("disparate treatment")? If yes, then some form of remedial preference is permissible, notwithstanding the seeming facial bar. If no, then affirmative action violates the equal protection mandate which it is supposed to enforce. This doctrinal dispute remains unresolved to this day.[6]

Here was a moral issue of the first magnitude. How was America to attack its long and abysmal history of invidious discrimination? Did not the moral premises of the equal protection clause oblige the country to invoke affirmative action for this purpose? Was it appropriate to limit the 1964 Act to curing disparate treatment?

Affirmative action won the first round of the battle. In the 1970s and 80s the civil rights lobby, and its allies in the executive bureaucracy, persuaded the High Court to rule that disparate impact is illegal,[7] and that affirmative action was available both under the 1964 Act,[8] and—in *Regents v. Bakke*[9]—under the equal protection clause of the Constitution. One opinion in *Bakke*— that by Justice Powell—went so far as to accept the use of race as a "plus" factor in university admissions for diversity purposes even in the absence of discrimination. Concurrently the Nixon Administration initiated a hiring regime permitting racial preferences in the enforcement of anti-discrimination in federal contracting. All told, it appeared that affirmative action was here to stay.

But then came the second round. In the *1989 Wards Cove v.*

Atonio opinion,[10] the Court decided to shift the burden of proof in disparate impact litigation to the plaintiff. Had this decision stood, affirmative action would have been dealt a paralyzing blow.[11] But Congress intervened. By amendments finally approved in 1991, disparate impact and affirmative action were incorporated in the 1964 Act, together with a qualified version of the old burden-of-proof law.

Nevertheless, it can be argued that the *Wards Cove* turn-around by the Supreme Court has continued. In the *1989 Richmond v. Croson*[12] case, the Supreme Court struck down a municipal plan ear-marking public funds ("set-asides") for the benefit of disadvantaged minority contractors. The Court held that the plan violated the equal protection rights of nonminority contractors because the asserted minority "disadvantage" was not attributable to past discrimination by the municipality. The past-discrimination rule was central to "strict scrutiny" judicial review imposed in *Croson* for the first time in connection with the adjudication of state affirmative action. And the past discrimination/strict scrutiny standard seemingly represents a major change in affirmative action case law; implicitly calling into question that policy's systemic-bias predicate. In *Adarand v. Pena* (1995),[13] the Court applied the past discrimination/strict scrutiny standard in deciding an appeal involving a *federal* set-aside. In both cases, the Court's majority appeared to express considerable doubt that group rights fall within the purview of the equal protection clause.

WHITHER THE SUPREME COURT AND AFFIRMATIVE ACTION?

At present, the tide appears to be running against affirmative action. Apart from the adverse trend in recent Supreme Court decisions, several states have enacted affirmative action bans, or are actively considering them. Three of the eleven federal courts of appeals have repudiated the "diversity" rationale which has been a fixture in affirmative action policy. Across the country many local school districts are winning or seeking release from court-ordered busing plans; the Supreme Court has even been requested to reopen the lead *Charlotte-Mecklenburg* school-busing decision which has been on the books for almost 30 years. A growing number of minority spokesmen openly espouse return to separate but equal. For better or for worse, affirmative action's moral journey may be ending.

Yet it "ain't" necessarily so. There is every indication that the government and the country at large cannot make up their mind about how to handle this "hot potato." In recent sessions of Congress, several bills for abolition of affirmative action have not been allowed to get to the floor; at least two attempts to terminate existing programs have suffered defeat in up-and-down votes. There remains an abundance of support for protected group preferences in academe, the governmental bureaucracies, private business, and the White House. Many state legislatures have rejected bans on affirmative action as did the City of Houston. The Supreme Court has refused to adjudicate a number of cases which have life-or-death implications for race, gender, national origin-conscious programs: e.g., (1) the status of non-remedial "diversity";[14] (2) the status of desegregation in higher learning, in particular the future of historically black colleges and universities;[15] and (3) the states' legal right to abolish affirmative action.[16]

Affirmative action should be considered unfinished political and legal business. It would be rash to rule out the possibility of developments that could offset the current trend. As we have seen, the history of minority rights has always been non-linear— X steps forward, Y steps back, Z steps forward again. Who is to say that this process is no longer in effect, particularly since the strict scrutiny doctrine is subject to a variety of firmer and looser constructions. An outstanding constitutional scholar—Ronald Dworkin— impressively argues that the opinions of the current Supreme Court majority conform more with a looser view—a view which regards race-conscious programs as incapable of passing strict scrutiny only when they are rooted in racial/minority group animus.[17] Surely, this approach to strict scrutiny might permit much affirmative action. Additionally, consider the creation of "minority-majority" electoral districts which has been promoted to increase the number of minority public officials. The Supreme Court ruled in 1993[18] that these districts are subject to strict scrutiny where race is the *predominant* factor in their creation. Of course, it is easy to imagine many situations where race can be a factor— but not necessarily the predominant one—in the drawing of district lines, thus allowing for more minority-majority districting. Further, the Court has yet to tell us whether protected group preference programs are appropriate remedies for segregation in residential housing, currently the hardiest variety of racial segregation and one hardly visited by affirmative action.

What affirmative action possibilities will materialize? In truth, nobody knows. Probably though, Supreme Court affirmative action clarification will be slow in coming, cautious, and incremental. This is understandable given the formidable analytical problems involved, and the fierce differences of opinion on the subject. The decisive moral question is how far "equality" can be stretched? How does the State resolve the inherent conflict between the citizenry's freedom of choice and its own moral duty to eradicate bias? Has government the legal right and moral duty to impose limits on the expansion of minority and female rights? There is no explicit guidance for the solution of these issues in the words of the Constitution. Given the absence of such guidance, the eye-crossing analytical problems, and the enormous political controversy, it should be recognized that affirmative action is a labyrinth in which even the most seasoned legal travelers easily lose their way. Consequently, those seeking a near-term, energetic High Court initiative for the adoption of specific and comprehensive standards in this area are likely to be disappointed. Those so affected will doubtless view the Court's moral authority as considerably deficient. On the other hand, a major Court historian—Robert McCloskey—praised the caution, deliberateness, and incrementalism which the Court has exercised, theorizing that this operational mode was the Court's most efficient way to exercise its moral authority and promote justice and decency. He wrote:

> Surely the record teaches that no useful purpose is served when the judges seek all the hottest political caldrons of the moment and dive into the middle of them . . . The Court's greatest successes have been achieved when it has operated near the margins rather that in the center of political controversy, when it has nudged and gently tugged the nation, instead of trying to rule . . . [C]onsider the long campaign on behalf of laissez-faire from 1905 to 1934, with its pattern of concession to the principle of regulation, dotted here and there with a warning that the principle could be carried too far . . . The Court ruled more in each case when it tried to rule less, and that paradox is one of the clearest morals to be drawn from its history.[19]

The question of whether the McCloskey thesis is applicable to the Supreme Court's treatment of affirmative action is a challenging one.

CHAPTER TWENTY ONE

Antitrust: A Codification of American Morality

THEODORE P. KOVALEFF

DIRKS AND COMPANY

IN MANY WAYS, the antitrust corpus is the best example of morality in the United States' legal system. The embodiment of fair play, protection for the weaker and unprotected, and with the goal of the welfare of the consumer, the body of laws that constitute today's antitrust corpus has a history that dates back to colonial times and its much revered English common law antecedents.

Essentially, the early laws were designed to ensure that persons would not be victimized by those who cornered a market or artificially set a price on an important commodity, the lack of which could make the difference between life and death. Today, while the consequences are not as dire, the concept is no different. To understand where we are today, however, it is necessary to look at the foundations of the laws; we must trace their evolution to today and their invocation in the Microsoft case.

In the colonial and early national days, when the economies were local, it was easy to interfere with the trade of essentials. Thus it was that in most of the original colonies and in the early states, there were statutes that prohibited regrating, forestalling, and engrossing of necessities such as food or firewood. A person who forestalled intercepted goods on the way to market with the intent of fixing the price of the item when it reached the market. Thus he was better able to make a profit. An engrosser would buy at wholesale (in gross) and later would resell, either at retail but usually in bulk with the intention of making a profit. Regrating was buying a necessity in one market with the purpose of selling it again in another market at a profit. Although the regulations were aimed at the attempt to corner the market, this clearly was not a time that was friendly to the arbitrageur!

These early laws reflected the deep-felt attitudes of the settlers. Those who came on their own volition to the Thirteen Colonies were far different from the settlers in French, Spanish or Portuguese America. Whereas the latter had come to work in extractive enterprises such as mining or fur trading, most of the former were settled by persons with highly individualistic attitudes. Although extant, especially as one journeyed southward, class distinctions were less prevalent than in contemporary Europe. As one went westward, they tended to diminish further. In sum, our forefathers were independent minded, somewhat ornery, goal oriented, and not very class conscious. Their religious outlook and the physical environment itself made personal responsibility primary. In retrospect, it is fitting that Adam Smith would publish *The Wealth of Nations* in 1776, the same date as the outbreak of the American Revolution.

In many ways, the American Revolution can be seen as the first battle against monopoly in America. While many of the colonies had benefited from specific monopolies granted to facilitate their growth, support for the British mercantile system was not widespread and many attempted to evade its regulations. Had it not been for the Boston Tea Party (a response to the British East India Company's plan to liquidate inventory at a price which undercut the ongoing cost of the smuggled product) and allied events in other colonies, there would never have been the repressive British response, the "Intolerable Acts," the Massachusetts colonial response, and then the ensuing Revolution.

Subsequently, with the advent of canal and rail transportation in the early nineteenth century, the movement of freight became easier and less expensive for all concerned. As a result, economies evolved from local to regional and then, later, after the Civil War, to national. As that transpired, enterprise grew and became more efficient. Yet, with that came the opportunity for obstruction of the free market on an ever larger and larger scale. As a result, early efforts at containing them were state-based responses. The first of these movements was the result of farm organizations or "granges"; their actions were often aimed at the railroads which came to have a stranglehold over the delivery systems, or the operators of grain elevators which stored the product for the farmers until they were ready to ship it. In *Munn v. Illinois* (1877), the Supreme Court upheld the right of states (in this case Illinois) to regulate what was, to the users, a public utility.

The Gilded Age was very much a two-party period. No president served two consecutive terms and neither the Republicans nor the Democrats controlled the presidency for more than four consecutive years. Some of the most compelling ideas of the period were first voiced by third parties and then were quickly coopted by one or both of the major parties.

Therefore, it is not surprising that although the Anti-Monopoly Party ran a presidential candidate in 1884, winning a minuscule less than two percent of the total votes cast, its influence was far more considerable. In the next election contest, the Republican Party platform inveighed against "all combinations of capital organized in trusts or otherwise to control arbitrarily the conditions of trade among our citizens." The platform then suggested legislation to "prevent the execution of all schemes to oppress the people." The Democrats also included a statement in opposition to trusts: ". . . the interests of the people are betrayed, when, by unnecessary taxation, trusts and combinations are permitted and fostered which . . . rob the body of our citizens.[1] That same year, Senator John Sherman introduced his first antitrust bill but it did not come to the floor for a vote. Neither, for that matter, did any of the numerous other bills on the subject.

Although in the *Wabash Case*,[2] the Supreme Court had invalidated state attempts to regulate interstate rail traffic, within a year, Congress had created the Interstate Commerce Commission, opening the way for the first federal attempt at regulation of business outside of banking. The federal government now had the power to regulate its first monopolies. How successful it was has been a matter of debate. Whatever its degree of success, it was placed in a position of becoming a countervailing power, with the responsibility of protecting the weaker party.

The result of compromise among the many who had offered legislation regulating trade, the Sherman Antitrust Act[3] was passed with but one dissenting vote in 1890. This was a time of Social Darwinism. The doctrine of the "survival of the fittest" had been applied to industry. Thus, "industry's biggest are the fittest."

The legislation was indeed a breakthrough; a qualifier had been added: the big entities had to have achieved their status fairly. To be specific, the statute prohibited every contract, combination, or conspiracy in restraint of interstate trade. To ensure that the private sector as well as the government would utilize the statute, nongovernmental parties were allowed to sue for treble repayment of damages incurred as a result of an illegal act.

Given the rhetoric of the debates over the legislation, one

would have expected that the statute would have been used immediately and often. Surprisingly, this was not the case. A good proportion of the early actions were brought against labor unions and farm cooperatives.

To ensure that the statute could accomplish the goals of its drafters, in the period after its passage, a number of provisions were added to broaden its ambit and to respond to adverse Supreme Court decisions. The most important of these were the passage of the Clayton Act and the Federal Trade Commission Act in 1914 during the administration of President Woodrow Wilson. Each significantly extended the antitrust coverage. Additionally, labor and farm cooperative organizations were protected from the Sherman Act provisions.

The Clayton Act did not change the thrust of the Sherman Act. Rather, it interdicted activities which Congress felt had been left uncovered by the statute. The concept of "incipiency" is key to the coverage of the new law. Whereas the Sherman Act was aimed at *present* evils, for the most part, the Clayton Act was directed against *potential* problems, whether or not the action(s) were presently illegal. As a result, it forbade such activities as price discrimination, exclusive dealer contracts, certain types of stock acquisitions or interlocking directorates, any of which could have the effect of substantially lessening competition or *tending to* create a monopoly. Again, the treble damage recovery proviso was included for private actions.

Almost simultaneously with the passage of the Clayton Act, Congress ratified the Trade Commission Act, establishing the Federal Trade Commission (FTC) to serve as an administrative body. Congress endowed it with quasi-legislative powers so it could define what was unfair competition. By logical extension, Congress allowed it to determine for itself the areas of its jurisdiction.

In many ways, the passage of the two statutes marked the first high water mark for antitrust. After President Theodore Roosevelt had resurrected antitrust and used it as part of his campaign to regulate big business, his successor William Howard Taft had continued his policy; and his administration, which lasted roughly half as long, initiated twice as many antitrust actions. Even on a sheer numbers basis, the eighteen actions initiated during his predecessor administrations were dwarfed by his filings.

It is instructive that the Supreme Court had not helped matters with their decisions and opinions. The *E. C. Knight*[4] case which held that the manufacture of sugar was not commerce, with the logical extension that the consolidation of the industry was out of the range of the Act, disappointed many who had hoped that the Sherman Act could halt the growth of trusts. After the *Trans-Missouri Freight Association* and *Addyston* cases[5] which had treated loose combinations and poolings, the Court did little to discourage full combinations into single legal entities.

Roosevelt's surprising and successful action against the Northern Security Company,[6] challenging a combination of rail giants in the northwest that had brought together J. P. Morgan, John D. Rockefeller, James J. Hill, and E. H. Harriman, a veritable *dramatis personae* of trustees, rallied popular support for the statute and led inexorably to a number of high profile actions, including the ones against Standard Oil, the Beef and Tobacco Trusts, all of which resulted in Supreme Court victories.[7] It is unquestionable that the outcome of the cases did have a lasting influence on jurisprudence and the economy in general.[8]

Within hours after the signing of the Trade Commission Act into law, World War I began. As a result, the exigencies of war preparation and supply muted the antitrust impulse.

In the twenties, widespread inventions and their quick acceptance brought prosperity to many. Few appeared troubled by the growth of industry associations. They were simply an outgrowth of the new prosperity. Economic historians Gilbert C. Fite and Jim E. Reese overstate it somewhat saying, "For all practical purposes the antitrust laws were suspended in the 1920s."[9] The Secretary of Commerce, Herbert Hoover, advocated protection from antitrust prosecution for industries that had "failed to prosper under the competitive system."[10] As president, however, he tended away from this stance, only supporting dilution of antitrust coverage when it would encourage the conservation of natural resources. An analysis of his actions shows that this applied most especially to the coal and oil industries.[11]

The Depression was not likely to foster attitudes in favor of the existing economic system, which was essentially one of competition. Franklin Roosevelt's response to the economic disaster followed no single policy. This is especially true in the case of antitrust and the regulation of business. At first the National Recovery Act experimented with the cartelization of industry. In order to return to prosperity, the idea was to remove obstructions to the free flow of business in interstate and foreign commerce and to foster the general welfare by promoting the organization of industries. To accomplish this the resultant National Recovery Administration (NRA) suspended many facets of the antitrust laws. It condoned and even encouraged the formation of more trade associations and it established Codes of Fair Competition which included pricing and production goals and limits. In some cases they even divided a market between competitors. Even after the unanimous *Schechter* decision[12] which declared the NRA unconstitutional, the thrust of the New Deal toward antitrust remained unchanged for several more years.

The 1937 Roosevelt Depression following his landslide election victory forced the administration to search for a way to extricate the country from a second major economic downturn. The appointment of Thurman Arnold as Assistant Attorney General in charge of the Antitrust Division of the Department of Justice (AAG) and his Temporary National Economic Commission in 1938, marked a change in new Deal attitudes toward antitrust. The thrust of the change was not to a trust-busting mandate, but rather to one designed for promoting growth and expanding the purchasing power of the consumer.[13] During his five-year tenure, the size of the Division grew from just over 100 to nearly 500.

When war broke out again in Europe, it dramatically affected antitrust policy. Roosevelt reversed course. In the antitrust sphere, the change in outlook was ratified in an agreement between the Attorney General, the Secretary of War, the Secretary of the Navy, and the AAG on March 20, 1942, in which many antitrust actions, including trials, were postponed until after the end of the conflict.

World War II doubled the Gross National Product—to $100 billion. Concomitant with this increase was a growth in industrial concentration. Larger companies had benefited inordinately from war production contracts. Additionally, to facilitate production of needed war material, the Government itself had acquired diverse properties. The antitrust ideal and the need for competition were not, however, casualties of the conflict. The Surplus Property Act of 1944 included directions that the government dispose of properties "as promptly as possible without fostering monopoly or restraint of trade"[14] as soon as the conflict had ended.

The government's interaction with the aluminum industry is a good example of the way postwar divestiture was supposed to proceed. Arising out of an investigation begun in 1934, the government had filed a Sherman Act suit in April 1937 against Aluminum Company of America (customarily shortened to Alcoa), charging that the company had sought to restrain competition, monopolize bauxite, water power, and various specific products including alumina and aluminum.[15] The case was dismissed in July 1943. Although the company was heavily involved in the war effort, the government had appealed immediately.[16] After the war, under the Surplus Property Administrator, the government aluminum plants were divested to Reynolds and Permanente Metals corporations. The only facilities sold to Alcoa were ones for which there were no reasonable bids. As a result, Alcoa was able to demonstrate satisfactorily that there was indeed competition in the industry and that there was no requirement that it be broken up. Thanks to the interaction of the Sherman Act and the Surplus Property Act, competition was finally adjudged to have come to the aluminum industry in 1955. As Whitney stated, "the application of antitrust laws to aluminum . . . must be rated as one of the several reasons for the rapid growth of the industry today."[17]

The attitude toward antitrust was more favorable after World War II than it had been after World War I. Instead of ignoring it, the corpus was strengthened as legislation was passed closing a loophole in the Clayton Act in 1950. The Truman Administration filed several important actions, including American Telephone and Telegraph (ATT), International Business Machines, and two against E.I. Dupont de Nemours & Company. While few of the suits were ultimately successful, the amended statute would play a major role in subsequent enforcement. Popular sentiment in favor of the corpus could not have hurt its chances with the successor Eisenhower administration.

Today, one must struggle to understand the temper of the immediate postwar era. On the international front, a war in which all the enemies had been decisively vanquished, the discovery that one of our former allies was now a threat to our way of life, was frightening. Domestically, after the Great Depression and the various attempts to solve its problems, and then the dislocations of World War II, there was the fear that the depression might return. It was only the war-induced mobilization that finally broke the depression. With the peace, that heritage, plus the worry that the dislocations of demobilization might lead to a return of the depression, led many to question how to ensure that job development could be national priority. In this climate, it would have been easy for antitrust to have become a casualty.

Luckily for our economic system today, the Eisenhower administration adopted a strong enforcement policy and in a number of instances, even strengthened portions of the antitrust corpus. Drawing on a careful study of the laws[18] and utilizing the newly amended Clayton Act for the first time, its antitrusters sought court decisions defining its coverage. These included the acquisition of the Hotels Statler Corporation by Hilton Hotels, and Snow Crop by Minute Maid Corporation. Had it not been for their interest and early actions, it is not likely that Bethlehem Steel would have abandoned its plans to acquire Youngstown Sheet and Tube Corporation after an unfavorable determination by the District Court.[19] Later, the administration became more activist appealing the *Brown Shoe* decision[20] and opposing the planned Texaco acquisition of Superior Oil Corporation.[21] In each case, the government would ultimately prevail; in the *Brown Shoe*, it was necessary to appeal a District Court decision to the Supreme Court; in *Texaco*, given the administration's strong enforcement record, the companies abandoned their plans, certain that they would have to spend significant resources in a time-consuming, and probably losing legal struggle.

The Eisenhower antitrusters took equally decisive action against long-standing business practices in the electrical industry which had consistently violated the Sherman Act.[22] The final count number 32 corporations and 48 individual defendants as defendants or co-conspirators in 20 separate conspiracies to fix prices or allocate contracts. It is noteworthy that the punishments were levied after the Kennedy administration has taken power; the fines of $1,785,000 for the corporations and $139,000 for their executives may seem small by today's standards, but, at the time and in the context of previous enforcement, they were gigantic and nearly bankrupted some of the smaller players.

In many ways, the most important result of the electrical cases was the growth of private actions, taking advantage of the treble damage provisions of the corpus. As the government had insisted on guilty rather than *nolo contendere* pleas in most cases, the record of each of the cases was admissible for private plaintiffs. The total costs of all the conspirators was never tallied, but with but four cases left unsettled, on May 13, 1969, Senator Philip Hart claimed that "the total paid [by the defendant electrical manufacturers] or agreed to" was $405,274,016.07. The sum was, for the most part, the result of private actions filed by persons or corporations. As a result, a private action-oriented antitrust bar developed which would play a major role in antitrust policy thereafter.[23]

That the Kennedy–Johnson Department of Justice followed through on the inherited actions is important in that it continued the momentum. Kennedy AAG Lee Loevinger did follow through with his successful attempts to bring regulated industries such as banking more directly under the supervision of the antitrusters. The Kennedy administration's landmark action opposing Philadelphia National Bank's acquisition of Girard Trust Corn Exchange Bank was finally victorious at the Supreme Court level[24] and provided a much-needed precedent for dealing with other similar mergers in the industry.

While there was an antitrust corpus, there was no official explanation or the interpretation of the laws. The *Report of the Attorney General's National Committee to Study the Antitrust Laws* had helped somewhat, but it was not an Antitrust Division document and thus it was still necessary to peruse speech and interview transcripts for clues as to Division policy and actions. It was not until the Johnson administration and Donald F. Turner's tenure as AAG that the first specific set of guidelines was promulgated. It specifically covered the area of mergers and acquisitions.[25] The attitude behind the promulgation of the guidelines is most important and represents an important shift in perspective: now companies were viewed as wanting to abide by the regulations. As a consequence, the Division should try to help them, rather than trap them.

During the late 1950s and 1960s a number of companies merged across product lines. While not a totally new phenomenon, the scope and magnitude of the conglomerate movement in the 1960s was unparalleled. Ironically, however, it was not until the Nixon administration that any action was taken to rein in the movement.

Absent the Watergate scandal, it is likely that the Nixon administration would have been heralded for its tough stance against conglomerates. One of his AAG's, Richard McLaren, filed a number of actions against conglomerate takeovers, including those involving Ling Temco-Vought, Inc. (LTV), and Northwest Industries,[26] and three separate actions against International

Telephone and Telegraph Corporation (ITT) for its acquisitions of Canteen Corporation,[27] Grinnell Corporation,[28] and the Hartford Insurance Group.[29] Although the government suffered setbacks on the District Court level with injunctions against the Hartford and Grinnell acquisitions being denied, along with substantive losses in the Grinnell and Canteen Cases, he was, nevertheless, able to negotiate a settlement which included major divestitures by ITT. From this point onward until the late 1990s, when Dennis Kozlowski of Tyco Industries practically reinvented the structure, there were few conglomerate-type acquisitions, and companies so-designated languished while others flourished. Were one to analyze the record carefully, one would conclude that in the 1980s and 1990s, the real profits were made in transactions involving voluntary divestitures of divisions of wholesale corporate breakups.

Early efforts to deregulate industry in the modern era began during the Carter Administration. The Antitrust Division took the lead in numerous proceedings before the Interstate Commerce Commission and the Civil Aeronautics Board (CAB). The Airline Deregulation Act,[30] which provided for the abolition of the CAB, was subsequently passed during Carter's presidency. While federal regulation had been hailed as a boon for the public welfare just a century earlier, by the late twentieth century, markets had changed and potential competition loomed from differing forms of transportation. Deregulation became the heart of "consumer welfare" and the successor Reagan administration would endeavor to remove controls from many other different industries as well.

The Reagan administration had come into office with a very simple agenda: The government must get "off the backs of the American public." A most important aspect of this was the deregulation of additional industry sectors, and that the continuation of the ongoing deregulation be fostered.[31] The Reaganauts also believed that the ruling body of laws must be understandable; companies should be able to predict with a reasonable degree of certainty what would be the consequences of an action. As a result, they made public the business reviews that the Division had been issuing for the previous three decades They also updated and expanded upon Donald Turner's guidelines.

Someone waiting in a heavily used airport might wonder how the crowding or convoluted routing structure could be viewed as having any relation to "consumer welfare." Nevertheless, the very increase of users is the best indication of the changes wrought by deregulation. In communications, the settlement of the Telephone case,[32] resulting in the splitting off from ATT of the Bell Operating Companies, has led to a revolution in telecommunications that could never have evolved so quickly or have been so beneficial to so many had ATT remained a regulated monopolist.

The Reagan administration has been accused of having allowed too many mergers to proceed that should have been prevented. His antitrusters believed that we had evolved from a national economy to a world-wide economy, thus potential competition could arise from just about anywhere on the globe. When assessing the administration's record, it must be remembered that the number of Sherman Act cases reached an all-time high; a record number of individuals were indicted for criminal offenses, and more days of jail time were served by more individuals for antitrust infractions than ever before.[33]

During the Bush years, antitrust policy was definitely directed to enhancing consumer welfare. As a result, it brought actions against members of professional services including architects, dentists, and various aspects of medical service delivery. With the rapid changes in medical technology, what had once been a highly individualistic enterprise had evolved to one with health maintenance organizations (HMO) and doctors' groups. Applying the Sherman Act to collusive activities of these new associations aided in ensuring that the costs of health care would not rise because of illegal activities. More broadly, with the advent of a truly global economy, consumer and corporate welfare demanded that antitrust not remain solely within our national borders. The Bush antitrusters took the first steps toward elimination of foreign anti-competitive barriers to commerce. Not only did this include pressure on various countries to lower barriers to American exports, it also involved cooperation and information exchange where bilateral issues were concerned.

The antitrust record of the Clinton administration has been uneven. While it has condoned many mergers in the health care industry, it did so ensuring that the consumer was adequately protected. In encouraging and/or sanctioning mergers in the military technology industry, the rationale for action did not take the consumer into account in the same way: here the consumer was the government and in many cases it was the only purchaser.

Thus the idea of cost savings from the elimination of overlapping competitive programs was acceptable, since the companies had to negotiate terms and conditions anyway. In short, this consumer was willing to trade lowered costs, knowing that it could deal with a monopolist on equal terms. On the other hand, allowing the top two oil companies, Exxon and Mobil, to merge raises many questions. The extent of the divestitures required for governmental approval has not yet been made public. Allowing two former "sons of Standard Oil" to merge is more than noteworthy. In the international sphere, however, the Clinton antitrusters expanded upon the Bush initiatives and protected the American consumer from various collusive practices including price fixing.

As technology evolves, so too must enforcement. When the issue of intellectual property rights was first debated, no one dreamed that it would come to apply to computer programs and to the means of access to an "Internet." At the heart of the ongoing Microsoft case is the desire to ensure that there will be continuing growth and innovation in the field based on consumer welfare and acceptance of, rather than the power of, a large already extant corporation. It is premature to conjecture as to the ultimate denouement of the Microsoft action. What is clear is that it and allied initiatives, such as that of the recently settled FTC case against Intel, are having results. Other large factors such as Sun Microsystems are not making information about how their products work available to programmers of other companies. The administration has a tremendous task on its hands: it must ensure that innovation can continue at the pace that has made the country the undisputed leader in the field. It must also ensure that those who have succeeded should be able to enjoy the fruits of their labors while, at the same time, not letting them take advantage of their position and stifle future innovation—in the process hindering consumer welfare in the future. As we approach the 2000 election year, this becomes a responsibility of major proportions for all candidates.

CHARACTER AND INTEGRITY

Moral Authority through Character and Integrity

MOORHEAD KENNEDY

CHAIRMAN
MOORHEAD KENNEDY GROUP

THE ESSAYS IN THIS CHAPTER address the relevance of individual behavior to the political process. Dr. John T. Casteen, III, President of the University of Virginia, introduces many of the issues addressed by other contributors.

Dr. Casteen observes that the distinction between the *polis*, or public space, and the household, the private place, goes back to Plato. In the private space, Socrates said, people can do what they want, as they cannot in public life. For Machiavelli, however, the ruler's quality of moral worth is "irrelevant because the prince's obligation is to be effective in pursuing self-interest, not to be good." Throughout our history, Casteen points out, "we have functioned comfortably . . . with the conception of 'reasons of state', including lying and espionage. In their essays, Senator Lugar and Dr. Mervin discuss the acceptability of reasons of State.

But, Casteen notes, traditionally the "personal goodness of a governor or king is correlative to the protective stewardship that most Western cultures have seen as the ruler's obligation." Like Mark Melcher in the next essay, Dr. Casteen goes back to biblical sources to sustain this identification.

Finally, in a South fighting desegregation, government's failure to do right taught a young John Casteen the moral responsibility of government. "Moral authority derives from moral action. . . . Good government earns its goodness. We know it by its acts." The Rt. Rev. Paul Moore, Jr., further develops these ideas in the final essay of this chapter.

Dr. Casteen's essay is followed by "Character in the First "Post-Modern" Presidency," by Mark L. Melcher, Managing Director, Washington Research, Prudential Securities. He takes immediate issue with a statement made by President Clinton in an Internet interview, that character is demonstrated "most effectively" not by what you do in your personal life, but "what you fight for and for whom you fight." Mr. Clinton implies that an individual's personal behavior is not relevant to leadership.

Melcher calls this a "victory cry for post-modern thought; a bold, public assertion that traditional American views on morality and ethics had changed so dramatically that they could be flouted with relative impunity by the president himself."

Melcher goes on to summarize the debate in language reminiscent of the "natural law" versus "positive law" discussion in the previous chapter, particularly in the essays of Marie Natoli and Judith Best. On the one hand, he notes, is the traditional "Judaeo-Christian" approach—morality based on "transcendental truths." This, he says, is basic to the traditional American understanding of leadership in terms of character.

The other approach argues that there are no absolutes, no transcendental truths. He quotes President Clinton's former Surgeon General, "everyone has different moral standards." All moral standards are therefore merely subjective.

After tracing the origins of this conflict back for many centuries, Melcher concludes, as did Judith Best, that liberty cannot exist where there are no transcendental truths. These are the basis for the moral authority of the government that, in turn, makes liberty possible.

In the next essay, "Is Government an Authority on Morality?" Dan F. Hahn, Professor of Culture and Communication, New York University, projects the postmodern approach that Melcher so deplores. "I am suspicious," he comments, "of the move from public virtue to private morality. . . ."

Melcher's "fundamental conflict" becomes, in Hahn's view, a liberal versus conservative debate. In the Lewinsky scandal, the liberals argued that Clinton's morality was irrelevant, since it was a private matter. The conservatives argued that "morality protection and promulgation" was a basic function of government. In the Lewinsky case, the public took the "liberal" position. Hahn separates personal moral questions from questions of civic virtue, and particularly how well an official does his job.

Hence, Hahn sees the "moral authority of government" in

terms of whether we "turn over to government the responsibility for being a/the moral authority." His answer is negative: ". . . government only can have 'moral authority' when the people it governs subscribe to the same morality . . . and that when all subscribe to the same morality, we have not a society of humans but a colony of automatons."

By contrast, Dorothy Buckton James, Professor of Political Science, Connecticut College, begins her essay, "The Once and Future (?) Consensus" with the assertion, "The United States of America began its national life with a strong consensus that government should exercise moral authority." Like Melcher, she argues that this consensus held firm until recently (according to her in the 1970s). It has been replaced by a "corrosive cynicism" about the moral authority of government.

Professor James examines this consensus, why it has broken down, and how to repair it. She points out that given the dark side of human nature, the Founding Fathers structured a government to restrain these tendencies "in order to protect the common good against the bias of organized interests. It was that protective role on which the government's moral authority was based." In addition to the limitations which government placed on its own power to abuse the governed, the virtue of the original leadership group, typified by George Washington, helped to establish its moral authority.

Professor James adduces as evidence the image of the presidency and government as portrayed in films. Until the 1970s, if there were bad guys in government, still the common good always triumphed. The president was projected as strong, dignified, and exercising moral leadership. In more recent films, he is seen as a bumbling weakling, while those who work for the government have been morally downsized to "the Feds."

Professor James summarizes the "six major changes" in American society that has brought about social fragmentation and weakened the moral authority of government. She argues that "a nation whose government lacks moral authority is a nation adrift, vulnerable to opportunists, demagogues, and charlatans . . ." She concludes with a discussion of ways in which moral authority can be rebuilt.

Dr. James P. Pfiffner, Professor of Government and Public Policy, George Mason University, in his essay "The Paradox of Government Power," seconds Professor James' view that the government embodies our collective ideals. After sketching the balances of power inherent in the Constitution, he argues that "officials (elected and appointed) have a particularly important obligation. They must discharge their duties conscientiously, as well as provide moral leadership to the polity. . . . In light of the power we grant public officials, citizens have a right to expect them to comport themselves above reproach. If their behavior does not conform to high standards of integrity, they . . . undermine trust in the polity itself. . . ." Professor Pfiffner concludes by emphasizing need for virtue among the citizenry.

In his essay, "On Telling the Truth," United States Senator Richard G. Lugar of Indiana addresses a problem which has done much to undermine the credibility of government, and hence its moral authority. To what extent is government required to tell the truth to the citizenry? When can a lie be justified? He cites Emmanuel Kant's dictum that truthfulness is an unconditional duty that holds in all circumstances.

The Senator served on the Select Committee on Intelligence, which deals with the moral ambiguities and dilemmas of covert activity, including lying. From this experience, he argues that "the immediate problem for government is that lying—or even 'spinning' the truth . . . unravels the code of conduct and confidence in which we are all bound by our assumptions that we are telling the truth to one another." He concludes, "if our government hopes to preserve its moral authority and the confidence of the people, establishing a much stronger culture of truth in public service is essential."

Dr. David Mervin, Reader in Politics, University of Warwick in England, in his essay "Deception in Government," takes a different view. His conclusion: "while dishonesty by the chief magistrate in judicial proceedings concerned with his personal behavior is unacceptable, deception in the cause of national security may be justified."

In support, Dr. Mervin refers to "deception on a grand scale" by Franklin Roosevelt. He cites with approval the president's use of "secrecy, subterfuge, duplicity, and deception to implement a policy unobtainable through the processes of open government. . . . to have been meticulously constitutional and entirely open in his actions . . . would have entailed an abdication of his solemn responsibility to guard the nation's security."

Raymond J. Saulnier, former Chairman of the President's Council of Economic Advisers, comes next with his essay, "American Politics, 1999 Style: Congestion in the Middle of the Political

Spectrum." He addresses the liberal/conservative split, to which many of these essayists have ascribed differences in attitudes toward moral authority. According to Saulnier, this split is less significant today. For example, when conservatives wanted a balanced budget, liberals often thought of a budget deficit as more stimulative of economic growth.

For the conservatives, the moral authority of government once depended in part on government's not living beyond its means. But today, with a large surplus, liberals are proposing debt reduction, while conservatives want tax cuts. Saulnier offers other examples of reversal of position, or common positions as conservatives and liberals both enter the center.

Saulnier does not raise a question that the reader might well ask: When it comes to the moral authority of government, are liberals and conservatives, as they approach the center, adopting more similar views? From these essays, apparently not.

In his essay, Hugh R.K. Barber, M.D., Professor of Clinical Obstetrics and Gynecology, Cornell University Medical College, defines morals as "the rules by which a society exhorts (as laws are the rules by which it seeks to compel) its members and associates to behavior consistent with its order, security, and growth." He adds that a society cannot sustain moral life without the aid of religion. "Without a state religion, but a respect for all religions, the moral authority of government has been established."

The Right Reverend Paul Moore, Jr., retired Episcopal Bishop of New York, subtitles the final essay "A Religious Perspective." His religious perspective is not, however, that of Mark Melcher or Hugh Barber. They see the moral authority of government as deriving from the truths of revealed religion. Rather, Moore's source of moral authority parallels that of President Clinton, "what you fight for, and for whom you fight."

Bishop Moore sees the Church as the conscience of the nation, fighting for the "powerless, voiceless poor." In his view, to issues such as drug-inspired violence, despair over employment, homelessness, inferior education, "our government responds with force: more police, mandatory sentencing, more prisons, capital punishment." Nor does the manner in which foreign affairs are being conducted escape his moral censure.

The Bishop wants to "call the religious community to our responsibility to speak and act more vigorously, so that our government might regain its moral authority by acting in a moral fashion."

CHAPTER TWENTY TWO

Moral Authority of Government

JOHN T. CASTEEN III

PRESIDENT
UNIVERSITY OF VIRGINIA
NISS GOLD MEDALIST

FEW ERAS, perhaps our own least of all, altogether maintain the notion that governors (or kings or presidents) differ from government itself. Consequently, we struggle when we must distinguish the virtues or vices of elected leaders from the capacity or incapacity of the government that we identify with them. Talking about government's moral authority without slipping into oversimplification or platitude can be difficult. Distinguishing leaders, individual persons whose personal qualities, quirks, and adventures receive constant journalistic and political attention, from government, the institution that presides over the public interest, seems sometimes to be beyond our reach. The discourse grows even more challenging in times of scandal and factiousness, when personal immorality may become a public concern.

Conceptions of the motives appropriate to leadership and the actions appropriate to statecraft distribute themselves on an imaginary line that extends roughly from Socrates to Machiavelli. Socrates distinguishes the *polis* or public place from household space, the private place. For him, the *polis* is the proper sphere of government, of the public trust or good, and of equity among citizens. In the *polis*, citizens meet as equals. In the exclusivity and sanctuary of the home, domestic hierarchies exist, and so does that privacy in which possessors or occupants can be what they wish to be rather than what, in the *polis*, they must be.

Machiavelli reasons differently in *The Prince*, a tract whose relevance is perhaps underscored by the fact that it is intended to be a courtesy book or primer for educating an ideal ruler of a new kind. First, Machiavelli rejects the concept of equity; all persons are *not* equal before the prince. The properly educated prince judges humankind by its lowest average of motive or intelligence. The prince's self-interest is the law applicable to affairs of state.

The prince may or may not be morally good, but the quality of moral worth is irrelevant because the prince's obligation is to be effective in pursuing self-interest, not to be good. Reasons of state override considerations of personal morality, and they do so with such finality that the prince has no reason to contemplate differences between the two. "It is frequently necessary for the upholding of the state," Machiavelli teaches his prince, "to go to work against charity, against humanity, against religion, and a new prince cannot observe all the things for which men are reckoned good." So governmental leadership is morally neutral. The prince has no reason to recognize the *polis* and to live by its rules; the nation itself is his domestic space. The prince has no reason to recognize or maintain loyalty to a community of persons created equal.

The prince stands aside from morality (or sentimentality). Ends justify his means, and he judges his own actions without regard to precedent, rule, or universal principle. The prince submits to no higher authority. He calculates his appearance in the world. Wisdom or goodness can have a place in the prince's actions only if he has uses for these qualities, and then only as apparent qualities, not as real or innate qualities. He is in most situations ruthlessly self-interested.

Our modern way of reading oversimplifies Machiavelli. Amoral is not evil in this scheme. Yet we have functioned comfortably for most of our history as a Republic with the conception of "reasons of state." Most citizens have understood and more or less accepted the necessity of governmental espionage, of occasional strategic misrepresentation, and perhaps even of lying to Congress. But in an increasingly conservative Republic as this century draws to a close, sins once left out of the news have become fundamental considerations of the fitness of leaders and, by association, of government itself.

Mr. Clinton's impeachment and Mr. Nixon's forced resignation in the aftermath of the Watergate burglaries perhaps define a new conception of the ruler's moral obligations to the state. Outraged popular views of morality or journalistic fervor, or more likely both, may not be well along in the process of drawing the nation away from something akin to Machiavelli's end of my imaginary line and toward Socrates' conception of the state as *polis*, as the public place where domestic privacy cannot mask those more venal varieties of personal evil or immorality that are not treated in *The Prince*.

This is not to say that our generation was the first to discover discontinuity between private and public moralities. With interesting exceptions, Western paradigms of good government prior to Machiavelli assumed that dispassionate, disinterested governance was a mark of godliness in the state and in the ruler. Solomon's widsom, Beowulf's goodness, or Solon's selflessness, or for that matter Caesar's characterizations of himself and the popular characterization of his wife, invoke the notion that the personal goodness of a governor or king is a correlative to the protective stewardship that most Western cultures have seen as the ruler's obligation. Shakespeare's representation of the costs to the nation state of royal folly, greed, lechery, or uxoriousness simultaneously reflect a richly mixed prior tradition and define many of our own assumptions.

The pattern is remarkably consistent throughout the Western literatures. Solomon's wisdom is contrasted to his venality and his pride. Confronting Goliath, the boy David is Israel's selfless protector. In his worst moment, he appears shamefully as the self-interested seducer of his captain's wife. Suetonius's evil Caesars act out of pure self-interest, with the occasional good rule of a Julius or Augustus rising above self-interest. In the great Anglo-Saxon history of the English church and people, the Venerable Bede has good kings act heroically, but always dispassionately, and perhaps especially so when they die in their people's service. Indeed, Bede's kings willingly accept their own deaths as means of atoning for national sins or weaknesses. Bede's words about rulers would just as well describe good abbots or martyrs.

Our modern view of government's moral imperatives derives in part from prototypes such as these. We may or may not distinguish Solomon's wisdom from David's bravery as separate traits of kingship, but we recognize that both qualities, when found in a ruler, strengthen the nation. Yet our perspective derives at least equally from the Enlightenment, particularly as that European movement influenced the creators of our American republic.

It derives also from other sources, including our propensity toward anachronism when we pass judgment on the sins of the past. In the early years of this century, historians divided over the character and personality of Alexander Hamilton, and more than one commentator overlooked Hamilton's role in shaping the republican component of our democratic republic. More recently, journalists and historians are divided over the personality of Thomas

Jefferson, with more than a few interpreting the genetic evidence of kinship between white males of the Jefferson family and some of the descendants of Sally Hemmings as the final and necessary personal invalidation of the shaper of the democratic component of this same republic. Both disputes manifest a particularly self-destructive form of deconstructionist reasoning, one in which the sins and eccentricities of Founding Fathers are ransacked for evidence of unsoundness in the foundation itself. Grievous though the sins or presumed sins are—and they are sometimes very grievous indeed—they do not invalidate or undercut the institution of the republic itself. Indeed, they may instead prove its fundamental durability, and in the process, the essential wisdom of its founders. They made it strong enough to survive human frailty.

Even as we recognize this irony, let us acknowledge also that our time has seen its share of government's capacity for immoral action. The governor standing in the school's door to keep out a black child is an enduring icon of the republic's agony in that period when the court and the national conscience came to recognize that separate is inherently unequal. For many of us, as this century draws to a close, that agony is intensely personal. I was a schoolboy in Virginia in the mid-1950s when that state's legislature and governor seized, closed, and locked public schools in localities where elected school boards voted to comply with the *Brown* decision. Initially, these actions made little sense to me. My own school remained open. I read the news and heard adults discuss it, but I was puzzled rather than outraged or thrilled. The news was not of my place.

Three persons, two ninth-grade girls whose parents brought them to my school because their own school had been seized and closed, and a morally indignant school principal, taught me the moral nature of government's failing in that time. Their outrage that state government would use schools and children as playing pieces in the game of constitutional impasse that occurred in the South, indeed across the country, in those years before the great civil rights acts of the 1960s became part of my own conscience. They held government itself responsible for threatening human freedom. They understood and told us that the value at stake was everyone's right to learn, to be a free citizen, not merely the isolated rights of the black children whose pictures in the newspapers documented their alienation from the world of learning.

Moral authority derives from moral action. Government's

actions are not moral because they are government's. They are moral because they conform to the principles of life in the *polis*, in the place where we are all equal. Perhaps this is the essential republican lesson about government's moral authority: for government, as for individual persons, righteous acts define righteousness itself, moral acts define morality itself. Good government earns its goodness. We know it by its acts.

CHAPTER TWENTY THREE

"Character" in the First "Post-Modern" Presidency

MARK L. MELCHER

MANAGING DIRECTOR, WASHINGTON RESEARCH
PRUDENTIAL SECURITIES, INC.

DURING THE OPENING DAYS of his reelection campaign in 1996, President Bill Clinton fired a shot in America's on-going cultural war that should have been heard round the world, but which went largely unnoticed. This occurred when he told news anchor Tom Brokaw on the new MSNBC INTERNET show that "character" is demonstrated "most effectively" not by what you do in your personal life, but by "what you fight for and for whom you fight."

Specifically, he said he believed that the goodness of his own character should be measured by "the fact that I've stood up for the American people for things like fighting for the Family Leave Law, the Assault Weapons Ban or the Brady Bill or the v-chip for parents, or trying to keep tobacco out of the hands of kids and a lot of other issues."

This was not simply a new twist on an old debate. This was a startlingly new and portentous argument. Many presidents before Clinton have contended that character is of less importance than other attributes. And many have argued that the public is wrongly measuring their character, that allegations against them of moral or ethical laxness are lies, or exaggerated. But no American president, to my knowledge, had ever before seriously asserted that "character" has nothing to do with personal behavior, but is instead a derivative of the verve with which one advocates "progressive" government programs.

Not too many years ago, few Americans would have taken such an assertion seriously, if for no other reason than their awareness of the fact that the history and literature of every civilization since the beginning of recorded time is replete with stories of the dire consequences to nations whose leaders lack "character." And while there would have been some disagreements over which specific qualities best define character, virtually all Americans would have agreed that the term implied some combination of Plato's classical virtues of wisdom, courage, temperance, and a sense of justice; the Christian virtues of faith, hope, and charity; and the Victorian virtues of work, thrift, cleanliness, self reliance, perseverance, and honesty.

In fact, the importance of these qualities to leadership was, until recently, so widely believed by ordinary Americans that an essay on the subject would probably not have argued the point directly, but would have taken the approach of Thomas Carlyle, in his famous little book *Heroes and Hero Worship*, or of President John Kennedy, in his best selling *Profiles In Courage*, and discussed how excellent character in specific persons reinforced what people already thought about the subject.

Today, polling data and a variety of anecdotal evidence indicate that a large number of Americans are either passively or actively in agreement with President Clinton's assertion that an individual's personal behavior is not relevant to leadership.

It could be argued, of course, that President Clinton's assault on the traditional concept of "character" was nothing more than a simple one-time contrivance to rationalize his odious personal conduct. But I believe otherwise. I believe it was a victory cry for post-modern thought; a bold, public assertion that traditional American views on morality and ethics had changed so dramatically that they could be flouted with relative impunity by the president himself.

In short, as I indicated in the opening paragraph, I believe it was a very loud and important shot in a long war between two competing moral systems that has been going on in Western society for almost seven hundred years, which has heated up in America since the 1960s, and which broke into hot combat when Bill Clinton moved into the White House.

One side in this conflict can be described as traditional Judaeo-Christian. The foundation of this belief system was established some three thousand four hundred years ago with the receipt and promulgation of the Decalogue by Moses at Mt. Sinai. It combines Talmudic truths and the teachings of Jesus Christ, as interpreted and clarified by such scholars as St. Augustine, Moses Maimonides, and St. Thomas Aquinas, each of whom introduced portions of Aristotelian philosophy.

This system embraces a host of traditions, customs and mores that developed in Western society over many centuries. It is emblazoned with a rich repository of art and literature, and historic struggles, both religious and secular. The twin, faith-based concepts of "sin" and "truth" help bind this system together, along with a respect for the rule of law, which protects the fruits of this system, among which are individual rights and liberties.

The opposing moral system espouses beliefs that are often referred to today as "post-modern." This system rejects the notion that there are transcendental truths. Concepts such as "right," "wrong," "truth," and of course, "character," are considered subjective. Jocelyn Elders, President Clinton's former Surgeon General, put a practical face on this system when she once approvingly noted that "everyone has different moral standards."

Under this system, traditional Western values, customs, and laws are viewed as "fetters," which impede the formation of a more "perfect" society. For example, the ancient Judaeo-Christian belief that human life is sacred is a thorn in the side of advocates of abortion rights and euthanasia. Laws and policies that favor traditional families threaten gay and women's "rights," as well as sexual license. The ancient Western tradition of respect for private property interferes with the visions of the radical environmentalists. The bedrock Western concept of "to each his own," is a flagrant affront to radical egalitarianism. And the list goes on.

It is important to understand that this is a real philosophical belief system. It is hundreds of years old. In fact, its roots can be traced to medieval times. It has its own heroes and icons. These include Jean.Jacque Rousseau, Friedrich Nietzsche, Jean Paul Sartre, and the post-modernist philosophers, people like Hans-Georg Gadamer, Martin Heidegger, Jacques Derrida, Paul de Man, Michel Foucault, and of course, Richard Rorty, a frequent guest at the Clinton White House.

It is also important to understand that we are talking here about a philosophy, not a political system. Nevertheless, it is worth noting that this philosophy has spawned some of the most destructive political systems in the history of mankind. These include communism, socialism, and fascism, all of which substitute arbitrary dicta for traditional ethical, moral, and legal prescriptions.

The modern-day origins of this system stem from the attempt by seventeenth century Enlightenment philosophers to establish a moral scheme based on reason alone, via the application of Bacon's "scientific method" to the study of human affairs.

Rene Descartes, highly influenced by the thoughts of Bacon and Machiavelli, was the first philosopher publicly to attack those individuals and their followers, who, he claimed, drew their beliefs from "the ancient books, their histories and their fables." These were, Descartes said, a "superstitious" lot, who had "weak minds," and consciences agitated by "repentances and remorse." Descartes argued that a "new method" must be found that is mathematical, or reason-based, and he thus became the "founder of modern philosophy."

The list of philosophers who tried to fulfill Descartes' charge of developing a new "moral science," is, of course, long, and I might add, for the most part, historically distinguished. But as the great American moral philosopher Alasdair MacIntyre points out, while this effort succeeded in beginning the process of eroding belief in the theistically based moral order of the Middle Ages, it failed to establish an alternative moral order that would stand the test of time.

In his remarkable book *After Virtue*, published in 1981, MacIntyre maintains that this failure was due to the fact that they had to reject, due to the nature of their project, the notion that life has a divine purpose, either in the Aristotelian sense that man must fulfill his role as dictated by "nature," or in the theological sense that man must fulfill God's will. Without such a teleological framework, MacIntyre argues, the whole project of morality becomes unintelligible, and moral philosophy becomes nothing more than an arena for competing notions that have no basis other than "logic," which is, of course, debatable.

This leads, he says, to situations in which "an agent can only justify a particular judgment by referring to some universal rule from which it may be logically derived, and can only justify that rule in turn by deriving it from some more general rule or principle; but on this view since every chain of reasoning must be finite, such a process of justificatory reasoning must always terminate with the assertion of some rule or principle for which no further reason can be given." (p. 20)

Nietzsche was the first philosopher who clearly recognized the failure of the Enlightenment philosophers. But instead of arguing for a return to the old "pre-modern" religious-based views, which he also rejected, he went post-modern, as some would say, and advocated razing to the ground all the structures of inherited moral belief and argument. He urged that mankind admit that all moral judgments are simply masks worn by persons too weak and slavish to assert, as he advocated, their "will to power" in aristocratic grandeur.

Sartre later played a different version of the same tune, arguing that all moral pronouncements were, for the most part, exercises in bad faith by those who could not tolerate the recognition of their own choices as the sole source of moral judgment.

So where does this lead? According to MacIntyre, the result of this assault on the traditional Western view of morality is widespread adherence to what he calls "emotivism," or the "doctrine that all evaluative judgments and more specifically all moral judgments are *nothing but* expressions of preference, expressions of attitude or feeling, insofar as they are moral or evaluative in character." (p. 11)

MacIntyre notes that by asserting that emotivism has become embedded in American society, he is not "merely contending that morality is not what it once was, but also and more importantly that what once was morality has to some large degree disappeared." (p. 22)

We still employ the ancient language of moral discourse, he points out, but it no longer means anything because the phrases used are merely "incoherent fragments of a once coherent scheme of thought and action." Under these circumstances, the statement "This is good" has come to mean nothing more than "Hurrah for this!" The result is that society becomes Nietzschean, as each individual pursues his or her own "will to power" in a moral vacuum. (p. 12)

In such a world, he says, it is unsurprising that politics "oscillate between a freedom which is nothing but a lack of regulation of individual behavior and forms of collectivist control designed only to limit the anarchy of self-interest. The consequences of a victory by one side or the other are often of the highest immediate importance; but, as Solzhenitsyn has understood so well, both ways of life are in the long run intolerable. Thus the society in which we live is one in which bureaucracy and individualism are partners as well as antagonists. And it is in the cultural climate of this bureaucratic individualism that the emotivist self is naturally at home." (p. 35)

It is not exaggeration, I believe, to say that the outcome of the war between this new moral system, as described by MacIntyre, and the traditional Judaeo-Christian one will decide the enduring question asked by Lincoln at Gettysburg, whether a nation that was "conceived in liberty and dedicated to the proposition that all men are created equal . . . can long endure." For liberty cannot endure in a society that recognizes no truths.

As MacIntyre points out, the vacuum created when truth disappears is inevitably filled with what he calls new pseudo-concepts. One of these is the concept that "experts" can solve all of society's problems, if they are just given enough power. This, he says, leads to the transfer of vast control over society to a central bureaucracy.

According to MacIntyre, government becomes a "hierarchy of bureaucratic managers, and the major justification advanced for the intervention of government in society is the contention that government has resources of competence which most citizens do not possess." In our culture, he says, "we know of no organized movement towards power which is not bureaucratic and managerial in mode." (p. 108)

MacIntyre doesn't say so, but it is worth noting that this Orwellian managerial class ironically actually gains power through failure, since its failures inevitably lead to more social chaos, which in turn leads emotivist society to demand more "experts" and "managers."

The second of MacIntyre's pseudo-concepts, to which he says people will cling in an emotivist society, is the eighteenth century idea that individuals have certain "natural rights," which guarantee that they will not "be interfered with in their pursuit of life, liberty and happiness." (p. 69)

MacIntyre argues that every attempt to give good reasons for believing that there are such rights has failed. But more importantly he notes that the concept of "natural rights," if widely believed, inevitably leads to a fragmented society in which individuals and groups of individuals aggressively assert their individual and group "rights" against those of others in a massive Nietzschean-like campaign of "will to power." (p. 69)

In such a society, government becomes nothing more than a set of institutional arrangements for imposing a bureaucratized unity on a community that lacks genuine moral consensus, and politics becomes a "civil war carried on by other means." (p. 253)

MacIntyre didn't, of course, predict precisely in 1981 that the United States would, in slightly more than 10 years, have a president who would feel comfortable publicly arguing that his character should not be judged by the fact that he had sex with a young subordinate and lied about it under oath, but should instead be judged by the "goodness" of his political projects. What MacIntyre did foresee, however, was the emergence of a type of society in which a large number of citizens would find such a claim to be unremarkable.

CHAPTER TWENTY FOUR

Is Government an Authority on Morality?

DAN F. HAHN

VISITING PROFESSOR OF CULTURE AND COMMUNICATION
NEW YORK UNIVERSITY

ALTHOUGH I do not know it to be the case, it seems a good bet that the topic for this volume was suggested by the argumentation swirling around the Clinton-Lewinsky scandal of 1998–99.

That argumentation was, as is usual in our society, rather neatly laid out on the liberal-conservative continuum, with the liberals arguing that Clinton's morality (or lack thereof) was irrelevant because (since it concerned his sexual behavior) it was his private morality, and conservatives arguing that morality protection and promulgation is a basic function of government and that one who is immoral in one sphere is bound to carry that immorality into any other sphere of that person's activity.

These are not only the liberal-conservative positions in terms of this scandal, but fairly summarize the normal disagreements about morality between the two sides of the political equation. For instance, conservatives are likely to argue that abortion is immoral, and that government should not allow immoral behavior, while liberals are likely to put forward the position that abortion is a private matter, none of the government's business. Yet there have been occasions when the two sides flip-flopped. In the 1950s the liberals argued that segregation was immoral and the government should put an end to it, while the conservatives took the position that how people did or did not "naturally" interact with each other was a private matter and that laws "could not change human nature." All in all, however, liberal endorsement of government-enforced morality is as rare as conservative endorsement of government-enforced economics.

But, it should be noted, there is a difference between "the president" and "the government." Hence, "the moral authority of government" and "the moral authority of President Clinton" are not precisely the same topic, although the two topics do interact and partake of each other. Therefore, I shall first address the question of the moral authority of President Clinton vis-à-vis the Clinton-Lewinsky episode, then turn to the broader question of the moral authority of government.

For the conservative it was obvious that Clinton lost his moral authority, either at the point where he engaged sexually with Monica Lewinsky or at the point where he lied to the public and the courts about it, and that that loss of moral authority meant that he could not do the jobs that a president has to do—lead the public to make tough decisions, provide moral leadership to the young, etc.

The public, however, did not agree; indeed, they seemed to take the position that the affair was unimportant precisely because it had not interfered with Clinton's ability to do his job. Undoubtedly that assessment was based partly on the people's satisfaction with how the country was doing, but another part of it probably came from knowing friends and neighbors who were having affairs and yet were doing their jobs competently.[1]

Because these citizens perceived Clinton to be doing the job he was elected to do, they found the Clinton-Lewinsky capers irrelevant. In one early national poll, 84 percent agreed that "someone can still be a good President even if they do things in their personal life that you disapprove of"[2] and even a poll among 252 (presumably Republican) senior executives, run by *Business Week*, found that "56% said his dalliance . . . was 'not relevant' to his ability to serve as President."[3]

In arguing for the irrelevance of Clinton's sexual history to his ability to do the job, citizens tended to point to other leaders who had had sexual liaisons and still provided superlative leadership, including Martin Luther King, Jr., the Duke of Wellington, David Lloyd George, Franklin Roosevelt, and John F. Kennedy.[4]

Without trying to put too Machiavellian a spin on the "he's dong his job" position, it is relevant to note that the portion of the public which supported the President seemed to agree with the position of Machiavelli that saints should stick to their convents and not get involved in matters of government. Citizen Alan Ryan, for instance, suggested, "We should be ruthless with leaders who weaken national defenses, steal from the public purse or subvert constitutions. But we should not expect to like what we see when we peer into our rulers' souls."[5]

The other major argument about the Clinton-Lewinsky case which impinges on the moral authority question concerns the relationship between disparate parts of one's life. Thus, conservatives tended to argue that you cannot "separate a person's private life from his or her public life";[6] that "if you'll cheat and lie to those you love, you'll cheat and lie to the American public";[7] that the Romans had it right in their phrase "falso in uno, falsus in omnibus," i.e., "if he lied in this, he lied in all."[8]

The public rejection of this argument seemed to be made up of three reactions. First, many people seemed to know people who had had affairs and then lied about them, yet had remained entirely constant in their professional lives, that is, who would never dream of lying in the business world or cheating a customer; thus they didn't believe that just because Clinton lied about his sexual life he would lie about other things. Second, it seemed obvious to many that committing adultery and then lying about it were only two of dozens and dozens of aspects of character and private life which might be utilized to make judgments about politicians, and were not necessarily two that they wanted to rely upon. And third, at least some citizens seemed to suggest that *public* character was more important than private character, that things like "indifference to the poor . . . tax avoidance and dishonest campaigning"[9] are more significant than adultery in evaluating public figures. Some who felt that way sneered that "the 'character' issue has been hijacked by a group of political peeping Toms who can't see or hear past the bedroom."[10]

Robert C. Solomon, a professor of philosophy at the University of Texas at Austin, examined the argument that a person who would lie about one thing would lie about another, and concluded that it just is not true. Rather, he suggested, "the demand for honesty is contextual. It depends on what the truth concerns."[11] Turning, then, to the case of President Clinton, he argued that "lying about sex, while it may have grave significance for people in an intimate relationship, has nothing to do with one's public credibility" because the person who has raised the question has violated the personal boundaries of the one under suspicion. And he concluded that "a lie or an invitation to lie that is provoked by a breach of sacred personal boundaries is in moral limbo, and no violation of a public trust."

While approaching the question somewhat differently from Professor Solomon, I essentially have arrived at the same point.

That is, I am suspicious of the move from public virtue to private morality, of what Communication Professor Josh Meyrowitz calls the shift from "resume criteria" to "dating criteria" for the evaluation of public figures.[12] Undoubtedly, I have been influenced in this assessment by my study of classical rhetoric, for Aristotle and other ancient Greek rhetoricians believed that "civic virtue" was the most important aspect of ethos. "It was unlike the Christian virtues of faith, hope, and charity . . . which are best practiced beyond the glare of publicity. They had in mind practical virtues that would help in forming prudent public decisions."[13] But in the latter part of the twentieth century we seem to have junked all that. While we have a "don't ask, don't tell" policy in terms of military sex, we have no equivalent in the political arena.

By now, then—and I would argue that this is the ultimate sadness about the public-private morality realm—we are more likely to see politics through a private morality than a public virtue lens. We are more likely to focus on Clinton's marital indiscretions than his public persona and acts, indeed, to perceive those public activities through a private, and dark, Puritan filter. We are more likely to insist that our own private moral standards—on abortion, on reading materials, on pre-marital sex, on family values—become public policy, and to evaluate politicians on their standards on those private morality beliefs, than we are to examine the justice or prudence of their public decisions or the temperance and magnanimity of their public utterances.

Some of this move, I must admit, is caused by the complexity of modern life, and the resultant complexifications of the public problem/public solution ecology. We seem to have arrived at a point where we think verifiable truth cannot be found, so we have retreated to our private lives, peering out fearfully at a seemingly ever-more-dangerous world.

So, I doubt if the coverage of private morality helps us understand public character. Further, it seems to me that the extensive coverage of morality questions has other disadvantages. If you assume, with me, that there is a sexual skeleton in practically everybody's closet, one result of focusing on sexual questions is going to be a weakening of their credibility, a weakening that is inevitable. As David Broder explains, "By probing so persistently into that one aspect of their lives, the press may force candidates to proclaim a degree of virtue which few . . . can sustain.

When those claims are debunked, their overall credibility suffers, and cynicism grows."[14]

This being the case, other inevitable results of the focus on sexuality come into view, such as that it scares many good people away from politics,[15] makes "greatness" impossible,[16] and converts all of us into an "adultery public"—that is, an electorate whose "insecurity about the 'faithfulness' of our representatives coincides with anxieties about the fidelity of the wider institutions of representation themselves."[17] So, in the little space remaining to me, let's turn to the widest of all those institutions, the government.

In trying to determine whether we want to turn over to government the responsibility for being a/the moral authority, it is necessary to understand what is meant by the word "authority." In common parlance, authority is of two types—role and knowledge. Some roles carry authority with them—parent, boss, teacher, etc.; that is, we heed those who play these roles because we think we ought to acquiesce to them. Knowledge-based authority, however, is based on information and intelligence; that is, the acquiescence is based upon recognition that the person knows more about the topic than do we.

The difference between being *in* an authoritative role and being *an* authority is important, for one does not presuppose the other, that is, the person in the role may not know what ought to be done and/or the person who knows may not be in an authoritative role. The distinction is especially important when we are discussing whether government should be granted any authority in the realm of morality. There is no reason to suppose that anybody in government has any special knowledge in that realm—politicians are not presumed to be particularly moral; they are mostly drawn from the legal profession, which is not normally perceived as partaking of morality; they are not elected/appointed to their positions because of either their personal morality or their knowledge about morals.

And, indeed, if you think about the history of governments in the world, it is difficult to be sanguine about the possibility of governments intelligently handling moral authority. That is, it would seem that the fact that governments have been just as likely to embrace immorality (racism, apartheid, anti-semitism, ethnic cleansing, germ warfare, etc.) as morality probably has weakened the call for governments to have moral authority.

Additionally, although it might seem to strengthen governmental power to give government authority over morality, the ultimate result would be to weaken government, or at least a government based upon respect for democratic principles. Consider that a basic democratic principle of our system is a receptivity to opposing views, an acknowledgment of the possibility that I may be wrong and the other person may be right. That principle clearly would be in trouble if the government took control of societal morality . . . yet morality itself would be in trouble if it could change after each election.

So would our much-vaunted individualism. This is because the development of a personality, including its moral components, results from talking about morality, talking through the possibilities, accepting some, rejecting others. Being silenced and cut off from that discussion by the prior existence of a societal morality formally adopted by the government is a kind of amputation, an oppression that is particularly vicious inasmuch as it precludes our development of our fullest potentiality . . . and maybe even precludes us from becoming fully human.

The more I try to sort through the various advantages and disadvantages of "the moral authority of government," the more it looks to me that government only can have "moral authority" when the people it governs subscribe to the same morality . . . and that when all subscribe to the same morality, we have not a society of humans but a colony of automatons.

Thus while I *do* understand why the Clinton years have made many of us nervous about the state of public morality, I have no choice but to resist the burgeoning movement for moral authority to be anchored in government. Clinton's personal moral authority may have been weakened by his actions, but at least his authority and actions were logically separable from the moral authority of the government, a separation from the moral authority of the government, a separation which would have been made more difficult if government had been a/the site for societal determination/promulgation of all or most moral authority.

CHAPTER TWENTY FIVE

The Once and Future (?) Consensus

DOROTHY BUCKTON JAMES

PROFESSOR OF POLITICAL SCIENCE
CONNECTICUT COLLEGE

THE UNITED STATES OF AMERICA began its national life with a strong consensus that government should exercise moral authority. Over the course of two centuries from the 1770s to the 1970s, that consensus held firm. There were times of scandal or corruption, but Americans believed that such periods reflected historical accident or individual failure, not inherent structural problems. They believed that their system of government was inherently self-righting.

Since the 1970s that faith has declined. A corrosive cynicism about government's moral authority dominates public and private discourse. Critics across the political spectrum find no dearth of villains to blame. Those on the political right tend to attribute the loss of moral authority to lifestyle issues of a permissive society that has abandoned "family values." The intensity of their animosity toward President Clinton is not simply a partisan matter. For political conservatives, he epitomizes everything that is most threatening in what they see as the self-indulgent, "baby boomer" lifestyle.

Writers on the political left tend to attribute the loss of moral authority to structural aspects of a government that has grown since the second World War in both size and complexity to the point that it is not amenable to popular control, but seems to have become a government of, by, and for the special interests. Its superpower status, its secrecy, and the coercive power of its sophisticated technology and vast sources of information about its citizens have alienated a wide spectrum of Americans. In fact, most critics, whatever their ideology, agree that the national government has become too big. At best, it is seen as lurching from crisis to crisis, lacking moral authority and out of touch with its citizens. At worst, it is seen as the enemy of its own people, a vast elite conspiracy.

Critics also agree that the failure or corruption of individual leaders has caused (or at least heavily contributed to) the growing cynicism about government. Conservatives point to President Kennedy's sexual peccadilloes (not widely known at the time of his presidency but disclosed with increasing salacious detail in subsequent decades), President Carter's weakness as a leader, and President Clinton's scandals—including Whitewater, Travelgate, Filegate, campaign finance scandals that also involved Vice President Gore, and sexual peccadilloes leading to impeachment. Their opponents point to the involvement of President Nixon and his staff in the Watergate scandal, his resignation to avoid impeachment, and the involvement of staff and possibly President Reagan and Vice President Bush in the Iranscam scandal. Each side can rattle off a litany of indicted or publicly disgraced Cabinet members and members of Congress from both parties to support the point that the government has lost moral authority, and that individual corruption or failure has been a major, if not the primary, factor in this loss.

This paper analyzes the Federalists' eighteenth-century concept of moral leadership, the underlying reasons for late twentieth-century slippage from that concept, and suggests a possible basis on which to begin rebuilding moral authority for the twenty-first century.

THE FEDERALIST BASIS
FOR MORAL AUTHORITY IN GOVERNMENT

Because the Federalists believed that humans are inherently selfish, short sighted, and factional, they maintained that government had to be structured to restrain those tendencies in order to protect the common good against the bias of organized interests. It was that protective role on which government's moral authority was based.

In *Federalist 10*, James Madison wrote:

> As long as the reason of man continues to be fallible, and he is at liberty to exercise it, different opinions will be formed. As long as the connection subsists between his reason and his self-love, his opinions and his passions will have a reciprocal influence on each other; and the former will be objects to which the latter will attach themselves.[1]

Madison defined faction as:

... a number of citizens, whether amounting to a majority or minority of the whole, who are united and actuated by some common impulse of passion, or of interest, adverse to the rights of other citizens, or to the permanent and aggregate interests of the community.

He noted that mutual animosities could occur over a wide variety of topics, such as differences in religion, political preference, or attachment to different leaders, but that ". . . the most common and durable source of factions has been the various and unequal distribution of property."

The elaborate structure of the United States Constitution was created to achieve two goals: to enable the government to control the factious tendencies of those it governed, and to control itself. As Madison wrote in *Federalist 51*:

... Whilst all authority in it will be derived from, and dependent on the society, the society itself will be broken into so many parts, interests, and classes of citizens that the rights of individuals, or of the minority, will be in little danger from interested combinations of the majority.

The new government's claim to moral authority was established by a fortuitous combination of this structure plus a number of leaders in each of the three branches (executive, legislative, and judicial) whose character, intellect, and accomplishments legitimized it. Above all, the first president, George Washington, was believed by an overwhelming majority of Americans to place the common good above other interests, including his own.

From those early years until the 1970s, there were periods of scandal, of individual failure of leadership, or of drift, but few Americans attributed this to systemic failure. Even when scandals like the Teapot Dome affair involved a wide swath of individuals in government, Americans believed that they were caused by "rotten apples," and the system would be self-righting.

Evidence of this belief can be found in the popular culture. For example, films from the dark days of the Great Depression, such as *Mr. Smith Goes to Washington*, or from the postwar era of the 1950s, such as *Born Yesterday*, showed individual Senators or Congressmen who could be bought and sold by special interests, but the common good always triumphed, even if it needed an improbable filibuster by Jimmy Stewart or recitation of the Declaration of Independence by William Holden to get the job done.

Attitudes changed in the aftermath of the protest movements of the 1960s and early 1970s, government's failure to respond to intense and sustained public opposition to our involvement in Vietnam, the resignation of Vice President Agnew for tax fraud, and the Watergate scandal and resulting resignation of President Nixon. From that period to the present, opinion polls indicate that public cynicism has become so widespread and corrosive that there is a general feeling that the government has lost its moral authority.

The cynicism is reflected in the mass media to such an extent that since the 1970s, American films and television have generally portrayed government leaders as incompetent or dishonorable. Senators and Congressmen have regularly been portrayed as corrupt, or at least self-serving. The president had traditionally been portrayed in films by an actor who projected strong, dignified moral leadership, such as Gregory Peck or Raymond Massey. He was photographed with back lighting and heavy over orchestration just as saints and religious figures were customarily portrayed. Since the 1970s, Presidents are preponderantly portrayed as weaklings, bumblers, or willing to stop at nothing to protect their power stakes, advised by equally flawed, self-serving staff who obsess about superficial questions of image or the next election rather than substantive policy questions. There is no longer a general perception that the system can be counted on to right itself. All those who work for the national government are tarred with the title that has become a universal term of opprobrium, "the Feds."

As cynicism grows, public interest and involvement in all aspects of the political process declines, particularly among younger citizens, with serious negative implications for popular government. After being perceived by the public for most of two centuries as exercising moral authority, how can the government have slipped so far in public perception in just two decades? Critics on the right and left are correct in pointing to a variety of concerns, but these tend to be reflections more than causes of the underlying changes.

UNDERLYING REASONS FOR RECENT SLIPPAGE IN THAT AUTHORITY

Clearly, the United States is undergoing a period of serious political stress that is reflected in high levels of public malaise. Starting with the family, every social and political institution is experiencing this stress. In the past few years, an unusually large number of books have focused on the nation's cultural crisis, questioning democracy's future. Recent publications include: Christopher Lasch, *The Revolt of the Elites and the Betrayal of Democracy*;[2] Samuel P. Huntington, *The Clash of the Civilizations and the Remaking of World Order*;[3] Lester C. Thurow, *The Future of Capitalism: How Today's Economic Forces Shape Tomorrow's World*;[4] Peter F. Drucker, *Post-Capitalist Society*;[5] and Mary Ann Glendon, *Rights Talk: The Impoverishment of Political Discourse*.[6] Some critics go so far as to suggest that America is having a national identity crisis as it sinks away from nationhood into "tribalism." (Similar occurrences are noted through all industrialized societies, but the situation in the United States is generally portrayed as the most seriously advanced.)

The social fragmentation reflects the impact of six major changes that affect us simultaneously at the end of the twentieth century. First, technology has created a social transformation that particularly undercuts community. Through developments in communication, transportation, and computer technology, our lives have become increasingly fragmented. Our work, friends, residence, and leisure pursuits have become geographically separated, leaving less time or incentive to identify with a specific community. Technological developments have also enabled us to disengage from community altogether, as we can communicate around the world on the Internet; be entertained within our homes through television, VCRs, video games, and home entertainment centers; and even work from our homes using the Internet. At its worst, this trend poses a threat of social isolation and alienation. Less extreme, yet still negative in their consequences, are the social biases inherent in being able to live, work, and play without regard to a broader, more diverse community. Such homogeneity encourages development of the very factions against which the Federalists struggled so intently, particularly those based on "the various and unequal distribution of property" that concerned Madison in *Federalist 10*.

Second, technological developments have also transformed society in ways that increasingly pit "knowledge workers" (elites defined by education and power of the mind who deal in information, concepts, and abstract symbols, such as lawyers, journal-

ists and media people, academics, consultants, and similar professionals) against everyone else. In a post-industrial economy
most jobs require either extensive education or formal training.
To join the "knowledge worker" elite requires at least a college
education and generally demands graduate work. Well-paying
service jobs may not require formal education, but increasingly
they require formal training. For example, repair of automo-
biles, electronics, computers, or refrigeration units now requires
technologically sophisticated skills and knowledge. Many other
service jobs require formal training to meet the increasing
demands of licensing organizations, such as food services or
beauticians. This need for educated or formally trained workers
is one aspect of change that is moving the United States danger-
ously away from a class system (which is permeable to able,
motivated, or fortunate individuals) to a system of caste that
traps the uneducated or untrained in a near-permanent underclass. In an agricultural or industrial economy there are jobs for
those who are willing and able to work, but in a post-industrial
economy the will to work is not enough. One must have an education or training that is too costly for most members of the
underclass to achieve. As social class drifts toward caste, income
differentials grow in a mutually reinforcing cycle. In short, the
same technological developments that enrich the "knowledge
workers" at the expense of others also undercut community.
The elite can live in homogeneous suburbs or gated "communities"; they can study, work and play with people like themselves;
and they can avoid any sense of shared stakes with less advan-
taged citizens. The negative consequences for democratic government are obvious.

The third factor presently dividing United States society is its
increasing racial, ethnic, and religious diversity. Both legal and
illegal immigration patterns in the last quarter of the twentieth
century have been dominated by peoples of color from Latin
American, Caribbean, Asian, and African nations. The resulting
racial diversity has been accompanied by increased ethnic and
religious diversity. These changes are perceived by some Americans as enriching the nation, but others find them threatening.
Many of the immigrants lack the education or training necessary
to get jobs that pay an adequate wage in the post-industrial economy, which contributes to the dangerous movement away from
class to caste system.

Fourth, the United States is dependent on externally controlled economic factors, the "globalization" of the American economy. The decisions of multi-national corporations and the impact of international economic forces undercut the ability of any nation to control its economy. Those groups and individuals who are marginalized in the process increasingly express frustration or alienation from their government. Their marginalization is another aspect of the movement from class to caste. Nevertheless, government has little effective control over economic globalization.

A fifth factor contributing to social fragmentation results from the fact that the massive federal deficit of the 1980s to the mid 1990s severely reduced the amount of disposable income available to support any government programs, whether existing, emergency, or new. Previously, socially activist presidents like Franklin Delano Roosevelt, John Fitzgerald Kennedy, or Lyndon Baines Johnson could count on a constantly expanding pie. During the recent period of massive federal deficits, presidents had no option but to play a zero-sum game in which money for a new or expanded program, or to respond to a crisis, had to come from an existing program. The politics of redistribution are always divisive. Congress and President Clinton agreed to a budget plan to put the deficit on what then Speaker Newt Gingrich termed "a glide path to zero." The plan called for further stringent cuts and caps on government spending to assure a balanced budget and attempt to reduce the national debt. That is a process that will continue to constrain spending on existing, new, or emergency programs.

Ironically, the final fragmenting factor is posed by the end of the cold war. Much as we may have desired that end for over forty-five years, it had the negative consequence of removing the sense of a common enemy. Anti-communism united people of different social classes, races, ethnic, and religious backgrounds across the country and gave shape to our foreign and military policy. It also legitimized heavy defense spending on grounds that protection from a potent enemy is in the common good. In a post-cold war world we seem, so far, to lack a clear sense of direction as we attempt to develop a new basis on which to determine our foreign or military policy. The sense of drift undercuts the perceived legitimacy of government decisions in these areas.

THE BASIS ON WHICH TO
REBUILD GOVERNMENT'S MORAL AUTHORITY

One lesson that history teaches with startling clarity, especially in the twentieth century, is the fact that a nation whose government lacks moral authority is a nation adrift, vulnerable to opportunists, demagogues, and charlatans who prey upon citizens whose critical faculties are fogged by a cloud of corrosive cynicism. Government can never be value-free. It is organized for a purpose, which reflects the society's fundamental values. For example, because the Federalists believed that humans are inherently factional, they organized a government whose purpose was to control the damage that factions could do to the common good.

How, then, can moral authority be regained under the present circumstances? It would constitute *chutzpah* beyond even the normal level among academics to pretend to be able to solve this complex question, particularly in a page or two. Nonetheless, intellectual honesty compels us to recognize the importance of that question, even if we must also recognize that the best for which we can hope is what, in *The Children of Light and the Children of Darkness*,[7] Rienhold Niebuhr termed "proximate solutions to insoluble problems."

The last third of the twentieth century has been the demonstration model of what Madison called man's inherent tendency toward faction. Since the 1970s, the United States has experienced an explosion of organized interest groups whose political action committees (PACs) have become essential elements in the election process (analyzed in Jeffrey M. Berry, *the Interest Group Society*).[8] Public opinion polls and an outpouring of books such as those mentioned above, demonstrate that most Americans are uncomfortable with the present situation and wish change. Many writers suggest specific structural changes such as: reinvigorating political parties, limiting the influence of campaign funding by interest groups, reducing the cost of running for office, reducing the negativity and superficiality of political campaigns and increasing their substantive engagement with relevant ideas and issues, and encouraging the best and brightest to dedicate themselves to public service. These, and many similar suggestions, undoubtedly have merit, but they do not help us to move much beyond the impact of the six fragmenting factors analyzed above. Three major approaches are relevant in that regard.

Economic problems and the caste system that is developing to separate "knowledge workers" from others can be significantly alleviated by a major national commitment to effective education or training to meet the demands of a technologically sophisticated, globally interdependent, knowledge and service society. This proposal might seem to fly in the face of the need to maintain a balanced budget and reduce the national debt, but a serious commitment to educational and training programs geared to twenty-first century needs would pay off handsomely in increased productivity, which would create a higher standard of living for the nation, produce revenues that more rapidly reduce the national debt, and create surplus to provide the safety net for those who cannot develop the necessary skills. In addition, some of the tensions resulting from increasing racial, ethnic, and religious diversity would be alleviated if newcomers were able to benefit from such educational and training programs. Widespread affluence may not level the playing field, but it can certainly smooth out a lot of obstacles along the way.

Similarly, much of the racial, ethnic, and religious tension would be reduced if we recognize that no matter how well-meaning the desire to protect previously disadvantaged groups, any such attempts are bound to be divisive and perpetuate inequalities if they focus on organized groups and protected categories rather than on individuals. Increasingly, the assertion of group rights is destroying the sense of community and the idea of the common good on which the nation was founded. As we lose our sense of community and civic duty, our commitment to democracy is undercut. We can alleviate this by focusing seriously on an *even-handed, rigorous* enforcement of the laws that require protection of the civil rights and civil liberties of *each* individual because that protects both the individual and the common good.

Finally, some of the harsh edge of each of the six fragmenting factors would be alleviated if, as a society, we pull back from the individualistic extremes of the recent past. An emphasis on individualism has always been a central American value. It is responsible for much of both our strengths and our weaknesses (analyzed in Seymour Martin Lipset, *American Exceptionalism: A Double-Edged Sword*).[9] However, until recently it has been tempered by the simultaneously held value of concern for the community and the common good. There are many hopeful signs that movement to restore that second pillar of our political values is underway: for example, opinion polls reflect a growing concern to redevelop a sense of community, and many public discussions, books, and articles are engaging with the issue.

It may be a daunting task, but there are clear signs that Americans wish to restore moral authority to their government. To do that, they will need to reevaluate the balance between organized interests and the common good. In developing a new consensus, they will have to acknowledge and take into account the factors that have undercut the old consensus. There is no turning back from the social transformation created by technology, increasing social diversity, a globalized economy, the limitations on government spending implicit in a balanced budget and debt reduction, and the loss of a commonly perceived enemy.

CHAPTER TWENTY SIX

The Paradox of Governmental Power

JAMES P. PFIFFNER

PROFESSOR OF GOVERNMENT AND PUBLIC POLICY
GEORGE MASON UNIVERSITY

IN THE UNITED STATES, our polity depends crucially upon three pillars: the constitutional system, the virtue of good leaders, and the vigilance of the citizenry. This essay will review the moral roles and obligations of each of these pillars and conclude that in the end the virtue of the citizenry is the bedrock upon which all else depends; that is, we will get the kind of government that we deserve.

THE MORAL ROLE OF GOVERNMENT

In the United States, government plays a moral role in several ways. The national government embodies our highest *collective* ideals, as expressed in the preamble to the Constitution: ". . . to form a more perfect Union, establish Justice, insure domestic Tranquility, provide for the common defence, promote the general Welfare, and secure the Blessings of Liberty to ourselves and our Posterity. . . ." But in order to fulfill these lofty ideals, the Framers had to create a government that possessed power (moral and material) sufficient to its purposes. The institutions created by the Articles of Confederation were not strong enough to do the job, and the new governmental structure was intended to overcome that lack.

As the authors of the *Federalist Papers* argued, a government capable of securing liberty must necessarily be delegated enough power to be effective. In *Federalist No. 1* Hamilton asserted that ". . . the vigor of government is essential to the security of liberty. . . ." Government must raise adequate taxes to support the governmental institutions necessary to protect our national security, create an infrastructure for a thriving economy, provide for those who cannot provide for themselves, and create a safe society. Government must also be strong enough to protect small businesses and consumers from exploitation by large business enterprises, such as the railroads and large trusts of the late nineteenth century. Our property rights and our right to privacy are not safe without a government strong enough to protect them. The terrible vision of George Orwell's distopia described in his novel, *1984*, has not come to pass in the West, despite the technological tools available. Ironically, now we need a strong government to be able to protect us from the invasion of our privacy by private enterprises who are capable of amassing huge amounts of personal data (medical, financial, marketing, etc.) and selling it to the highest bidder. The good news is that the government is not Big Brother; the bad news is that the private sector has some of that potential.

But in seeking a stronger government, the Framers were also skeptical of a government with too much power. Thus as Madison said in *Federalist No. 21*: ". . . the great difficulty lies in this: you must first enable the government to control the governed; and in the next place oblige it to control itself." The Framers intended the "auxiliary precautions" of the separation of powers and checks and balances built into the Constitution to create the necessary self control. In addition, the first ten amendments to the Constitution, the Bill of Rights, was intended to ensure that the government would not infringe a specific (though not exclusionary) set of individual rights as against the government. The Supreme Court over the past century has extended these fundamental rights of citizens against state governments as well, through the incorporation of the due process and equal protection clauses of the Fourteenth Amendment to the Constitution.

The Bill of Rights, as imperfect as our implementation of its ideals may be, is a moral statement about individual freedom and the limits of governmental power. These limits along with the other checks and balances are intended to keep the government from being captured and used by those who would use governmental power to enforce their own sectarian or narrow moral or religious values. The First Amendment assures the freedom of citizens to exercise their religion at the same time that it prohibits the establishment of religion through the government. The moral role of government here is to ensure that no one set of sectarian or narrow definition of morality is imposed by the government on unwilling citizens.

Thus the Framers intended to create a government with just

the right amount of power to be capable of governing, but not enough to allow the government to oppress its citizens: a very delicate balance to achieve.

THE OBLIGATIONS OF GOVERNMENTAL OFFICIALS

In our system of government, officials (elected and appointed) have a particularly important obligation. They must discharge their duties conscientiously, as well as provide moral leadership to the polity. Their obligations are special because we the people grant them power over us, whether it is the cop on the beat carrying a gun, an Air Force officer in charge of nuclear missiles, or the welfare official deciding who qualifies for government aid. It is their obligation to use that power wisely and in the public interest. They are rightly expected to uphold higher standards than we expect in the business world; their power is delegated from the people, and the stakes are much higher. As Elliot Richardson argues, the "State" is "only a label for the arrangements by which we the people delegate to some among us responsibility for things that concern us in common."[1]

Not only must officials make wise and just decisions, but they must also care for and preserve the institutions of government for the next incumbents, regardless of political party. Thus they are responsible for the preservation of our democracy as well as the apparatus of government. In the zeal of elected officials and political appointees to fulfill the campaign promises they have made, they ought not destroy the infrastructure or institutional memory of the government necessary for the next set of officials to change the direction of public policy. That is, government officials have fiduciary obligations and guardian roles as well as instrumental duties.

In light of the power we grant public officials, citizens have a right to expect them to comport themselves above reproach. If their behavior does not conform to high standards of integrity, they not only do an immediate injustice in specific matters but also more generally undermine trust in the polity itself, a much more profound loss.

The fulfilling of this high level of expectations entails a special attitude toward one's position in government. Those performing the official functions of government have more than a job; they have a public trust. Their approach to their profession should be considered a calling, not merely a means of earning a living. The further up the hierarchy a person is, the more we have a right to expect of them. Positions of authority, as Hugh Heclo argues, should be seen as an office, not merely a job.

> Jobholding implies no larger vision beyond the working self and the task at hand. In a deep sense the concept of office subordinates self to larger normative responsibilities that cannot be captured by a list of job tasks to be performed. The skills package of a job are not the same thing as the duties of an office. A job is discharged by performing in accordance with assigned specifications. An office is discharged by understanding its customary and proper functions. There is therefore a fiduciary quality in office-holding that is missing from job-holding. One is expected to understand what is expected of an office in light of the purposes of a large scheme of things. It is something qualitatively different than "only doing my job."[2]

But just as virtue in our governmental leaders is important, the Framers knew that they could not always count on such virtue in government officials. From their knowledge of human experience, from classical history to that of contemporary Europe, they were appropriately skeptical about the innate virtue of people who would be in government. So they set up a structure of "auxiliary precautions" that could survive bad leaders and thrive under good leaders.

If we take the presidency for instance, we see that our system cannot survive without virtuous leaders, but we cannot always count on getting virtuous presidents. External constraints must act as a safeguard in our search for virtue. The checks and balances built into the Constitution ensure that bad presidents cannot go too far. Thus if their own character is not virtuous, they are checked by a fixed term of office, by the Congress, by the judiciary, by public opinion, and by a vigorous media. But these same checks also operate on virtuous presidents. Good presidents can never go as far as we would like them to, and bad presidents may go further than we want them to. These limits are inherent in our constitutional arrangements of limited government.

These limitations are frustrating when we agree with the president in office, but remember, we Americans can never seem to agree on who are the good presidents and who are the bad ones (though history sometimes forges a consensus). Only Washington, among all presidents, seems to have enjoyed almost universal respect in his own time, and even then the anti-Federalists fought the creation of the new government he would head. Since we cannot agree upon policy goals, we must adhere to the rules under which we have agreed to govern ourselves, regardless of which political party is in power.

The Constitution created a resilient system, but it depends on the virtue of the people and its leaders. The presidential office, like the government itself, must be strong, but not too strong. The preservation of the Republic depends on our finding virtuous leaders. We can limp along for a while with poor leaders, but only for a while. When virtue fails, the external checks can save us, but only for a while. The systems of checks and balances can thwart a bad leader and voters can use elections to throw out a bad leader, but only the people at the ballot can choose a virtuous leader.

THE MORAL OBLIGATIONS OF CITIZENS

The bedrock upon which the Republic stands is the citizenry, for the highest office in our democratic republic is that of citizen. The Framers knew that the success of the new Republic would depend upon the citizenry for performance of the essential functions of 1) vigilance in maintaining the liberties guaranteed to them, 2) selecting those to whom they would delegate power, and 3) participating in the shaping of governmental policies.[3]

Madison argued in *Federalist No. 51* that "A dependence on the people is, no doubt, the primary control on the government. . . ." He also argued in the 1788 Virginia ratification debate:

> But I go on this great republican principle, that the people will have virtue and intelligence to select men of virtue and wisdom. Is there no virtue among us? If there be not, we are in a wretched situation. No theoretical checks—no form of government can render us secure. To suppose that any form of government will secure liberty or happiness without any virtue in the people, is a chimerical idea. If there be sufficient virtue and intelligence in the community, it will be exercised in the selection of these men. So that we do not depend on their virtue, or put confidence in our rulers, but in the people who are to choose them.[4]

Clever governmental arrangements cannot guarantee virtue in government. Virtue must come in the form of wise and virtuous elected public officials, political appointees, and competent and virtuous career civil servants. But all of these depend on the virtues of an informed citizenry. Vigilant citizens will ensure that only good leaders are elected. As Abraham Lincoln said in his first inaugural address, "While the people retain their virtue and vigilance, no administration, by any extreme of wickedness or folly, can very seriously injure the government in the short space of four years."

Virtuous elected officials will ensure that good laws are enacted and faithfully executed. While these ideals are not always achieved, they must be achieved often enough or we will lose our Republic.

We, as citizens, have the obligation to make moral choices about the direction of public policy and reflect these moral deliberations at the ballot box and in civic discourse. The moral content of our civic obligations come not from the content of our policy positions, but in our commitment to participate as citizens in the process of governance. Our acceptance of the rules of the game, that is, the constitutional process, is crucial to the civic health of our polity.

We must be careful not to idealize the governmental process too much, for politics is often a dirty business, and we must strive to conduct our part of the process virtuously. We must also be careful, when we observe the seamy side of politics, not to fall into the trap of cynicism. Attitudes such as, "they all do it" or "all politicians are liars and crooks" are irresponsible and harmful. But uncritical idealism leads too easily to disillusionment and cynicism. We must be realistic, but not cynical; idealistic, but not utopian. This takes effort and energy. It is not easy to gather the necessary information to make informed choices. Nor is it easy to make the necessary nuanced judgments that are often called for. Seldom are important issues of public policy black and white; more often they are subtle shades of gray. But that is our duty as citizens.

Only with concerted and sustained effort by citizens and public officials will we be able to maintain freedom, liberty, and representative government. To paraphrase Benjamin Franklin: "we have a republic . . . if we can keep it."

CHAPTER TWENTY SEVEN

On Telling the Truth

RICHARD G. LUGAR

UNITED STATES SENATOR FROM INDIANA

NISS GOLD MEDALIST

IN ARTHUR MILLER'S PLAY, *The Archbishop's Ceiling*, the characters assumed that every word uttered in the central room would be monitored by listening ears of an authoritarian government. Each conversation was structured to meet those conditions as opposed to being allowed to flow into normal channels of human discourse. Each speaker was very careful about the use of language in the presence of overwhelming authority.

How many of us are prepared for our private conversations to be monitored by outside authority? Is our speech truthful, compassionate, and wise enough to stand outside analysis? Are we morally tough enough and courageous enough to stand the consequences of inspection of our judgment calls and deeply held opinions?

At some point in a course of liberal arts and sciences, most students will contemplate the possibility that we are all in a vast room in which God listens to everything we say. As each one of us raises such a question, we are tempted to dismiss it rapidly because we will find the implications truly unsettling if not downright terrifying. Who among us would want to be held responsible for every word we utter.

To believe that God is listening to each word and to discipline patterns of thought and speech accordingly is to confront basic questions regarding our responsibilities as human beings.

Immanuel Kant pondered over this predicament and finally stated, "Truthfulness in statements which cannot be avoided is the formal duty of an individual to everyone, however great may be the disadvantage accruing to himself or to another." Sissela Bok in her important work, *Lying, Moral Choice in Public and Private Life*,[1] contends that Kant regards truthfulness as an unconditional duty that holds in all circumstances—that a lie, even if it does not wrong a particular individual, always harms mankind because it vitiates the source of law.

TRUTH IN A DANGEROUS WORLD

During the early days of my service in the United States Senate, I learned that vacancies on the Senate Select Committee on Intelligence needed to be filled. I volunteered for active duty. In the post-Watergate period, the president of the United States is compelled to share with the Senate and House Committees what intelligence agencies know about foreign governments and how we plan to know more about their activities.

The check and balance relationship in the intelligence field is an uneasy one fraught with potential dangers to the lives of intelligence personnel and to the security of our country. We have spent much time in the committee over the years listening to complaints about alleged abuses to the civil rights and to the physical well being of many American citizens, in addition to persons of other nationalities. During the debate within the Senate Intelligence Committee on legislation authorizing wire-tapping of aliens, we were aware that the words of an alien spoken in conversation cannot be separated from the words of others, possibly innocent American citizens, whose lives may become involved in dramas beyond their control.

Nowhere in government are questions of truth and what constitutes a justifiable lie more intimately connected with issues of life, death, and basic human freedoms than in the intelligence field. Indeed, some Americans believe that we should not be involved in intelligence collection efforts that occasionally require men and women to lie, cheat, steal, and violate moral codes in pursuit of advantages for our country.

Reinhold Niebuhr once wrote, "Our idealists are divided between those who would renounce the responsibilities of power for the sake of preserving the purity of our souls and those who are ready to cover every ambiguity of good and evil in our actions by the frantic insistence that any measure taken in good cause must be unequivocally virtuous. We take and must continue to take morally hazardous actions to preserve our civilization."

Our world remains an extremely dangerous place, even in the post-cold war era. Ethnic and sectarian conflicts rage in several regions of the world and rogue nations and terrorist organizations that wish us harm are intently seeking weapons of mass destruction. Our personal spheres of activity also are dangerous. We build defenses to protect our persons, families, and property. We are willing to tolerate what we regard as harmless untruths as we carry on with our lives in these insecure public and private environments.

The solution of Immanuel Kant seems extreme to us because it may be justifiable in many scenarios to tell a lie in order to protect some greater good. Who among us would condemn a lie intended to save the life of a fugitive from totalitarian secret police, to comfort a tiny child or dying loved one, or to preserve a congregation's opportunity to worship by establishing a protective front.

And thus we are drawn by the rhetoric of a political candidate who says, "I will never lie to you," but equally attracted to the idea of deceptions, misinformation, and covert operations designed to protect Americans from terrorism, war, and even less catastrophic misfortunes.

Truth and Public Service

Generally, as a nation, we are willing to struggle consciously with difficult moral issues of truth when they involve clandestine efforts such as intelligence collection. Unfortunately, we are not nearly as sensitive to the impact of lies in more ordinary government and political endeavors.

The ultimate problem for an individual may be one of responsibility before God and eternity. But the immediate problem for government is that lying—or even "spinning" the truth, which is so often seen as a necessary practice—unravels the code of conduct and confidence in which we are all bound by our assumptions that we are telling the truth to one another.

We have long been accustomed to post-mortem comments of reporters following televised official statements by the president, members of Congress, or other officials. It is assumed that the words spoken by leaders were words spoken for the record, to achieve a certain mood or effect, and to mask what truly is the larger unspoken message. Speech writers, public relations specialists, legal counselors all serve as professional craftsmen to produce words that will suffice for the purposes intended, leaving other commentators to render translations.

During the cold war, this type of translating reached its zenith with the development of "Kremlinology." This was the minute analysis in the West of statements and esoteric information emanating from the Kremlin. The machinery of the Soviet leadership reduced all sentences uttered for alien consumption to boilerplate cliches. Kremlinologists would look for significant change when new phrases or even new shading sprouted from an otherwise predictable paragraph. What does human dignity mean in such circumstances and what impact does such an evasion of the truth have on the moral authority of government?

While admitting the complexity of truth telling in public service, we must not allow ourselves to evade responsibility in a sea of excuses and exceptions. As individuals and as public servants, we must take as given that it is important to tell the truth, that telling the truth is standard conduct, that each lie requires justification and sensitive probing as to why we told it.

The unfortunate reality of public life is that the telling of lies is such a prevalent norm that persons who tell the truth with any degree of consistency are found to be peculiarly meritorious and exceptional leaders. Often they are of help to us as singular pillars on whom some reliance might be placed in the midst of a crumbling superstructure of millions of words. The bulk of public words have become nonsense because both those who have spoken and heard them have come to expect that they mean little. Like Kremlinologists, we believe that the words often mean nothing in the absence of revealing analysis of the inflection of the speaker and the words left unspoken.

President Clinton's problems with the truth have expanded the nation's attention to what is a lie. Unfortunately, it has also reinforced a long-held cynical presumption that public officials lack integrity and that politics is a dirty game. Most people give low marks for integrity to public institutions because they have a feeling that most of those in charge of these institutions lie systematically.

Men and women of prudence may counter that we have escalated our standards to impossible levels, that lying is no more prevalent now than in the past. Furthermore, we may protest that those who are tenacious in telling the truth might be perceived as having far too little knowledge of human relationships and might be failures as husbands or wives, parents, or neighbors, lacking common sense and even a redeeming sense of humor. Some citizens may point out that a certain amount of lying may be the oil that lubricates the machinery of getting things done in this world, and that human beings can tolerate only certain limits (often fairly low limits) of unvarnished truth.

Some analysts of democratic institutions have suggested that democracy does not work if individual citizens of average or below average knowledge are overwhelmed by super-sophisticated arguments, vastly conflicting and complex sets of data, and too many issues.

Yet, I am persuaded that the importance of telling the truth comes home in a dramatic form if you find yourself writing laws for other people to observe—laws which may involve loss of freedom, property, or dignity. The importance of telling the truth comes home with force when you have shared responsibility for the lives and reputations of persons in the military and intelligence activities of this country.

TRUTH AND MORAL AUTHORITY

I am convinced that we need a first-rate intelligence capability combined with an equally first-rate defense establishment. Both of these objectives may require on many occasions the use of covert and clandestine action shrouded by the highest degree of secrecy that the president and a bi-partisan group of Senate and House members must study and justify.

Yet, I have become more and more attracted to the idea of attempting to tell the truth on all occasions and of thinking much more carefully about what I am saying. I am increasingly sensitive about falling short in this quest and about the consequences of telling something less than the truth. I cannot assume that anyone else is telling the truth, but I am intent upon establishing confidence with others that I can be counted upon to tell the truth or to say nothing when that seems most appropriate. What might have been evaluated as abnormal conduct in other times and circumstances may now hold increasing importance as an imperative in public and private life, which otherwise begins to approximate the biblical Tower of Babel.

We must return to a presumption that telling the truth is good and important. Our falls from grace must be exceptions. We must become more thoughtful about the reasons for those falls and take time to state our justifications.

The dangers of our public and private worlds will require

every talent and many more well developed strengths to cope with difficult circumstances. The individual who prevails under such conditions is likely to be one who is the least encumbered with the self-destruction of systematic deception or whose personal dignity has not been corroded by a habitual resort to cover-up and dishonesty.

In other words, telling the truth as standard conduct may be good for your family life, for your general health, for your relationships with people in politics, business, and neighborhood causes. On a larger scale, if our government hopes to preserve its moral authority and the confidence of the people, establishing a much stronger culture of truth in public service is essential.

Anybody who suggests that this is either obvious or easy is very wrong. Moving from our present trend will mean that telling the truth with consistency and courage is likely to be an acquired taste for most of us.

We may be dealing with something more than the lubrication of human institutional machinery. God may be listening, too. But his compassion is profound for the teller of truth who is cheated and deceived daily, for the one honest student taking a test in a room of cheaters, or for a nation that advances the basic principles of truth and decency in a difficult world. The indispensable element of both a person affirming human dignity and a government establishing moral authority is the free will choice of telling the truth.

CHAPTER TWENTY EIGHT

Deception in Government

DAVID MERVIN

READER IN POLITICS
UNIVERSITY OF WARWICK

A PRESIDENT'S FAILURE to tell the truth in judicial proceedings in an effort to conceal embarrassing personal behavior is indefensible even if it hardly merits removal from office. It does not follow, however, that there are no circumstances where deception by the chief executive can be justified. Indeed, it is arguable that the very nature of the American political system actually compels presidents, in some situations, to engage in deception. As Hans Morgenthau put it a long time ago, in reference to the making of foreign policy, "No president of the United States, handicapped as he is by constitutional and political conditions, is capable of translating his judgment and that of his advisers into action without overcoming grave difficulties, running grave risks, and resorting at times to evasion, subterfuge and manipulation."[1]

Executive leadership in the United States is infinitely problematical, and in seeking to ensure that his judgment prevails in the policymaking process a president must come to terms with a political system that verges on the ungovernable. It is marked by an anti-authority political culture; it includes a very real separation of powers, has a formidable array of pressure groups and sports a virulent, remarkably uninhibited media. Unaided by consequential parties, at the mercy of a notoriously undisciplined bureaucracy and often unable to rely on the loyalty of cabinet members—or even of his own staff—the presidency is indeed a "beleaguered office."[2] In domestic affairs the many checks and balances, the centrifugal distribution of power, and the individualistic ethos that pervades the political system are relatively harmless disadvantages, but that cannot be said of vital matters affecting the relations of the United States with the outside world.

Notwithstanding the ambiguities of the Constitution, there is no doubt that the president is ultimately responsible for national security, a concept that has been appropriately defined by former

Secretary of Defense, Harold Brown, as "the ability to preserve the nation's physical integrity and territory, to maintain its economic relations with the rest of the world on reasonable terms, to protect its nature, institutions and governance from disruption from outside, and to control its borders."[3] Given these onerous demands, and the problems of governance in the United States, it is not surprising that chief executives should, on occasion, resort to deception in endeavoring to meet their daunting foreign and national security policy responsibilities. And to be absolutely clear, it should be stressed that the issue under consideration here is not deception aimed at confusing enemies, which most would find unobjectionable. My focus here is rather the use of such strategies by presidents in their relations with the public, the media, Congress, and the bureaucracy as they strive to ensure that foreign and national security policy outcomes coincide with their preferences.

One president who engaged in deception on a grand scale for such purposes was Franklin Roosevelt. During the 1930s, he became increasingly convinced that the German militarism represented a serious threat to American national security, yet neither Congress nor the public were receptive to his warnings. The national legislature remained committed to a policy of neutrality and opinion polls repeatedly demonstrated the public's unwillingness to become involved in European affairs. The president, however, was not to be deterred and his administration, over and over again, used secrecy, subterfuge, duplicity, and deception to implement a policy unobtainable through the processes of open government.[4]

It has been often argued that many of Roosevelt's actions in the Atlantic theater in the years before Pearl Harbor were of dubious constitutionality and violated the norms of democratic government. These charges are undeniably true, yet surely a persuasive case can be made in deference to his behavior. As president, he above all other public officials was responsible for national security. Based on the sources available to him, he had identified what he perceived to be a serious threat to that security and was obliged to do whatever he thought necessary to meet that threat, even in the face of congressional opposition and public apathy. To have done otherwise, to have deferred to those who opposed him, to have been meticulously constitutional and entirely open in his actions, would have jeopardized the policy he had embarked upon and would have entailed an abdication of his solemn responsibility to guard the nation's security.

Forty years later, Ronald Reagan was similarly pilloried for engaging in deception in the making of foreign policy. In Roosevelt's case, his policy toward Nazi Germany was ultimately vindicated by victory in war, whereas the Iran Contra affair remains a disastrous episode in the history of American foreign policy. Nevertheless, one strand of the 1980s crisis invites comparison with the events that took place earlier. Like his predecessor, Reagan became convinced that a serious threat to the national security of the United States was developing. As he and others saw it, Nicaragua was on the verge of becoming another Cuba and, as such, an additional bastion of Soviet influence in Central America.[5] The United States therefore needed to sustain the Contra rebels in their struggle against the Sandanista regime in Managua. In much the same way that Roosevelt strove to aid the British in staving off the threat to American national security posed by Nazi Germany, Reagan endeavored to help the Contras "keep body and soul together."

Like Roosevelt, Reagan's stance faced fierce opposition in Congress and did not enjoy public support. Furthermore, Reagan's persistence with his policy of aiding the Contras, in such circumstances, did not meet with the approval of senior members of his own cabinet such as George Schultz, the Secretary of State and Caspar Weinberger, the Secretary of Defense. Given the widespread antipathy toward his policy, Reagan was bound to proceed with stealth, concealing his actions behind a cloak of secrecy; and for implementation purposes, utilizing National Security Council staff, people who could be relied upon to respect the president's priorities.

Secret government however, is not only anti-democratic by definition, it also strikes at the very heart of the American constitutional settlement. As good republicans, the Framers were bent on creating a polity where decisions were not monopolized by the executive, but were subject to consultation with the representatives of the people. More specifically, when it came to warmaking, the constitution-makers recognized the need to allow presidents the freedom to "repel sudden attacks"—to take defensive action in emergencies—yet they were determined to exclude the possibility of chief executives embarking on offensive military action without the approval of the legislature.

By contrast, it is being suggested here that the imperatives of national security in the modern age sometimes require Presidents to act on their own initiative, and in doing so they may well find it necessary to dissemble, to utter falsehoods, and to conceal their actions from both the people and Congress. This is, of course, doubly controversial. First, it implies that the constitutional strait-jacket carefully constructed by the Framers needs to be set aside in some situations. And second, it suggests that democratic forms, while acceptable for domestic policy purposes, are not really workable when it comes to national security.

There is no doubting that these are truly awesome implications, but the realities of modern warfare have to be faced. Antique distinctions between defensive and offensive war are no longer valid and the isolation of the United States from the rest of the world is now no more than a distant memory. Presidents today must be alert to threats to American interests, not just at the nation's borders, but also to those that may be gestating thousands of miles away. The lightning speed of modern weaponry and the extraordinary intelligence resources available to the man in the White House create situations where he is entitled to say, as both Roosevelt and Reagan effectively did, "I have identified a threat to the national security and it is my duty to respond accordingly even if both the public and other political leaders do not share my view that such a threat exists." The contentious nature of the situation coupled with the many opportunities available to those who may wish to thwart the president's policies, in my view, legitimize his use of deception as he struggles to fulfill his most important responsibility of all, the preservation of the security of the nation.

Those who find the foregoing analysis unacceptable need to provide an answer to the following question. What is a president to do if he believes that the national security is at risk, but cannot convince Congress, or the public, of the validity of his fears? He surely cannot be expected to defer to his opponents and to abandon the position he has adopted. It is reasonable to expect him to do all he can to persuade those who disagree with him on the merits of his policy, and both Roosevelt and Reagan have been rightly criticized for doing less than they might have done in this regard. But what if, despite a president's best efforts at persuasion, his opinion does not prevail? Is it really sufficient for him to leave the matter there, to do nothing, to abdicate his responsibility to lead, as constitutional and democratic theory purists seem to suggest?

Ultimately, what is at stake here is the place of leadership in the American system. As Theodore Sorensen observed some years ago:

> A President cannot afford to be modest. No one else sits where he sits or knows all that he knows. No one else has his power to lead, to inspire or to restrain the Congress and country. If he fails to lead, no one leads. . . .

> The nation selects its President, at least in part for his philosophy and his judgment and his conscientious conviction of what is right—and he need not hesitate to apply them. He must believe in his own objectives. He must assert his own priorities.[6]

When Roosevelt and Reagan struggled to assert their own priorities in the face of congressional and popular opposition, they were endeavoring to meet the responsibilities Sorensen refers to; they were trying to exercise leadership; they were attempting to do what they were elected for in the first place.

The American political system was originally built on a healthy and entirely understandable mistrust of political leaders. It is this lack of trust that underlies all the checks and balances and all those restraints on those in authority. Some would argue, moreover, that the palpable evidence the presidents have engaged in widespread deception in recent decades only serves to confirm the wisdom of the Founding Fathers. However, I have argued here that while dishonesty by the chief magistrate in judicial proceedings concerned with his personal behavior is unacceptable, deception in the cause of national security may be justified.

In that policymaking arena it is inappropriate for all the usual constraints to apply and there has to be a degree of trust between the rulers and the ruled. Edmund Burke famously argued that legislators owed their constituents their best judgment rather than subservience to their wishes, and it may be that chief executives need to be accorded the same freedom. Given the uniquely daunting problems of governance in the United States and the president's ultimate responsibility for the fate of the nation and the safety of is people, he has to be conceded some leeway. He cannot always be bound hand and foot by rules and it is unreasonable to expect everything to be out in the open.

CHAPTER TWENTY NINE

American Politics, 1999 Style: Congestion in the Middle of the Political Spectrum

RAYMOND J. SAULNIER

FORMER CHAIRMAN
PRESIDENT'S COUNCIL OF ECONOMIC ADVISERS

As THE NATIONAL INSTITUTE of Social Sciences celebrates its 100th birthday, what seems to me most notable about contemporary government in the United States is the blurring of long-standing differences on major economic policy issues that has occurred recently between conservatives and liberals. In this process, points-of-view that have long been distinctive, to all intents and purposes exclusive, with conservatives have been accepted, in fact eagerly embraced, by liberals who have long been severely critical of them. And because the main body of conservatives remains in the centrist position that has traditionally been its location, the result has been to create congestion in the middle of the political spectrum.

There is no settled view as to what this realignment of political parties relative to one another should be called. "Triangulation" has been suggested, but that implies that the result has been to create a third position, somewhere between left and right, a "middle" that did not exist before, when that is obviously not what has happened. There has been a strongly-supported, conservatively-oriented middle-ground in American politics throughout the country's history, and quite clearly so in the last fifty or sixty years. From time to time it has needed to be reinforced and given a more focused direction, which is what General Eisenhower undertook to do in a carefully crafted paper, "The Middle of the Road: a Statement of Faith in America," read to the October 1949 convention of the American Bar Association. President Eisenhower held consistently to the centrist course sketched in that paper, remarking to Sherman Adams on leaving the White House that he felt good when attacked from both sides because it "showed he was on the right track."

There was widespread support in the 1950s for this centrist, middle-of-the-road position, just as there is convincing evidence today in public opinion polls and in what is learned from so-called focus groups that it is consistent with the basically moderate political leanings of the great majority of American people. Thus, the current changing of position by liberal elements in American politics is not so much the shaping-up of a new political position as a recognition by them of a basically conservative bent in American public opinion and a decision to associate with it. There having been essentially no movement by conservatives away from their traditionally centrist position, the result has been to diminish differences between the two major political parties on a number of public policy questions, notably on those involving economic policy.

Attitudes toward the federal budget are a good example of what has happened. Fifty years ago, there was an unmistakable difference between what the two major political parties stood for in this regard. On both sides the top object of economic policy was to achieve a high and sustainable record of economic growth, from which one could expect to achieve high and improving levels of income and welfare; but there was a distinctive cast to the conservative approach. In that approach you achieved the growth goal not by trying to manage or manipulate the economy from above but by creating an economic environment favorable to its operation, and having the federal budget in structural balance (income and outgo so related through time as to be in balance when the economy was operating satisfactorily) was an essential feature of such an environment. Thus, a balanced budget goal was central to the "sound finance" which became the hallmark of what conservatives stood for.

As with conservatives, the ultimate goal on the liberal side was also to achieve a high and sustainable rate of economic growth, but achieving this result might or might not involve a balance in the federal budget. Indeed, in the macroeconomic logic that came to dominate liberal economic strategizing in the 1930s, and has continued to do so apparently until very recently, a budget surplus is a negative and a deficit is a positive in the determination of economic growth. In the full-employment strategy that liberals favored and followed consistently, the mechanisms most relied on for increasing or retarding the economy were not what government could do to create a growth-promoting economic environment but what government could do to influence the pace of activity directly through its spending programs and indirectly through the manipulation of tax rates. Putting downward pressure on interest rates through credit easing was a third possible expansion-promoting tactic, acceptable to the liberal side even at the risk of increasing the inflation rate.

Understandably, there was a collision between these two strategies when General Eisenhower, newly elected as president of the United States, delivered to Congress a State of the Union Message in January 1953 in which it was declared that eliminating the deficit in the federal budget would be his administration's "first order of business." It inaugurated the regime of "sound finance," put a strikingly new and challenging face on federal economic policymaking, called for a reversal of what had been happening for years in federal finances (in all but five of the twenty-four fiscal periods beginning in 1929 and continuing through 1952 the federal budget had been in deficit) and ran completely contrary to conventional wisdom on how federal fiscal affairs should be managed.

Conservatives had weighty reasons for putting this accent on achieving a budget balance. In the first place, the moral authority of government was at stake. If "setting a good example" is what we mean by exercising one's moral authority constructively, then government exercises its moral authority constructively when, in the management of its fiscal affairs, it seeks to match spending with income, at least over some reasonable period of time. Conservatives have typically been acutely conscious of this responsibility, and Eisenhower especially so. When it was suggested at a press conference late in his presidency that his administration had made a "fetish" out of balancing the budget, he dismissed the charge as ungrounded, which it was, but then went on to say, moralizing a bit: "I think it is rather a good thing to be a bit frugal and to say that we can live within our income."

In the 1950s, to feel as Eisenhower did about the management of federal fiscal affairs was considered by many to be at best a little naïve. A more severe but not uncommon judgment was that it was simply wrong. But nothing succeeds like success, even in intellectual matters, and to have had the economy growing strongly in the 1990s while the federal budget was moving into surplus in very large amounts has made believers in the principles of sound finance and in the merits of a balanced-budget goal out of many long-time critics of both. Liberals are now eager to join conservatives in celebrating the benefits that accrue from these twin developments, expunging a difference that formerly separated their parties.

But as we know, harmony is not the normal state of affairs in politics where, as they say, "you are nothing if you are not different," and at this writing harmony appears to have broken down on the interesting question: What disposition should be made of the budget surpluses that are pouring in nowadays on a federal government?

One would think that the principles of sound finance would give instantly an answer to that question. With 5.5 trillion dollars of federal debt already outstanding, with actually no ground beyond simple extrapolation for counting on surpluses necessarily in the future, and with the current surplus due not to the "on budget" operations of the federal government but to the "off budget" operations of the Social Security system, sound finance would seem to imply that the funds be used to retire public debt. In any case, using them to fund tax cuts that would permanently reduce the revenue-raising capability of the tax system would be particularly ruled out.

To date, the issue is not yet settled, but debate on it is taking shape entirely contrary to what one would expect on the basis of the traditional views of liberals and conservatives, with the former proposing a program of debt reduction and the latter favoring tax cuts! This odd and historically-inconsistent state of affairs does nothing to clarify the middle ground in American politics—indeed it confuses it further—but to have all parties joined in celebrating the benefits of having the federal budget in surplus is in any case a happy result for America.

A second set of questions on which liberals and conservatives have typically differed widely but on which they are now less apart than formerly has to do with inflation and how to combat it. Again, budget management is involved in this, having to do with (i) increases in the money supply, (ii) how these can occur (in many aspects a fairly arcane matter), and (iii) what can follow from them. Briefly, for the federal budget to be in deficit does not guarantee an increase in money supply greater than would otherwise occur—that depends mainly on how the deficit is financed—but it makes such an increase distinctly more likely than when the budget is in surplus; and while an increase in money supply—however it comes about—will not necessarily cause an increase in the inflation rate, it raises the chances of that coming to pass.

In the past, questions arising out of these connections have been at the bottom of heated and deeply partisan debate. Because of the stress conservatives put on price stability as a necessary condition of an environment favorable to growth they have typically been more alert than liberals to the inflation risk. And because they have been definitely more disposed than liberals to view inflation as basically a monetary phenomenon they have been more consistently supportive of monetary and credit restraint, administered by a strictly independent central bank (in our case the Federal Reserve System), to control it. It follows also that conservatives, contrasting sharply with liberals, have been typically opposed to the use of wage and price controls to cope with an inflation danger.

But events have altered much of this. Even if it is unclear to the most schooled and experienced technicians why inflation has been so tame of late in the face of long-continued and vigorous economic growth, the fact that that happy combination has prevailed now for a long stretch of time, along with a growing popular conviction that price stability has been somehow important to achieving the high growth result, has robbed the issue of monetary restraint versus direct measures for inflation control of any significant relevance or interest. Indeed, price stability in the face of vigorous growth has made anti-inflationists, possibly even monetarists, out of everyone.

There would doubtless be sharp differences again between liberals and conservatives on how to control inflation if prices were to begin rising noticeably, but as things stand inflation-control is not an issue dividing the major parties. Satisfaction on both sides with monetary control as a means for keeping inflation in check is at least presumptively the order of the day. It is another circumstance that lessens differences between left and right, contributing further to congestion in the middle of the political spectrum.

Third, and finally, differences between conservatives and liberals in American politics appear to have diminished also on the question of what constitutes a proper balance between governmental and private responsibility in economic affairs, in fact quite drastically so. Conservatives have always taken a hard, pro-private position on this question. Adhering to individualism as a philosophy, their reliance for achieving economic growth and improvement has always been on the creative powers of free citizens working through a privately-funded, competitive, market-directed economy. Liberals, on the other hand, have typically been comfortable with a higher level of governmental responsibility for achieving economic growth.

But times have changed. The interest in "national planning" and "national economic budgeting" that cropped up in the United States following World War II has long since disappeared. Collectivized and centrally-controlled economic systems have collapsed just about everywhere overseas. And in the United States, the enterprise system's success in increasing employment opportunities and lifting levels of living up and down the income scale had by the 1990s so transformed opinion on this question that leadership on the liberal side was ready to proclaim that "the age of big government is over."

A variety of factors has contributed to this shifting of positions. Disarray in one major government program after another was doubtless one of them. So also must have been the widespread collapse of centrally-controlled economic systems elsewhere in the world, already noted. But principally responsible for it must have been the increased confidence of most Americans, confirmed by public opinion polls and the previously mentioned focus groups, in the superior capacity of the enterprise system—in short, of capitalism—to make the improvements in individual and family welfare that are desired on all sides. In any case, like the new respect for sound finance and for stable prices, this heightened respect for private effort and "the market" has lessened differences between political parties on a whole host of economic issues and thereby contributed heavily to congestion in the middle of the American political spectrum.

It is an open question whether these changes in how major political parties in America stand relative to one another will last for long, or will at some point lessen and perhaps disappear. There is almost no chance of this latter happening if the economy continues on a good-growth, low-inflation track. On the other hand, if the economy were to go into recession, even to enter an extended period of noticeably sub-par growth, political alignments would almost certainly return quickly to something like their earlier status. The year 2000 seems to me the outer edge of what is reasonably visible in these things, but I believe the odds are measurably better than 50/50 that the economy will continue at least through that period on its present good-growth, low inflation track. It being a virtual certainty that in such a context liberals will continue in their present laudatory stance regarding the ability of a market economy to resolve the problems of employment and income favorably, and there being no grounds, whatever happens to the economy, for conservatives to change their basic position on that question, the likelihood is that congestion in the middle of the American political spectrum will continue for the foreseeable future much as it is today.

CHAPTER THIRTY

Moral Authority of Government

HUGH R. K. BARBER

PROFESSOR OF CLINICAL OBSTETRICS AND GYNECOLOGY
CORNELL UNIVERSITY MEDICAL COLLEGE
NISS GOLD MEDALIST

THE SUBJECT PRESENTS A REAL CHALLENGE and can be discussed from any angle. Morals relate to dealing with or being capable of making a distinction between right and wrong in conduct. Morals are the rules by which a society exhorts (as laws are the rules by which it seeks to compel) its members and associates to behavior consistent with its order, security, and growth.

Lincoln said, "And that this government of the people, by the people, for the people shall not perish from the earth." It may be too simplistic but it can be said that we, the people of the United States, are the government. The decision must be made in discussing this topic—whether it should be explored in breadth rather than in depth. Government is the exercise of authority over an organization, institution, state, or district. Following the Revolutionary War, the authorities disbanded the Army, Navy, and all the armed services. It was feared that a standing army could take over control of the government. The democratic form of rule that exists in the United States has been internally and externally aped from its very beginning. Each challenge has made it a stronger nation. The Constitution was flawed from the beginning and needed ten amendments before it was approved as the guiding document for the country. However, it was the motivation of the people and their integrity that allowed it to survive, and not only to survive, but to prevail. Civilized men consume one another by due process of law. It is important that checks and balances are in place and, with the executive, judicial, and legislative branches, this has been achieved.

It is my opinion that England reached its peak at Waterloo and has been slowly decreasing in power since that time. The United States reached its peak at Surabachi and, by the form of government in the United States, has continued to improve and progress. Roman moral history would favorably judge the accuracy of this statement. Unlike the aristocracies, the United States did not oppress its people with selfish and myopic exploitation nor did it retard the growth of the nation by a blind addition to ancestral ways. At the beginning of our country, the excluded banded together in wild revolt and, with an unselfish attitude, established the United States, establishing world obligations for the leadership. There is no significant example in history, before our time, of a society successfully maintaining moral life without the aid of religion. Without a state religion, but a respect for all religions, the moral authority of government has been established.

Although the original rules for the United States were directed for an agricultural society, the country was able to adjust to an industrial society and now an information society. The Industrial Revolution brought with it democracy, feminism, birth control, socialism, the decline of some indigents, loosening of morals, liberation of literature from dependence upon aristocratic patronage, replacement of Romanticism by Realism in fiction, and economic interpretation of history. Each advance has improved the moral authority of government in the United States. Insecurity is the mother of greed and the United States, with the support and motivation of its people, has never suffered widespread insecurity. The reaction of the government must be interpreted in the time in which it occurred. Probably every vice was once a virtue. That is a quality making for the survival of the individual, the family, or a group.

Criticism is now rampant about the lack of morals, and indeed, perhaps, an amoral government. It must be appreciated that man's sense of morals may be the relics of his rise rather than the stigmata of his fall. Since the people and the government are one and the same in the United States, the moral authority of the government must be interpreted through the morality of its people. Lincoln said, "You can't fool all the people all the time, but you can fool enough of them to rule a large country." Civilization is a social order promoting cultural creation. However, the Ten Commandments are silenced when self-preservation is at stake. Civilization is a social order promoting cultural creation, and, therefore, challenges must be met. Political order is secured through custom, morals, and law, and economic order is secured through continuity of protection and exchange. If the leadership has achieved this without endangering the nation, then moral authority of government must be judged favorably.

The morals of our leaders are sometimes attacked and challenged. Those entrusted with the moral authority of government are human beings. If you tickle them, they laugh; if you cut them, they bleed; and, if somebody near to them dies, they cry. The question is not individual morality of a leader, but rather that the moral authority of government has been maintained and respected.

The government of the United States started in 1933 to follow Solon's peaceful methods and accomplished a modern and pacifying redistribution of wealth; perhaps someone had studied history. The upper classes in America cursed, complained and resumed the concentration of wealth. In Proverbs, it is stated, "The path of the just is as the shining light, that shineth more and more until the perfect day."

Historian Arnold Toynbee says, "it is characteristic of advanced societies to substitute license for liberty, irresponsibility for obligation, comfort for challenge, and self-interest for brotherhood." A balance that does no harm reflects the moral responsibility of the government.

This nation must protect its leaders and democracy, otherwise creeping fascism will be the rule of the day. Every great nation and empire rose and then declined. Following this, history reviews their contribution to society. It is my hope that, when history is reviewed for the United States, it will not be said that we rose from savagery to decadence and the only culture we left was rock 'n roll and drugs. However, the moral authority of government in the United States will never permit this.

CHAPTER THIRTY ONE

The Moral Authority of Government: A Religious Perspective

THE RT. REV. PAUL MOORE, JR.

RETIRED EPISCOPAL BISHOP OF NEW YORK

NISS GOLD MEDALIST

IN THESE DAYS, when so many peoples are seeking the security of religion because of the increasing insecurity of their lives, religion has become a most dangerous, as well as most positive, factor in the foreign and domestic policies of government.

The religious instinct is part of human nature. When it is repressed or ignored, this instinct can issue forth in ugly shapes. For instance, Germany, after World War I, was generally lacking in vital religious life. When the terrible aftermath of the war brought shame and despair to the German people, they were seduced by the quasi-religious Nazi movement, which almost destroyed the civilized world. In the early twentieth century, the Russian Church, wedded to the Czarist regime, ignored the suffering of the serfs and the workers. The Communist Revolution filled the vacuum left by a weak church with the zeal of Marxist Leninism. The fall-out of this religious explosion distorts the world even today.

As we enter the twenty-first century, people in the developing countries, uprooted from their cultural securities by the disruptions of fast-changing technological and economic Western imperialism, frequently are refugees from their homeland, sometimes near starvation, but in every case are shaken by the tectonic shifts in the world. In despair, they turn to a fundamentalist (for lack of a better word) Islamic, Jewish, Hindu, or Christian religion, as a secure place to fix their lives. The less secure they are, the more absolute their religious needs become. Whatever the economic, historic, and political origins of the struggle, when it is reinforced by a mixture of religion and chauvinism, compromise and reconciliation become almost impossible.

Given these religious dangers, what is the positive role of religion? I am not knowledgeable enough to speak of religion's role in other countries, but I would like to comment on religion within the United States. I feel that here, when it is a movement of integrity and generosity of spirit, religion can make an enormous difference in the destiny of our country. A sane, outspoken religious tradition can stand against seeming abuses elsewhere with integrity. To maintain this integrity, the religious community must be willing to be critical of the society around them, critical of the state, and self-critical as well.

The discrepancy between a humane society and the conditions found in the United States is glaring. But we are so used to these conditions that we take them for granted. Several years ago, the problem of homelessness first appeared, a direct result of inhumane federal policies on housing and inhumane policies on the part of the state in emptying the mental hospitals without the promised follow-up care for disturbed patients. I said at the time that New York City would become the Calcutta of the West; that commuters, on their way to work, would step over bodies sleeping on the cold marble floor of Grand Central Station without giving it another thought. I was called an alarmist at the time, but unfortunately that prophecy came true. No country in the history of the world has ever been as rich as we, no city as wealthy as New York. And yet we still have homeless in the streets; we still have major unemployment in the ghetto; we still have undernourished children, school buildings in shambles, inadequate health care, and over a million people in prison, mostly minorities. A high percentage were convicted of nonviolent drug-related crimes.

Our foreign policy is no better. We have a huge military budget, driven not by international security pressures, but by political response to the needs of the defense industry. In the last several years, our foreign policy has led to the virtual destruction of several Latin American countries, and through unwise greedy loan policies, our financial institutions have imperiled the world economy.

These policies are directly due to the overweening influence of commerce and industry on domestic and foreign affairs. The dream of globalization has become a nightmare to our "downsized" workers and to the poor countries of the world. They see our prosperity as often gained at their expense; their resentment grows, and, as we stated above, this resentment often finds its power magnified by a rigid, anti-Western religion.

It seems to me that the religious community must take note

of the human suffering that results from globalization and unfettered free enterprise. We are not experts who presume to dictate the structures for a more just economic order, but we are in a position to draw our nation's attention to unnecessary, massive human suffering, and to challenge government and corporate policy to set it right.

Is this the church getting involved with politics? Is this kind of action a breach of the wall of separation between church and state? By no means! The reason for "separation" is not only to keep the state out of the affairs of religion, but also to allow the church to be free enough to criticize the state, free to be the conscience of the nation.

Sometimes this privilege is abused. I believe the ideological warfare of the Christian Right is a case in point. But if the religious community does not take the part of the powerless, voiceless poor, who will?

The present silence of the majority of religious people in the United States is the equivalent of the silence of the Russian Church in the beginning of this century and of the German Churches before the rise of Hitler. Not only is this silence immoral, indeed sinful, this silence imperils the survival of the world as we know it. If the widening gap between the rich and the poor in this country and the rest of the world is not lessened, a massive social explosion is inevitable. The local wars and terrorism so prevalent today are the ominous chill breezes of the coming storm.

The responsibility for reform rests with all persons of good will, but it is urgent that the churches and the Jewish community lead the way. Our silence indicates to the rest of society that needless human suffering is admissible.

Without reform, without confronting the economic and accompanying social forces which cause injustices, government tends to deal with anti-social behavior by force. When eruptions occur in the ghetto due to drugs, despair over lack of employment, homelessness, or inferior education, our government responds with force: more police, mandatory sentencing, more prisons, capital punishment. Such measures are expensive, largely ineffective, and inhumane. Prevention is cheaper and longer lasting. For instance, funds for drug rehabilitation and education are slim, but money to build more prisons seems to be always available.

By the same token, our response to social revolutions in other countries has been to use military power, direct or indirect, to support the status quo, however corrupt it might be: Iran, Chile, the Dominican Republic, Nicaragua, El Salvador, Cuba, Guatemala, Indonesia, Panama, Grenada, to name a few. Even Iraq might have been dealt with more sensibly in the years leading up to the present crisis.

The burden of this essay is to raise the danger signs in today's conditions and to call the religious community to our responsibility to speak and act more vigorously, so that our government might regain its moral authority by acting in a moral fashion. If our commitment to justice and peace could become as zealous as the Fundamentalists' commitment to their causes, we could begin to close the gap between the rich and poor, begin to lessen the causes of violence, begin to build a more just and less dangerous world.

INTERNATIONAL AFFAIRS

Moral Authority in International Affairs

R. GORDON HOXIE

FOUNDER, CHAIRMAN EMERITUS
CENTER FOR THE STUDY OF THE PRESIDENCY

JOHN DONNE, the seventeenth century poet and priest, wrote so well, "No man is an island complete of itself. . . . We are part of the main." Anthony Eden, the British prime minister, stated in a volume I did in 1951, "No nation in the world can stand alone for more than a very limited period, unless it declares a state of siege with all its suffocating conditions." And Eden concluded, "I do not believe that it is morally possible to defend such a violation of the natural heritage of man."[1]

Frank E. Taplin, Jr., Fellow, Morgan Library, arrives at the same conclusion as Eden, stating, "a government that does not reflect the moral values shared by those who have established it . . . cannot long be maintained." Taplin concludes what Eden predicted of the Soviet Union, that with its claims "for ideological purity," the Soviet Union fell "into the trap that defeated communism." Indeed Taplin warns that "we must not preach to foreign governments about the virtues of a moral order we ourselves practice only imperfectly." He concludes, "Let us lead by example and not by precept." And Eden's prediction of a half century ago has proven right, "this sense of interdependence is the heart of the business."

In the first of a series of essays on the United Nations, William J. vanden Heuvel, Chairman, Franklin and Eleanor Roosevelt Institute, asserts, "One of our greatest opportunities and responsibilities is to make the United Nations an effective part of international governance." The cold war between the Soviet Union and the United States precluded the hopes of the United Nations founders from being realized. But as former President Reagan declared in December 1992, "With the end of the Cold War the UN was . . . liberated." However, Ambassador vanden Heuvel asserts that to be more effective, the United States needs to more fully "commit our power and prestige" in support of the UN efforts.

In like spirit, while serving as the United States Permanent Representative to the United Nations, Madeleine Albright contended, "We can believe that people do have the ability to rise above past hatreds and live together in mutual respect and peace." Further, she emphasized "the reason we cherish the principles embodied in the UN Charter is not because they are easy to realize, but because they are terribly hard."

Ambassador Albright recalled the bipartisan United States effort to draft the UN Charter, with the Republicans being led by Senator Arthur Vandenberg. She concludes: "The Truman-Vandenberg generation understood that although the noble aspects of human nature had made the UN possible, it was the ignoble aspects that had made it necessary."

One of our nation's business leaders, John K. McKinley, Chairman and CEO (Ret.), Texaco, Inc. makes some discerning observations about United States ethical and moral actions. He finds them on occasion contradictory. For example, he inquires whether there are "strategic considerations in providing food and medicine in support of one nation, but not to another in equal or greater need."

As a long-time respected leader in the nation's energy policies, Mr. McKinley contends, "Had the moral authority of the United States government been exercised to achieve economic fair treatment of its citizens, a far better American strategic oil position would be the result today and a much greater respect for United States investments abroad." In keeping with the adage that "people who live in glass houses should not throw stones," he concludes: "it seems unlikely that others would willingly accept the United States as an arbiter of moral behavior."

One of our nation's most distinguished historians, Professor Robert H. Ferrell, Indiana University, perceives three moral principles in the United States conduct of foreign policy. One of them, from the outset of the infant nation, was independence. While yet weak militarily, the United States fought a second war for independence, the War of 1812, and thereafter audaciously enunciated the Monroe Doctrine warning the Old World to stay out of the affairs of the New. A second moral principle was expansion "from sea to shining sea." And third, to borrow a phrase from President Wilson, was to "make the world safe for democracy." In his *Democracy in America*, written in the 1830s, the French visitor Tocqueville perceived similar forces in American history and a dedicated volunteerism in associations which he found good.

The concluding essay is that by Moorhead Kennedy, Secretary, National Institute of Social Sciences. He perceives dangers to moral authority in hypocrisy, autonomy, and too much diversity. He believes the United States exhibited hypocrisy in Iran by supporting the Shah, despite his extreme violations of human rights. He finds domestic militant groups claiming autonomy and demanding concessions based on diversity and what they claim as sovereignty. These subnational groups defy what we term "ordered liberty."

The author emphasizes that "ordered liberty" with its foundation in sovereignty coupled with moral authority must be preserved. But to the extent "that the sovereign state loses its moral authority," its foundations are threatened. He concludes that as we approach the new millennium, the "indications of diminishing respect for government bode ill for the moral authority of the United States, and for its ability to maintain the ordered liberty on which civilized existence depends."

CHAPTER THIRTY-TWO

The Moral Authority of Government

FRANK E. TAPLIN, JR.

FELLOW
MORGAN LIBRARY
NISS GOLD MEDALIST

IF THE AUTHORITY OF GOVERNMENT rests upon the consent of the governed, a government that does not reflect the moral values shared by those who have established it for their common good cannot long be maintained. What is the "common good?" It is a system of liberty based upon justice, equity, and truth—a social structure designed to permit diverse individuals to live their lives and realize their potential without infringing on the rights of others.

History has been marked by man's efforts to achieve this goal—Magna Carta, the British Civil War, the Constitution of the United States of America. The concept of power as residing in the people rather than in the sovereign, or in a privileged class of nobles, or in Plato's "guardians" of The Republic, has marked the evolution of the state in the direction of a government endowed with moral authority in the service of the people.

We cannot separate this moral authority of the government from its source in the people. We cannot anchor our hopes and aspirations solely in a constitution or in a system of laws. As Judge Learned Hand said (*The Spirit of Liberty*, p. 190), "Liberty lies in the hearts of men and women . . . [It] is the spirit which is not too sure that it is right; . . . which seeks to understand the minds of other men and women . . . which weighs their interests alongside its own without bias. . ." It is the skeptical spirit which reflects Cromwell's plea before the Battle of Dunbar (1650), "I beseech ye in the bowels of Christ that ye may be mistaken."

Moral authority, then, must be open to the spirit of inquiry. We cannot know the Truth (with a capital "T") in an absolute ideal sense. If we see the world in black-and-white terms, if we claim absolute moral virtue for our policies, we shall fall into the trap that defeated communism, with its claims for ideological purity and absolute truth. Our policy toward Cuba, for example, is deeply flawed, a policy not shared by most of the world's democracies, a view that we alone know the Truth. Wouldn't a policy designed to maximize trade as well as academic and cultural exchange of all kinds do more than our present sterile policy to advance the moral authority of our government among the Cuban people and encourage them to demand the freedoms we cherish?

Our experience in Vietnam is a distressing example of a policy carried out by our government without the moral backing of our people. The pendulum finally swung to reflect the people's views, and President Johnson resigned rather than face the people's outrage in the 1968 election. President Nixon did no better when he carried the fight into Cambodia, revealing again a policy divorced from the moral values of our people and showing finally in himself the lack of character and integrity that forced him to resign in the face of impeachment.

In this search for morality in government, based on the authority of the people, we cannot have perfection. Compromise is an essential element, as those who labored in 1787 to produce our Constitution well knew. Lincoln understood this when he argued in his last public address to his fellow citizens (April 11, 1865) that it would be better in the long run to accept Louisiana back into the Union with all her imperfections than keep her out until she met higher standards: "Concede that the new government of Louisiana is only to what it should be as the egg is to the fowl, we shall sooner have the fowl by hatching the egg than by smashing it."

We can never achieve absolute perfection or instant satisfaction in striving toward our ideals of good government. But we must still carry on the good fight. As Jefferson said in the Virginia Statute of Religious Liberty, "Truth is great and will prevail if left to herself; . . . she is the proper and sufficient antagonist to error, and has nothing to fear from the conflict, unless by human interposition disarmed of her natural weapons, free argument and debate . . ."

We might well apply this to our relations with China, where the demands of international trade may conflict with our views of a moral order based upon human rights and responsibilities. In this conflict, let us not underestimate the power of public opinion in a world increasingly bound by global communications.

Above all, we must not preach to foreign governments about the virtues of a moral order we ourselves practice only imperfectly. Let us lead by example and not by precept.

In the long run, the authority of government will go hand in hand with the moral values of society itself—in our case those humanistic values that reflect our Judaeo-Christian heritage.

CHAPTER THIRTY THREE

The United States and the United Nations: The Moral Authority to Preserve Peace

WILLIAM J. VANDEN HEUVEL

CHAIRMAN
FRANKLIN AND ELEANOR ROOSEVELT INSTITUTE
NISS GOLD MEDALIST

THE MORAL AUTHORITY of our government derives, as must all of the powers of governance, from and by the authority of the people. Our government was instituted, our Founding Fathers remind us, to create a more perfect union and to provide for the general welfare of its people. The scope of that obligation changes with each generation. To maintain peace, to contain violence, to assure our security, to provide the framework for the expression of freedom and opportunity—that is the basic obligation of government in a democratic society. Those whom history has judged to be great leaders have accepted that responsibility, challenging those they govern to strive for a better world.

The United States is blessed by its Constitution which has never been challenged as the basic social contract between its people and its government. It establishes the dominance of civilian authority. Its Bill of Rights is the charter of freedom defining the rights of citizens which no government can infringe. Its flexibility has allowed us to grow from a revolutionary republic isolated from the empires of the world into the dominant political, economic, and military power on earth. The rule of law has been our national commitment. It has given the nation its core of moral authority.

The administrations of Franklin Delano Roosevelt were the transforming years of the American Republic, when—reluctantly—we accepted the responsibility of international leadership. Never in modern history has the world's most powerful nation—as we are today—sought no territorial gain, wanted no Empire, had no overriding ambition other than world peace and social justice. Benjamin Franklin once said that America represents the conscience of Mankind. That has been our historical purpose. It must remain as our mission.

One of our greatest opportunities and responsibilities is to make the United Nations an effective part of international governance. Leading a country that was deeply isolationist, President Roosevelt took the political risk of confronting Hitler, of telling Americans that we had a rendezvous with destiny, that our security and well being depended upon the quarantine of the aggressors, that our national interest was to build a world where the Four Freedoms were paramount—let us remember them—Freedom of Speech and Expression, Freedom of Worship, Freedom from Want and Freedom from Fear. Before America entered World War II, Roosevelt was already planning the international structure that he knew was needed if the military victory of the democracies was to have lasting meaning. The United Nations was the culmination of his efforts. In his last newspaper interview, he said: "We cannot afford to let disappointment over specific solutions pull us back again from the course we have to take, however hard it is. If we all go our own ways, there will be no guarantee of peace, no justice for any nation."[1] The United Nations would not have come into existence without bipartisan support. Roosevelt welcomed and cultivated Republicans like Arthur Vandenberg and Warren Austin who understood the necessity of the United Nations and supported its creation.

Weeks after Franklin Roosevelt's death, President Harry Truman went to San Francisco and addressed the assembly that had adopted the charter of the United Nations. President Truman told that gathering and his fellow Americans:

> If we fail to use the Charter and the organization we have created with it, we shall betray all those who have died in order that we might meet here in freedom and safety to create it. If we seek to use it selfishly for the advantage of one nation or small group of nations, we shall be equally guilty of that betrayal. But oh, what a great day in history this can be! The Charter is no more perfect than our own Constitution, but like the Constitution, it must be made to live! . . . The powerful nations must accept responsibility for leadership toward a world of peace.[2]

The cold war paralyzed the United Nations and prevented the hopes of its founders from being realized. But the ending of the cold war gave us the opportunity to give substance to those hopes. Former president Ronald Reagan understood that. Speaking at Oxford University in December 1992, the former president told of a dream that he had long had and said:

> Just as the world's democracies banded together to advance the cause of freedom in the face of totalitarianism, might we not now unite to impose civilized standards of behavior on those who flout every measure of human decency? Are we not nearing a point in world history where civilized nations can in unison stand up to the most immoral and deadly excesses against humanity . . .

President Reagan went on to say:

> In the past the divided world of the Cold War paralyzed global organizations. It was virtually impossible to achieve global cooperation on most subjects. But with the end of the Cold War, the UN was also liberated—and with it, the noble vision of the UN's founders is now closer to realization.[3]

We all know the weaknesses and the vulnerability of the United Nations. It is not a sovereign body. It can only do what the Security Council orders it to do—and the Security Council can only do what the United States approves because of our veto power. The Congress can diminish the United Nations by rejecting our constitutional obligation to pay our assessed obligations and focusing on its weaknesses to prevent its effectiveness. Or they can work to correct its faults and provide American leadership to carry out its mission. The cost is infinitesimal compared to military budgets and the costs of war. Our assessed annual budget obligation is less than the cost of a flight deck of a new aircraft carrier. The United Nations has brought peace to Namibia, to El Salvador, to the killing fields of Cambodia. With our leadership and military support, it taught the lesson of collective security to Iraq and its dictator. Its intervention in Bosnia stopped the brutal systematic murder in the former Yugoslavia that had already claimed 250,000 lives. Again with American leadership, it ended the famine murder of Somalia and threw out the gangsters who had taken over Haiti.

Civilization needs a police force just as every one of our communities looks to its local police for security and protection against the lawless. What would our cities be like if gangsters held the power of life or death over us, threatening our children, our homes, our property? If thugs control the streets, forget the hopes and dreams of civilized society. Adolf Hitler and his Nazi hoodlums brought the world to the precipice of destruction. The tin-horn dictators who challenge democratic values today when they carry out ethnic cleansing and assault innocent people, destroying their lives and their hopes, are in the same gangster tradition. The United States does not want to be nor should it be the Policeman of the World. The United Nations provides a forum for confronting these gangster terrorists, and as in Iraq, it has an ability to provide a shield for collective action. But for the United Nations to have the ability to enforce its moral authority, the United States must participate and lead. The moral authority of the charter of the United Nations, of the Universal Declaration of Human Rights, of the rule of law, depends on the effective organization of political economic power—and yes, military power. If these values are only rhetoric unworthy of defense and sacrifice, they will not prosper and most certainly will be diminished.

If we had a small, disciplined, armed rapid deployment force with a United States flag in Rwanda—many experts believe—it could have stopped the massacre before it became a genocide. NATO, a multilateral defense organization, has great possibilities, at least in Europe, if its intervention in Kosovo is successful. Other regions may be organized to police themselves, which means not allowing arbitrary sovereign borders to protect a government in a criminal assault against its own people. Diplomacy, discussion, negotiation, patience, are the watchwords of peace, but to make them successful in the expression of moral authority, they must have the possibility of the intervention of effective force behind them. Because of its complex politics, the UN cannot always be successful in this way, nor can NATO, but we must continue our efforts to make them more perfect instruments of international governance.

America, which has always welcomed the adventure of the new frontier, must approach the millennium excited by the prospects before us. We have created a nation based upon the consent of the governed and respectful of the opinions of Mankind. We have amassed wealth that has never been equaled. We have brought together all of the world's races and creeds and shown that we can live together in peace and common purpose. We have spent our treasure and spilled our blood to prevent tyrants from destroying the possibilities of freedom and liberty. We must commit our power and prestige to the support of international governance based on the rule of law and the principles of collective security. Historic achievements were accomplished because we had courage, vision, compassion, strength, purpose—and yes, moral authority.

These are the qualities and values we will continue to need to achieve the better world that is our purpose.

CHAPTER THIRTY FOUR

The United Nations and the Moral Authority of Government

MADELEINE K. ALBRIGHT

UNITED STATES SECRETARY OF STATE

NISS GOLD MEDALIST

IN MY PREVIOUS LIFE, with the Center for National Policy and as a Board Member of the National Endowment for Democracy, I spent a great deal of time presenting awards to others. Because it is more blessed to give than to receive, I always felt very blessed. Now, however, I am learning that receiving is a lot more fun.

So thank you very much for the Gold Medal. Coming from *this* organization, and to receive it in such distinguished company, is a great honor—and I appreciate it very much.

Looking down the list of those who have received these medals in the past, I note a special relationship between this award and the United Nations.

I count among the recipients no less than seven of my predecessors as U.S. representatives to the UN, plus Ralph Bunche, who may have been the greatest American to actually serve at the UN.

There are also two members of the U.S. delegation to the conference that drafted the UN Charter, including the only woman member, Virginia Gildersleeve, then Dean of Barnard College.

At the time, Dean Gildersleeve argued that because technology had brought the world closer together, "a world-wide attempt must be made to control maverick nations and their outlaw brotherhoods wherever, in our interlocked societies, they strike to conquer." This was, she said, the "main highway toward peace."

One of the tools we use in that effort is the United Nations.

Now, it is no secret that some Americans are not comfortable

Editor's Note: These remarks by Hon. Madeleine K. Albright, were presented on December 2, 1996, on the occasion of her receipt of the NISS Gold Medal Award.

with our participation in the UN. Either they think the UN is trying to become a world government, which is ridiculous; or they dislike the organization because it is so full of foreigners, which really can't be helped.

The truth is that the UN cannot tax us; cannot entangle us in conflicts without our consent; and is not about to descend upon us in black helicopters and invade Montana.

Over the past half century, the UN has done much to make our world safer, more humane and more just than it otherwise would be.

Its peacekeepers have helped to create new democracies and to prevent conflict.

It has imposed sanctions against lawless regimes, such as those now in power in Iraq and Libya, and previously in South Africa.

It has sheltered refugees and waged war on hunger, poverty, and epidemic disease.

And through its specialized agencies, it helps to ensure that wings don't fall off airplanes, oil tankers don't leak, imported foods don't make us ill, and hurricanes don't take us by surprise.

The UN matters and it will matter more. As Dean Gildersleeve observed, the world is increasingly inter-locked.

But there is no guarantee that the UN will be equal to the challenge. During the cold war, it developed an elephantine bureaucracy. Now we are asking that elephant to do gymnastics.

It is because our expectations of the UN have increased that we feel so strongly and have pushed so hard for UN reform. It is why we believe the organization needs new leadership. And it is why we are working with Congress to see that our UN bills are paid. The number one power in the world can—and should—meet its obligations.

The UN is one part of the network of institutions, alliances, and arrangements that we rely upon to keep our globe from falling apart. The viability of this network matters to us as a nation, and as people.

Over the past few years, as U.S. Ambassador to the UN, I have seen what happens when civil society breaks down.

The result is a militiaman's paradise.

There is, after all, no infringement upon the right to bear arms in Liberia.

There is no ban on assault weapons in Burundi.

There is no capital gains tax in Nagorno-Karabakh.

There is no FBI harassment in the Balkans.

And for those who truly want to keep their distance from annoying neighbors, you have the opportunity in Angola to live in a house fully encircled by land mines.

One is reminded often, especially where I work, about the limits of what we can do. And there is much truth in these reminders. But we must be willing, when the stakes warrant, to push against those limits. As the president has said, the United States remains the world's indispensable country.

Obviously, we do not rely on the UN alone to defend our interests, enhance global stability, and keep us on the highway toward peace. We are fortunate to have other more powerful tools, including our armed forces, key alliances such as NATO, the world's most productive economy—and, of course, Richard Holbrooke.

Ultimately, however, our future will depend not on any single organization or individual, but on all our people. If we are lulled into a false sense of security, or a belief that we need not remain vigilant in our commitments and attention abroad, we will invite disaster.

We should never forget that the United Nations emerged not from a dream, but from a nightmare.

In the 1920s and 30s, the world squandered an opportunity to organize the peace. The result was the invasion of Manchuria, the conquest of Ethiopia, the betrayal of Munich, the depravity of the Holocaust, and the devastation of world war.

It has been fifty years since the Nuremberg trials. It is the first year of war crimes trials in Rwanda and the Balkans. A cynic might say that we have learned nothing; changed nothing; and forgotten the meaning of "never again"—again. We cannot exclude the possibility that the cynic is right. We cannot deny the perverse duality of human nature.

But we *can* choose our own role; to see our reflection not in Goebbels, or Karadzic, but in Anne Frank, Nelson Mandela, Vaclav Havel, Aung San Suu Kyi and others who have made history by refusing to become prisoners of history.

We can believe that people do have the ability to rise above past hatreds and to live together in mutual respect and peace.

And we can recognize that the reason we cherish the principles embodied in the UN Charter is not because they are easy to realize, but because they are so terribly hard.

When Republican Senator Arthur Vandenberg returned to Washington from the convention in San Francisco where the UN Charter was drafted, he was challenged by those who thought it too idealistic, even utopian. He replied that:

> You may tell me that I have but to scan the present world with realistic eyes in order to see the fine phrases (of the Charter) . . . reduced to a shambles . . . I reply that the nearer right you may be . . . the greater is the need for the new pattern which promises . . . to stem these evil tides.

The Truman-Vandenberg generation understood that although the noble aspects of human nature had made the UN possible, it was the ignoble aspects that had made it necessary.

It is up to us in *our* time to do what they did in *their* time: to accept the responsibilities of leadership; to defend freedom; and to expand outward the potential of institutions like the UN to extend law, promote development, protect human rights, and keep all of us on the road to peace.

CHAPTER THIRTY FIVE

The Moral Authority of Government

JOHN K. McKINLEY

CHAIRMAN AND CEO, RETIRED
TEXACO, INC.
NISS GOLD MEDALIST

THESE COMMENTS relate to the moral authority of the United States government and to ethical standards of this nation. Morality and authority by definition stand at the opposite ends of the playing field. Morality pertains to right conduct—the distinction between right and wrong without the power of law—while authority implies the power to adjudicate—the power to determine and command.

There is no Department of Morality. There is no cabinet-level position responsible for articulating the Moral Standards of Government.

It is reasonable to ask: "Is there a United States policy of moral and ethical behavior that is being followed by the government of the United States; if so, who knows what it is?" "To whom does it apply?"

If such a policy is not clear, easily understandable, known to the voters and taxpayers, how can the citizens of the United States, and for that matter, other governments, understand the United States government's actions. How can judgment be made whether there is any consistent moral authority being exercised.

Confusion and inconsistency are too often the major characteristics of moral and ethical actions by the United States.

If the use of tobacco is a health "demon," how can tobacco production be subsidized on one hand, and use castigated on the other, while at the same time be legalized and used as a major source of revenue? All of this is government's attempts to control advertising, selling, and which age groups may be allowed to smoke and where. What is the morality of the government's action in allowing its judicial system to sue the sellers of tobacco for outrageous sums while paying subsidies to producers of tobacco.

Consider this government's record on alcohol. It ranges from legal to constitutionally prohibited, back to legality with heavy taxation and efforts to control its use by age groups and now blood concentration. Clearly, if a blood level is set low enough, it would criminalize an individual for exercising a so-called constitutional right to use alcohol.

Governmental positions on population control, individual birth control, and abortion are riddled with confusion, inconsistency, and partisanship. Federal flood and storm disaster relief is provided in some areas with great political fanfare while smaller, less politically sensitive situations are ignored.

The moral standards of the United States, as they relate to foreign relations, are certainly not understood by many people of the world. In fact, large numbers of non-U.S. individuals consider the United States government as a representative of immorality— a Satan in world affairs.

Even in areas of health, which are generally accepted by all people as "a good thing," and help to others in health matters, thought of as charitable and on a high moral plain, we seem to be unable to explain our actions on a moral or ethical basis to other nations because they are constrained and limited by partisanship and political agendas.

This nation's actions in moral and ethical matters are perceived by many other nations to be motivated by self interest and expediency rather than a basic desire to help. What nation does more for humanity outside its borders than the United States? Probably none. Yet that is not a reasonable standard of judgment, as the United States has the military and economic power that permits it to afford humanistic goals that few can aspire to.

Without a known moral policy of the United States, separate actions often by relatively low level government employees, can set in motion that individual's ideas relating to humanitarian goals and apply them only in areas where that individual perceives there is a strategic national interest. An example is the strategic considerations in providing food and medicine in support of one nation, but not, to another in equal or greater need.

This inconsistent behavior is not limited to foreign nations. The government claims to hold the moral high ground in recognition of the national sovereignty of smaller nations, at the same time claiming to support the property rights of its American citizens. It encouraged investments abroad. In recent years the

United States government, under the guise of supporting the sovereignty of such nations as Saudi Arabia, Kuwait, Venezuela, Libya, tacitly supported nationalization of American stockholder oil assets and property without any effort to see that fair and reasonable compensation was paid to these American citizens. There was no expression of moral indignation, much less use of economic or military power, to assure fair treatment of United States citizens. This shortsighted decision, in abandoning the property rights of its citizens for some unstated political goal, must bear a portion of the responsibility for America's weakened position in the world of energy and the ongoing costs of such things as Desert Storm. The United States, providing the leadership and most of the military force, was victorious in Desert Storm. It clearly had the power to make meaningful changes, yet what it did was return to the non-democratic monarchy the control of and the revenues from oil—even though it was clear that the rulers of Kuwait did not fight, but in instances even left the country. The United States, risking American manpower in battle, saved the monarchies and the oil of surrounding nondemocratic nations from invasion, left the oil reserves under their control (control by very few people), but did nothing to save or recover the property rights of American citizens. Had the moral authority of the United States government been exercised to achieve economic fair treatment of its citizens, a far better American strategic oil position would be the result today and a much greater respect for United States investments abroad.

Morality should be founded on the fundamental principles of right conduct and concern for mankind rather than on legalities or custom.

In a world of instant communication and better informed populations, the United States government would be well served by clearly stating and pursuing its own national strategic interests and that of its individual citizens. It should conduct these activities in an ethical manner when such is consistent with accomplishing its national strategic goals. Practice morality where you can, but don't claim positions of morality that no logical person can accept.

The United States would be better accepted and understood by other nations if it claimed no moral "authority," no moral high ground, and pursued its legitimate governmental goals, leaving to individuals, institutions, and the religious community the field of morality.

The United States' efforts to promote moral conduct domestically and internationally will be more effective if done by example of government actions and that of its leaders. Among the leaders of the present administration and the Congress, there is widespread publicity given to acknowledged adultery, and in more than a single specific incident, suggestions that it is acceptable conduct and in fact normal conduct for United States leaders when many other nations and religious groups consider such conduct a major ethical fault. Is lying under oath satisfactory conduct for America's national leader but not for their citizens? This reeks of monarchy.

Given that such conduct may be commonplace and even normal, it is not acceptable to flaunt it before others, because it destroys morals and results in a situation where men of true quality will not want to devote their lives to service of such leaders and governments. Such leaders who use their office to distort the legal system and outrageously display their immoral conduct, will find adequate numbers of followers made up of those who serve themselves, receivers of government largess rather than payers, and of partisan politicians seeking at all costs to sustain themselves in office. But these will not be the men who serve their country in times of greatest need.

The United States will not succeed by claiming the high moral ground, the moral authority, the right to command, while acting in highly immoral and inconsistent ways. The humanitarian actions have too often been determined and carried out by each federal administration in response to variable political winds, as observed by those then in office.

The United States government High Road of Morality is filled with potholes of political expediency and misconduct of individuals. Until major repairs are made, it seems unlikely that others would willingly accept the United States as an arbiter of moral behavior.

CHAPTER THIRTY SIX

Moral Authority in Government

ROBERT FERRELL

DISTINGUISHED PROFESSOR EMERITUS OF HISTORY
INDIANA UNIVERSITY

IT MAY SEEM DIFFICULT TO BELIEVE, but the foreign relations of the government of the United States from the time of the American Revolution, have always given much evidence of moral authority. The three great principles by which the leaders of the Republic have conducted their country's diplomacy are naught but expressions of moral authority.

The first concern of the nation's leaders in the era of the Articles of Confederation, beginning in 1776, and then the initial half century of government under the Constitution, was independence. It is a principle that now appears so self-evident it needs no expression, but in the country's first years the very notion of independence—independence from Europe, especially Europe's monarchical ways—was a novelty, and its survival in the New World was not altogether clear. The wars of the French Revolution and Napoleon threatened to subvert independence. What the two major powers of Europe, Great Britain, and France could not arrange by seeking to dominate the American nation, they sought to force by capturing American merchant ships. Independence was very much a moral issue, because of what might have happened if one of the major powers had forced its system of government upon the government of the United States. The authority of the new nation of the New World was necessarily a moral authority because it was administratively as well as militarily weak. The Founding Fathers therefore sought to embody moral authority in the Articles of Confederation and especially in the Constitution, their great governmental design. In long retrospect, and despite the antagonisms after appearance of a party system (the Federalists and Jeffersonians), it was clear that the new nation envisioned its independence as morally superior to anything the European powers could have fastened upon government on this side of the Atlantic. The feeling was strong enough to cause the United States to survive the military defeats in the War of 1812 that included even the burning of the national capital.

The Monroe Doctrine announced by President James Monroe in 1823 was a suitable end to the initial era of American foreign policy that championed independence. It came not merely at a time of the survival but the flourishing of independence. It was true that Monroe, at the urging of his Secretary of State, John Quincy Adams, gave voice to a proposed freedom for the entire Western Hemisphere that was only possible because of British policy, which favored independence in Latin America. But because of the by-then established moral position of the United States, based upon independence from the monarchical system of Europe, it appeared advisable for all the American nations. Monroe and Adams were quite ready to recommend such a course and, although they would not have admitted what they were up to, force the European powers, with British assistance, into agreeing with it. The British foreign secretary, Edward Canning, presumptuously put the situation in terms of balance of power: "I called the New World into existence to redress the balance of the Old." It was a vain boast on the part of Canning, who found the American nation ready to twist the British purpose (which was not balance of power but hope of seizing the trade of the Latin American states) into a policy celebrating independence of the entire Western Hemisphere from all the European nations, not least from Britain. What Canning could not prevent, he proposed to justify. He had nothing to do with the independence of the Latin American nations, which had revolted from their allegiance to the Spanish crown because of the invasion of Spain by Napolean in 1808. When he spoke the phrase by which history has remembered him, there was a titter in the House of Commons, where all the members knew he was grossly exaggerating.

A second principle of American foreign relations that flourished during the nineteenth century was continental expansion, and American leaders of the time did not hesitate to place the moral authority of their government behind it. Europeans, horrified at what seemed the territorial appetite of the unruly Americans, called attention to the self-interest with which their American cousins acted, and did not hesitate to make remarks about how moral authority could cover cupidity. When President Thomas Jefferson presided over—he hardly arranged the matter, for it was so unexpected—the purchase of the Louisiana Territory in 1803, there was talk about a more perfect union. Settlers in the trans-Appalachian area desired to push on across the great river. Possession of the Mississippi basin allowed the American nation to keep out the territorial enterprises of Britain, France, and Spain. Jefferson perhaps had his own purpose, a great new territorial accretion that would ensure the future of his own political party against the merchants of New England. The purchase gave opportunity to Jefferson's political successors, notably General Andrew Jackson, to resettle the eastern Indians in the new territory. Still, despite all the obvious advantages, there surely was a sort of obvious necessity that surrounded the Purchase of 1803 in which it extended the authority, the moral authority, of the Republic of the New World. The sheer size of the United States after inclusion of the Mississippi Valley gave protection against European intervention, ensured independence.

Because of the land hunger of so many Westerners in that time, it might seem a near impossibility to contend that the War with Mexico and its enormous addition of territory—the last third of the American subcontinent—had much to do with moral authority. But one can argue that the territories taken from Mexico in 1846–48 were possible to acquire, not because they offered land but because they again extended the area of independence. With this acquisition, the American nation became so powerful, even at that time—and of course later when the country's population had grown to fit the territory—that throughout the world its purposes, which its countrymen believed were moral purposes, were bound to prevail.

One must mention what later historians have described as "the new manifest destiny," the yearning for noncontinental territory, that became so obvious at the time of the Spanish American War and for a few feverish years afterward; a time of dominance if not sovereignty in the area of the Caribbean, including acquisition of a Panama canal route. The hegemonial and territorial pretensions of the United States in the years from 1898 onward, until the opening of World War I in Europe, did not partake of much moral authority; although President Theodore Roosevelt was willing to announce that they did, using the "big stick" to advance the moral authority of his country. This turn-of-the-century imperialism (for it surely was that) did not last, and in the 1930s its protectorates were for the most part given up—sovereignty given back to the peoples who so reluctantly had found their countries supervised by *imperialismo yanqui.*

The third and last of American principles in foreign relations, and again an expression of moral authority, might be described as the great purpose of—to use the phrase of President Woodrow Wilson—making the world safe for democracy. When Wilson spoke of this purpose, he was greeted at first by enthusiasm, for America was entering World War I. Afterward, feeling against it deepened, and during much of the rest of the twentieth century the very notion that it was advisable for Americans to sponsor democracy elsewhere than in their own country seemed wrong; for it was intervention, the critics said, and there was nothing moral about that. In the years after World War II, the cold war often brought complaints that it was one thing to arrange for allies, sometimes having to pay for them, and something else to present them with advice favoring democracy, a form of government to which their politics, economics, and societies might be hostile. The nay-sayers said that we should take our allies where we found them, and of course acquire as few as possible, and in any event let them have their own forms of government; it was not our moral authority and should be no one's, to make them admire democracy.

In the last years of the cold war the belief that the United States was overextended, that it had sought to advance its moral authority further than its national pocketbook would allow, also dominated thought—and in a real sense action—in foreign relations. So that when, in Africa, a series of repressive dictatorships appeared, the word became fashionable that it was no duty of the United States to step in or for that matter, even give advice in favor of democracy. The repressive white regime in South Africa did not appear to be a concern, either, for it was only the inverse of the native tyrannies. In East Asia, the government in Cambodia of the infamous Pol Pot murdered millions of inhabitants of the country and the American nation deplored what was happening but did nothing to expel the murderers, again in belief that it was impossible to police the world.

But at last, with the cold war over, when a petty dictatorship in Serbia had the temerity to institute a new genocide in that centuries-old area where inhabitants had murdered neighbors as matters of course, the American government exerted itself—with the assistance of its NATO allies—and after a bombing campaign that raised again the talk of over-commitment, proved able to force the Belgrade government into leaving the area of oppression (Kosovo), allowing NATO peacekeepers to take over.

This good result was altogether in accord with the Wilsonian assertion of the moral authority of our governmental form, on the basis that no other form can be true to the wishes of any country's inhabitants. It accorded with the course of American foreign relations for more than two centuries, in which the principles of independence and continental expansion made possible President Wilson's moving words favoring democracy. In combination these principles have offered a new era for people everywhere. For moral authority, as Tocqueville wrote long ago, is the only authority that can form a basis for good government.

CHAPTER THIRTY SEVEN

The Moral Authority of Government

MOORHEAD KENNEDY

CHAIRMAN
MOORHEAD KENNEDY GROUP
NISS GOLD MEDALIST

THE MORAL AUTHORITY OF GOVERNMENT can be undermined from many sides. The following dangers, drawn from my own experience, need particularly to be guarded against. One has to do with *hypocrisy*. Another is the danger of too much *autonomy* and *diversity*. Still another is the misunderstanding of the implications of *sovereignty*. Let me begin with hypocrisy.

HYPOCRISY

When I was taken hostage in Tehran, in November, 1979, many Americans, besides being angered, were bewildered by the rage of our captors against the United States. The United States had become the *Great Satan,* an epithet our captors also applied, with vitriol, to President Carter.

The incoming Carter administration had made human rights a centerpiece of its foreign policy. Iranians—both the Shah's government and its growing opposition—had taken this commitment, and its implications for Iran, very seriously. Members of the opposition came out from hiding, and the government left them alone.

Then, gradually, it became clear that the United States, for a number of reasons, was prepared to support the Shah no matter what. The government cracked down on the opposition. By September, 1978, a group of students demonstrating in Jaleh Square were gunned down by the Shah's Imperial Guard. Jimmy Carter capped this appalling event by repeating his support for the Shah.

This was an example of most hypocritical policy, for which we in Tehran paid a price. The United States was prepared to enforce human rights in countries such as Chile, where we did not have strategic interests. Where, however, we did have such interests—as in Korea and Taiwan as well as Iran—human rights could be ignored, and those who relied on our supposed commitment to them could be sacrificed.

There is a critical need for an ethical ingredient in our foreign policy. At the same time, we owe it to ourselves to advance and defend our strategic interests. When these appear to be in conflict, we at least do not hold out assurances that we do not intend to keep. We avoid the appearance of denying to others what we claim for ourselves.

As in ordinary life, we have to consider the interests of all the other stakeholders in whatever we decide to do. It means putting ourselves in others' shoes. Others may disagree with the judgments we reach, and the decisions we take, and they may be adversely affected by them. They should not be in doubt that their interests were at least considered. All this is of the essence of the moral authority of government in foreign affairs, and thus of effective foreign policy.

AUTONOMY AND DIVERSITY

The taking of the United States embassy in Tehran was the precursor to a series of hostage holdings, most notably the taking of American journalists, clergy, and other communicators in Beirut. But, at least, terrorism was happening over "there," not "here."

Then came two explosions: in the World Trade Center in New York, and the Murrah Federal Building in Oklahoma City. Denial was rampant. Since the same explosive material was used in Oklahoma City as in New York, that meant the Middle East was somehow involved in Oklahoma City. A local businessman who happened to have been born and raised in the Middle East was duly thrown into jail.

When the perpetrator was found to be native-born, right-wing, and of "Christian identity," then the public opinion swung the other way. No connection was perceived between the two events. In fact, however, the two explosions were not only chemically, but conceptually related. Both send us messages which had much to do with the moral authority of government.

Both groups argued their case in terms of a double standard. The Islamic militants on trial for blowing up the World Trade

Center argued that the United States was more concerned with Israel's security than with that of the Palestinians. If the United States does not behave even-handedly, why should they not feel free to make their case known, in any way they considered effective?

The Oklahoma City defendants cited the federal assaults on the Branch Davidian Compound in Waco, Texas. They argued that the United States government, by the use of an unreasonable degree of force, not used in other situations, had forfeited its claim to moral authority.

Far more serious, however, than these specific grievances are the issues of *autonomy* and *diversity* that they raise. Oklahoma City was brought about by those sympathetic with the militias. These include the *Aryan Nations*, the *Covenant, Sword and Arm of the Lord*, even one with the delightfully sympathetic name of *Up the IRS*.

In 1996, to take one example, a federal jury in Georgia convicted three members of a militia group calling itself the *112th Regiment of Militia-at-Large, Republic of Georgia*. They expressed their demand for autonomy through a list of potential targets: bridges, vehicles, power lines, and Federal law enforcement officials. They justified their means of attaining autonomy as a defense of the moral high ground which, they argue, the federal government has abandoned. They would rather govern themselves.

Similarly, many Islamic militants uphold traditional values not that dissimilar from those espoused by the militias. They, however, demand another form of autonomy; not territorial, but rather one which represents, as Bernard Lewis, the eminent orientalist has pointed out, a basic difference between Islamic and modern Western views of the nature of law and authority, and of the function and jurisdiction of the State.

Muslims do not find in the United States the legal and cultural autonomy that would permit them to function satisfactorily as Muslims. In strict theory, they are forbidden, or at least discouraged, from residing in countries where Islamic law is not enforced. To satisfy them, there would have to be, as there is in varying degrees in the Middle East, one law for Christians, one for Muslims, one for Jews—an impossibility here.

They can still argue, however, that they are not being treated equitably. Similar concessions, after all, are being made to other groups, most notably to Hispanic Americans who enjoy considerable *linguistic* autonomy.

Both groups, militias and Islamic militants, have similar complaints. Both feel powerless, subject to ridicule. They vent their anger on symbols of power—economic in New York, administrative and political in Oklahoma City.

To the extent we give way too easily to demands for autonomy, and overdo concessions based on diversity, we give yet another group an argument that they are being left out. By such concessions, we weaken core allegiances, common standards, and basic feeling that we are all one. Common allegiances give the state the support it needs in dealing with terrorism.

SOVEREIGNTY

On June 14, 1985, TWA 847 from Athens to Rome was hijacked by terrorists and flown to Beirut International Airport. In that transit, one of the hijackers ran up the aisle of the plane shouting "New Jersey." A passenger, obviously not very sophisticated, shouted, "Hey, I'm from Joisey."

The reference, of course, was to the bombardment by the *U.S.S. New Jersey* and other units of the United States Navy, of Lebanese villages. The bombardment had caused extensive casualties, fatal and otherwise. Mutilated survivors were exhibited to the passengers, by then disembarked and held hostage. As an act of retaliation, one hostage, a United States Navy diver, Robert Dean Stethem, was murdered.

Probably at least as many innocent persons were killed by the United States Navy in the villages as by these Islamic terrorists that year. Stethem's murder was denominated terrorism, the shelling by the Navy of innocent villagers the legitimate action of a sovereign state. And correctly so.

The difference is that we impute to the sovereign state an ultimate degree of moral authority to which the subnational group, like these terrorists, cannot aspire. In the pursuit of its broad national interests, which are presumed to be moral, a sovereign state, *even when it may be mistaken,* is justified in using violence in ways not tolerable in subnational groups.

Upon this difference depends the future of ordered liberty, and of our society. For if every subnational group felt justified in realizing its individual aspirations or redressing its grievances through violence, anarchy would take the place of national and world order.

THE MORAL AUTHORITY OF GOVERNMENT

The ultimate moral authority of the United States is not diminished for long by mistakes in foreign policy like Lebanon, or domestic mistakes like Waco and Ruby Ridge. These things happen. From them, we need to learn lessons and adopt correctives. To the extent that the government continues to be perceived to be a font of moral authority, then those with unsatisfied aspirations and grievances hopefully will maintain the hope that, in time, right will be done.

To the extent, however, that the sovereign state loses its moral authority, its actions become harder to distinguish from those of the subnational group. "Taking the law into one's own hands," often in the form of terrorism, becomes more and more acceptable.

As we approach the next century, lower and lower electoral turnouts, tabloid stories about the White House, financial scandals, and many similar indications of diminishing respect for government, bode ill for the strength of the moral authority of the United States, and for its ability to maintain the ordered liberty on which civilized existence depends.

PHILANTHROPY AND SCIENCE

Moral Authority as Exercised through Philanthropy and Science

MOORHEAD KENNEDY

CHAIRMAN
MOORHEAD KENNEDY GROUP

THE FINAL SECTION of this collection of essays discusses two non-governmental institutions in American society that also exercise moral authority. The first, philanthropy, often influences and supplements governmental functions, or else fulfills functions that in other societies would be performed by government.

Several of the philanthropies discussed in this section are concerned with science. A final essay discusses the moral authority exercised by the scientific community.

The opening essay, "The Moral Authority of Government; The Role of Foundations and Philanthropy," is by Abby O'Neill. A granddaughter of the late John D. Rockefeller, Jr., Chairman and CEO of Rockefeller Financial Services, Chairman of the Board of Rockefeller and Company, Inc., and active in personal philanthropy, Mrs. O'Neill believes that this background has given her a deeper understanding of the moral authority of government.

Mrs. O'Neill respects "the moral authority of government as a desirable value and a helpful tool in an open and democratic society . . ." At the same time she deplores its seeming erosion, which "raises perplexing questions about the future of governance."

That said, Abby O'Neill describes the work of the Rockefeller Brothers Fund (RBF), particularly in developing and strengthening governance overseas. RBF has helped groups with legislative training and development, voter education, environmental assessment, "strong, free media," policymaking skills, and negotiation, among other accomplishments.

Through developing nongovernmental organizations (NGOs), RBF has sought to "build a flourishing civil society in these countries as a balance to government and business sectors." Besides the goals that they help accomplish, NGOs "encourage and provide a means for a wider and different kind of public participation than is possible through government and business. . . . [They] can be an insurer of public accountability and greater transparency, both of which are important aspects of good governance."

As a result, she sees in these newer countries "a far broader public involvement in government and a growing respect for its role. This newly gained credibility is enabling these still struggling governments to achieve public goals . . . through the assertion of moral authority . . ."

Like Mrs. O'Neill, Anthony Drexel Duke, the founder of The Harbor for Girls and Boys, sees his philanthropic efforts as helping government to fulfill functions it owes to the citizenry. "[T]he people," he points out, "require government to serve the interests of all its people equitably. This implies standards of ethics and morality."

Mr. Duke's principal concern is public education, which should equip "youth of every generation and every race . . . to compete on a level playing field . . ." He notes that, "In many parts of the country, it is evident that segments of the 'underclass' remain trapped in bad schools. This fosters frustration, violence, and other negative results that weaken our society." Hence government has a moral responsibility to children at all socioeconomic levels to provide them with "a solid academic start in life, early on, at that sensitive age when the cycle of learning and the cycle of failure both begin."

"Tony" Duke is nationally known for his work with inner city youth. He calls for private sector cooperation with government to bring about educational reforms. "It behooves government to recognize and support what works," he concludes.

Another well-known philanthropist and conservationist, Howard Phipps, Jr. has titled his essay "American Government Steps for Global Conservation Hobbled by Nostalgia." Mr. Phipps posits that all would agree that "the moral authority of government's actions rests on its clear duty to ensure a world for future generations with beauty, varied natural resources, a healthy livable environment, and on its sharing of a common view of the dangers facing such a world . . ."

American attitudes towards nature, however, were formed by a combination of wide-open spaces and a Puritan religious heritage, leading to a "moralistic view of the relationship between man and nature." Americans, therefore, who see an abundance of resources "have a tendency to see protection as the only morally appropriate action . . ." Elsewhere, "beautification and the active control of nature and man's activities in it are more widely recognized as appropriate governmental responsibilities."

In fact, America's former leadership role in conservation is challenged: ". . . we are now often the reluctant holdouts at conferences which deal with pollution, population, or the allocation of resources." While other countries devote a greater percentage of their budgets to environmental concerns, "America is, ever more regularly, seen as a principal cause of conservation problems elsewhere . . ."

Mr. Phipps concludes that America's past experience, based on self-sufficiency, growth, and access to natural products, hinders us from providing much-need moral leadership in international environmental issues.

Richard Boies Stark, MD, FACS, has submitted "Altruism, an American Characteristic?" Like Abby O'Neill with RBF, Dr. Stark cites his work with the Educational Foundation of the American Society of Plastic and Reconstructive Surgery, to illustrate the role that philanthropy can play. He describes "luring" twenty-five plastic surgeons to Vietnam at their own expense, to correct deformities. His conclusion: "We cannot rely on lovable traits exhibited en masse to salvage the human race, but rather on the few individuals who give altruistic love."

Beverly Sills Greenough, known from her operatic past and chairmanship of the Lincoln Center for the Performing Arts, has provided an essay titled "Breaking the Genetic Code." With her two children having suffered from genetic defects, Miss Sills calls for greater public understanding and support for new genetic technology and gene therapy.

Finally, William C. Spragens, Research Director of Spragens and Skinner, Associates, Communications and Policy Research, has contributed "Scientists and their Moral Authority in Government." As discoverers of knowledge, inventors, and theoreticians, and detached from government, scientists help to provide moral authority to government.

Dr. Spragens defines "moral" as "helping individuals to make choices between right and wrong." He continues, "moral authority leaders guide the citizenry in choosing the correct path, using influence rather than legal sanctions." Scientists are leaders who set good examples.

Dr. Spragens cites the examples of Albert Einstein, Robert Oppenheimer, and Edward Teller. The hard choices they made show "how great is the moral authority or moral suasion of American scientists—backed up by the extensive facilities for 'hard science' research and by the expertise of the American scientific community."

CHAPTER THIRTY EIGHT

The Moral Authority of Government: The Role of Foundations and Philanthropy

ABBY O'NEILL

CHAIRMAN AND CEO
ROCKEFELLER FINANCIAL SERVICES

CHAIRMAN OF THE BOARD
ROCKEFELLER AND COMPANY, INC.

NISS GOLD MEDALIST

TODAY, WHEN PEOPLE SPEAK of the "moral authority of government" in our country, it more often than not is with a tone of dismay or an expression of regret. In conversations and in the various media, government's moral authority is being described in such terms as declining and diminishing, compromised and eroded. Indeed, it is said that government, in a variety of situations, by its action—or, for that matter, its failure to act—has yielded its right to assert moral authority. It can no longer act effectively in achieving certain goals simply by exhortation, inducement, or example without the need for legislation, regulation, or a specific mandate.

This situation, which has become aggravated over the last quarter century, is generally described by those speaking or writing as something to be deplored. By comparison, references are often made to earlier periods in American history when the exercise by government of moral authority was seen as clear and unambiguous, and when, importantly, it was accepted as useful in addressing the long-term best interests of the nation. This was so even when particular outcomes might not have served the immediate needs of all the population. While I think we tend sometimes to look back on history and see what we want to see, I am especially struck in this instance that we have in America experienced a change—one that raises perplexing questions about the future of governance.

Since I respect the moral authority of government as a desirable value and a helpful tool in an open and democratic society, these discussions about its erosion are a reminder to me that a government's moral authority does not exist in a vacuum. To the contrary, its effectiveness is subject to abuse and misuse in the same way as other powers of government. Like these other powers, it can be trampled and turned to personal advantage by the very people who have been elected, authorized, or delegated to exercise it in the interest of a larger public good. And it can just as easily be damaged and undermined by a population, or segments of a population, acting in behalf of narrow self-interest.

There is, I realize, debate among political and moral commentators about the use and value of the moral authority of government at the end of the twentieth century. My own experience has been at the practical, grass-roots level, which I have gained through my long association with our family's foundation, the Rockefeller Brothers Fund (RBF), and through my personal philanthropy. In my reflections on the moral authority of government, I look back on some of these activities as helpful to my understanding of its meaning and importance.

A considerable portion of the Fund's grant program over a number of years has been involved with organizations and projects outside the United States. As a Fund trustee, and for a time as its chairman, I have followed this work closely. Some of my personal philanthropy has been in response to similar needs and opportunities overseas. We have worked with individuals, organizations, and governments, and in my travels, I have had a chance to meet with many of those with whom the Fund has been associated in their home countries and at their places of work. In thinking about the moral authority of government, I particularly recall the Fund's work in South Africa prior to and after the apartheid years, and in Eastern and Central Europe just before and after the fall of the Soviet Union.

In all of these countries, we were working in an environment in which new governments were attempting to establish themselves in order to build their countries—through political, economic, and social development—in ways that would serve their citizens and allow them to play an active role in the world. These fledgling governments were all challenged by a past in which governments were hateful and destructive and most often served only the private interests of a small, self-perpetuating elite. It was necessary for the new leaders to start with the foundations—the basic elements of nation building in every respect. Moreover, the predecessor governments, through their actions, had so thoroughly undermined government's moral authority that the new governments began their difficult work in an atmosphere of distrust and suspicion at best. They faced enormous obstacles.

In these circumstances, the RBF, often in partnership with other private donors and initiatives, supported a large number and great variety of projects aimed at assisting in the arduous task of nation building. We helped groups that were involved, for example, in legislative training and development; voter education; national, regional, and community planning; environmental assessment; consensus building; strong, free media—print, radio, and television; policymaking skills; and negotiation and mediation training.

On a broader basis, we devoted a great deal of time, attention, and funds to developing nongovernmental organizations working in a variety of fields—an NGO sector. The goal was to build a flourishing civil society in these countries as a balance to government and business sectors. Private nongovernmental organizations not only help to accomplish certain goals, but more generally, they encourage and provide a means for a wider and different kind of public participation than is possible through government and business. In addition, and most significantly, the NGO sector can be an insurer of public accountability and greater transparency, both of which are important aspects of good governance.

I would summarize the Fund's work in this way: it has helped to strengthen the processes and institutions of government, and it has helped citizens to work co-operatively toward accomplishing public goals through both government and NGOs.

In South Africa and in the countries of Eastern and Central Europe we have seen tremendous progress. A great deal that is positive has been—and continues to be—accomplished. To be certain, the RBF and other philanthropies working in these same areas are not responsible for the achievements in South Africa or in the countries of Eastern and Central Europe. Of course, the people of those countries have done the work, but I do believe the assistance, both technical and financial, of the RBF and others has been useful—perhaps in some ways critical—to the effort.

What we now see in all of these places is a far broader public involvement in government and a growing respect for its role.

This newly gained credibility is enabling these still struggling governments to achieve public goals through legislation and regulation. Moreover, they increasingly can act through the assertion of moral authority in ways that their predecessors had sacrificed. As a consequence, we see effective government action being taken without the need for coercion and the threat of penalty. I recognize that in two of these countries, South Africa and The Czech Republic, the heads of state—Nelson Mandela and Vaclav Havel, respectively—are able to exercise considerable moral authority in their own right that has been of great value in rebuilding their countries. These personal achievements, however, do not tell the whole of the story with respect to the development of government in either country, although one certainly hopes the future will produce more such leaders. Over time, the actions that these young governments and their leaders are able to take through such assertions of moral authority should help to build renewed respect for and trust in government, thereby overcoming lingering suspicions. This ultimately will contribute to stronger and more open democratic societies.

The projects I have mentioned of the Fund and other donors have been instructive. They demonstrate to me that the moral authority of government, even if it has been abused and compromised, can be nourished, enhanced, and protected by the very citizens it is intended to serve.

As I think about what I see as the erosion of the moral authority of government in our own country on the eve of the new millennium, two very different situations are of special interest to me. The first is single-issue politics and the commanding role this now plays in our governance at all levels. I do not quarrel with the importance of individuals and institutions having their own specific interests and objectives. I am concerned, however, that these increasingly are being asserted in such ways and so aggressively as to rule out accommodation, consensus, and a balanced resolution whether through legislation or some other means. Much of the decision making on issues of broad public interest is now being made on a win or lose battlefield with little appreciation of the value of give and take in attaining social political goals.

The result, it seems to me, is an increasingly pervasive cynicism toward government at all levels that is eroding the moral authority of government even though it may not be directly under attack. This puts at risk a fundamentally important aspect of American society: popular trust in government and respect for its institutions and mechanisms. I am interested to see whether what we have learned from our grant making in aid of building young governments overseas—albeit in entirely different circumstances—might be usefully applied in helping to rebuild the moral authority of government here in the United States. And if so, is there a role foundations and the NGO sector might play in this process?

Second, in the several countries I have mentioned, I have witnessed the change that creative energy and innovative approaches applied cooperatively can bring to finding solutions to difficult matters that have become deadened and stymied by individuals seeking personal security in the status quo. Today we are confronted by numerous problems that do not respect national borders and can only be resolved through transnational action. These problems, already severe, are becoming more critical and pose a growing threat to our well being and our security, both nationally and globally. Examples include exploitation and overuse of resources almost across the board—water, air, fish, forests, and on through the list; climate change; migration and immigration; terrorism; ethnic and religious hostilities; infectious diseases.

These problems will not be successfully addressed through responses that serve only special narrow interests either of individuals or national governments acting alone. But they can, I believe, be dealt with through cooperative action based on an understanding of history, an appreciation of what can be achieved, fairness, and an open process. While some of this cooperative action can be gained through legislation, regulation, and formal international agreements, much of it cannot. It will be dependent instead on governments being able to act through other means—through exhortation, inducement, and by example; that is, through the effective exercise of moral authority. From the perspective of my experience at the RBF and through my personal philanthropy, one way to think about restoring the diminished moral authority of our government so that it could be helpful in solving some of the difficult looming transnational problems would be to turn to our own advantage what we have learned in helping to build new governments in other parts of the world. There is, I feel, much we can adapt, but often overlook, from the experiences of others. Again, I ask myself, is there a role the foundations and the NGO sector might play in this process?

CHAPTER THIRTY NINE

The Moral Authority of Government

ANTHONY DREXEL DUKE

PRESIDENT AND TREASURER
HARBOR FOR GIRLS AND BOYS

NISS GOLD MEDALIST

THE MORAL AUTHORITY OF GOVERNMENT, in a democracy like ours, comes directly from the people. "Government by the people and for the people" was most likely envisioned to be workable inside the context of an ethical and moral society, the absence of which, to whatever degree, creates space for "might makes right" and tyranny of some sort.

Our 200-year experiment inaugurated by our Founding Fathers continues to survive only inasmuch, and long as, the people require government to serve the interests of *all its people equitably*. This implies standards of ethics and morality.

Government in education is an anathema to some because of its potential to color course content to reflect current political persuasions, doing damage to the classic rudiments of education. This is a bona fide concern.

However, government involvement in education to the extent that it facilitates the broader concerns of the people to insure that the youth of every generation and every race has equal access to an education that equips them to compete on a level playing field, should appeal to all sides. This does not mean that some will not have greater advantage than others, depending on their raw talent or resources to secure elite support systems in an educational environment. The government has, however, the moral authority to allocate resources across the population to insure that the fabric of society is adequately woven to support the common good of everyone.

Government exercises its moral authority to serve the will of the people by using the resources of the commonwealth to support those entities, organizations, and agencies committed to meeting the needs of those who, by virtue of living in an imperfect world, run the risk of being left out or relegated to an inferior version of the education system. In many parts of our country, it is evident that segments of the "underclass" remain trapped in bad schools. This fosters frustration, violence, and other negative results that weaken our society.

Entities like charter schools and special schools, such as the Harbor, with which I am affiliated, have missions to empower young citizens through the education they deserve, to move upward in our society. They prevent weakening of democracy's fabric by focusing on the chaos of America's inner cities and contributing, in part at least, to a solution to this condition.

From my own long experience working with inner-city youth, I conclude that particularly when it comes to education, equitable theories and practices must be delivered to the population as a whole. For our democracy to stand up as a strong model, its government has the moral responsibility to see that the educational needs of citizens at all socioeconomic levels be addressed by its school system. This implies that all American children, including those in our inner cities—the disadvantaged, at-risk children—should be provided with a solid academic start in life, early on, at that sensitive age when the cycle of learning and the cycle of failure both begin.

As a democratic government has received its moral authority and mandate from its populace to serve the common good, it is, or should be, the government's moral responsibility to keep in place standards under which special attention is paid, and support given, to inner city schools and agencies in poor areas in which teachers must truly and provenly recognize that *all* children are endowed with the genetics they need to master their destiny in life. Philosophically and pragmatically speaking, unless these children are taught in the right atmosphere—which should be a sympathetic, caring, respectful, and at the same time a disciplined kind of learning place—all the potential inherent in their genetics will go to waste.

Certain special schools, both inside and outside the public school system, display respect and understanding of the diverse backgrounds of their students. This involves knowledge and appreciation by staff and teachers of who these young, at-risk American children are and what their heritage is. Good teachers demonstrate care and respect. As home environment should complement school work, they recognize that further attention should be given to families of these children.

Long experience with the Harbor, its school and myriad after-school programs, have irrevocably instilled in me the conviction that there are no barriers when it comes to intelligence, or the ability to learn.This concept works at the Harbor as it does in other institutions and organizations with which I am familiar.

Alumni and alumnae ultimately tell the story. The ways we have of protecting what we have in this great country may differ.

There are many problems and weaknesses throughout our American education system, but there are also many reforms and changes taking place around the country involving private sector cooperation with government. It behooves government to recognize and support what works, what practices produce the best results. Through such recognition, government takes responsibility for instilling supportive and pertinent educational standards across the boards.

CHAPTER FORTY

Conservation Beyond Preservation

HOWARD PHIPPS, JR.

CHAIRMAN EMERITUS
WILDLIFE CONSERVATION SOCIETY
NISS GOLD MEDALIST

AMERICA'S UNIQUE INITIAL ENCOUNTER with nature in the New World, with its vast and lightly populated spaces and its abundance of wildlife, to which it brought a Puritan religious heritage, a democratic spirit, and a love of technology, helped produce a characteristically American moralistic view of the relationship between man and nature. This view still underlies the moral authority of our government when it acts in the name of benefiting the conservation of nature despite the fact that more recent experiences and a wider awareness of global problems lead many conservationists, at home and abroad, to believe it gives insufficient support to required new initiatives. While all may agree that the moral authority of government's actions rests on its clear duty to ensure a world for future generations with beauty, varied natural resources, a healthy livable environment, and on its sharing of a common view of the dangers facing such a world, Americans have a tendency to see protection as the only morally appropriate action because we still see our nation as a place filled with natural blessings which only need saving. In many other countries, where man has been shaping the landscape for centuries, manmade scenery is more widely appreciated, and beautification and the active control of nature and man's activities in it are more widely recognized as appropriate governmental responsibilities. Because of the past seeming abundance, we take a broad sharing of resources as natural, while in other societies, scarcity and appropriation by a few has always been the norm. With the difference in our histories, it is easy to see that restoration, reclamation, and beautification are controversial, and any restrictions on our use of natural products or on our lifestyle are grudgingly accepted and the government's actions regularly challenged.

Our position as the world's leader in conservation is challenged today. While for many years our actions were not only applauded but copied, and we were the first to identify issues which would receive worldwide attention, we are now often the reluctant holdouts at conferences which deal with pollution, population, or the allocation of resources. Many other countries now devote a greater percentage of their budgets not only to the now traditional conservation issues, including the creation of parks and reserves, but to the emerging issues of how to slow down population growth, how to reduce energy use and the production of greenhouse gases, how to develop ways to reduce consumption of tropical forests, the disposal of waste, and the ways to develop economic initiatives for the responsible use of wildlife. America is, ever more regularly, seen as a principal cause of conservation problems elsewhere by shipping our waste to Third World countries, promoting the drainage of irreplaceable, and biologically diversified wetlands elsewhere for the creation of pastures for cattle to supply our fast-food chains, through mining practices which pollute, by consumption of tropical woods which lead to the cutting of rain forests, by distributing insecticides and agricultural products which are banned at home, by the lack of support given to international organizations promoting family planning, and most especially to our profligate use of energy.

A quick look at the history of our first encounter with nature helps to reveal why we have certain distinctive attitudes which we regard as having great moral significance in our behavior toward nature. When the first settlers came, they found the land new and strange, hostile and threatening, and looked for guidance in the Bible they brought with them. In it they read that man was explicitly given dominion over all creatures, both plants and animals, for him to use for his own benefit. This was a perfect justification for all sorts of destructive exploitation. Yet the same Bible was equally explicit in calling man's a fallen nature, and this teaching led to the rise of a particularly American respect for whatever is pure and unspoiled, for anything uncorrupted by the hand of sinful man.

With the expansion of discovery and the growth in our knowledge of the previously unexplored wilderness, grew our wonder at the abundance of wildlife, at the multitude of great rivers, prairies, forests, and mountains. Fueled importantly by the widespread public exhibitions of huge dramatic canvasses by visionary artists from Europe, and by the impassioned descriptions of the new landscape by a generation or two of writers with a highly developed romantic and poetic style who found a mystic virtue in unspoiled nature, a new and very American sensibility arose. Building on the already present ideal of purity, an enormous moral value was attributed to places which were seen as coming directly from the hand of the Creator. Undefiled by sordid human activities or ambitions, sacred and uncorrupted, these places seemed miraculously able to refresh our souls and to inspire our spiritual development through their beauty and awesome grandeur. From this experience, grew the creation of National Parks, an activity widely approved here, and soon followed in other countries.

If we had the first National Park at Yellowstone in the Rockies, the Argentines, where the Andes produced similar reactions of wonder, moved quickly to create the second, and soon parks were ubiquitous. The ideal of preserving and protecting virgin areas is a great and largely American contribution to conservation.

The moral authority connected with the creation of parks is so strong that it has helped other countries prove their moral seriousness to us by the setting aside of land for this purpose. Costa Rica, which has set aside 11 percent of its nation for parks, is the largest recipient of foreign aid from Latin America, although tiny in comparison to Brazil. Everywhere, places which can preserve some value are designated as parks, generally for natural beauty and wildlife, but occasionally to preserve other values— even peace, as in the cases of Peru and Ecuador and of Argentina and Chile, which have been able to settle border disputes by the creation of international parks.

However, America has also, because of its religiously inspired attitude about the purity of certain places, taken at the same time the unspoken position that anyplace to any degree touched by man is spoiled forever and not worthy of respect or attention. In this country, the contrast between protected and unprotected land is extreme, and if America were respected for its leadership in the protection of nature within parks it was to become notorious for the hideousness of many of the abandoned or disregarded places, often on the very outskirts of parks. As a nation, we are often accused of seeing things in black and white and our division of lands into worthy and unworthy is one of the examples cited.

Toward animals, too, Americans developed a moralistic approach which seemed unusual to others with different histories. Combined with what, at first, seemed to be an unlimited abundance of game with which to supply the diet and the warm furs for the early colonists, was the democratic spirit which demanded free access to hunting, fishing, and trapping. While private ownership of land carries with it the right to exclude hunters, fishermen, and trappers, most land and game was public or unposted; and a fundamental right existed to bear arms and many people did for hunting and not defense. What was an aristocratic pursuit elsewhere, was Everyman's right, and the protection of game preserves which was a special duty and prerogative of the few in other countries, was left to the masses. We escaped what has been a major source of class resentment, and until the decline of many species became obvious, there were few restrictions to hunting and fishing—and the government's role was only grudgingly accepted. Even today, among the laws which people take a delight in stretching, those related to limits, or restrictions on the methods for the taking of game, rank next only to those related to speed limits. Once, however, we saw a need to protect animals beyond the park boundaries, we did what we had done before with land, and divided species up into the good and the bad, as Noah had done with the animals he was to put into the ark. Deer were good, coyotes were varmints; quail were good and the hawks which killed them, reprehensible; nice young salmon and trout needed to be saved from the wicked mergansers which delight in gobbling them up; and we extended our benevolent protection to the furbearers and the birds with beautiful feathers.

In contrast to the tradition in other places, we chose in this country to protect animals primarily through restrictions, even though they were often considered an obstacle to be avoided by the sportsmen, and never tried to restrict access to game to one economic group. While the fly fisherman may feel the social and moral superior to the bait caster, the latter is free to change over to a fly anytime and have a chance to fish on the rivers which may be reserved for that sort of fishing only. Our government has carried this spirit into negotiations with other countries, with mixed success. Early on, agreements were reached on migratory waterfowl and on the exploitation of birds for their plumage where America was in a strong position to force agreement with economic sanctions. Where we would like to set limits on fishing techniques such as long lines or require the use of special nets to release turtles, porpoises, and small fish caught inadvertently in the process of fishing, we have not been nearly as successful as when we extend the boundaries of national ownership of waters, which goes contrary to this tradition. Our arguments with Canada over salmon stock and the collapse of the cod fisheries are examples of our failure to persuade or to understand foreign attitudes. The waste of by-catch (the dumping of unwanted fish at sea) which now approaches 30 percent of the total catch, is a problem which our government has not been able to address, since it would seem to require severe limits on the freedom of fishermen to pursue their legitimate prey. Our government can take strong positions when the creature is perceived as good, as are the big-brained whales and dolphins, but when the need is as great but the animal is not highly regarded, as is the case with the sharks, it is slow to act indeed.

Along with the division of the world into spoiled and unspoiled spaces, of animals into good and bad or useless, the American preoccupation with health has made us conscious of another split, between the pure and the impure. Clean water for drinking and swimming in, clean air and food without harmful chemicals, are the excuse for giving enormous power to the government over our lives. And thanks to our technical skills we have been able to bring the monitoring and filtering to standards not possible only a few years ago. In this area, as in the others, the absolute moral division makes us want 100 percent purity at whatever the cost. Politically, it is hard to favor any compromise, and the resulting high cost or extreme delays in implementing programs are only beginning to be recognized. America, too, is so large that we were able to forget the degree to which our well-being depended on others. Acid rain, greenhouse gases, the importation of foreign fruit and vegetables with the inadvertent release of exotic insects, our own desires to ship out garbage and nuclear waste to distant places, and the realization that the demand on natural resources of all kinds grew under increasing pressure from the exploding world population, made us a bit less parochial; while at the same time we were being seen by others not as the leaders for a cleaner planet but as the great polluters of it.

In creating parks, America has begun to find that they are never big enough. They almost inevitably attract people and development to their borders, often destroying lands and animals which should be left as an important part of the park's natural environment, converting the parks into small islands unable to provide adequate habitat for the creatures they were supposed to protect. The Everglades, where drainage and the control of the water flowing through the park has caused a drastic loss in the number of many species, is an important test for our belief in protection, and of the government's ability to control huge regions beyond parks for their benefit.

The world's biggest parks are being created today in places like Tibet, Mongolia, Brazil, and the Congo, where there still exist numbers of spectacular creatures, often large mammals, in a natural state. Ironically, the impetus to create them is coming in large part from America and not from the local areas, because of the success of our zoos and of nature films which have brought these animals to the public attention. Pandas, tigers, elephants, and gorillas are seen here as creatures which must not disappear, and support here is stronger than in their homelands, where the idea of good animals may not resonate as it does in America.

Along with the westward expansion of America, grew a strong belief in the beneficial effects of growth. So strong has this belief been, that we have been slow to see the negatives which came with it, and we have never been comfortable with having the government place limits on development. The effect of the automobile on America has been profound, including the advent of suburban sprawl, the carving up of natural habitats for roads, noise and air pollution problems, extravagant energy use, and many more. Yet while these are issues recognized by many here, and by almost everyone in other countries, the support for government regulatory programs has been largely limited to those involving health and safety and the feared dependence on foreign oil.

The country welcomed the population growth which helped us establish economic leadership. While there is a wide recognition of the problems of unlimited growth in population and a general uneasiness over the 30 percent growth in this country alone since 1970, at the same time strong moral views prevent the government from taking very strong steps to promote family planning. Conservation science is new and its message that everything is interrelated with everything else and especially its concern with the importance of bio-diversity runs contrary to our history, where we have seen ourselves as big enough to go it alone and where the proposition that all species and all habitats deserve respect and attention, seems contrary to our selective favoritism. That we are coming up against limits to grow, seems to be merely a lack in the redeeming faith we share, thanks to past successes in the possibility of finding a technological fix to almost any problem.

In summary, our government has the moral authority to protect unspoiled spaces, good animals, valuable habitats, and pure air and water. With a little bit of ingenuity, it can stretch its role considerably, but its authority is weak when it comes to the big international issues. We will be unable to provide the leadership we must in such fields as global warming, bio-diversity, and population, if we continue to depend on our past experience where self sufficiency, growth, and a democratic open access to natural products worked well. Fortunately there is another, perhaps saving, belief in this country which has to do with the power to learn. Education is high on our national political agenda and, if it translates into the teaching of good science, we may be able to preserve and protect and restore our planet.

In the end, we will conserve only what we love.

We will love only what we understand.

We will understand only what we are taught.

—Baba Dioum

CHAPTER FORTY ONE

Altruism: An American Characteristic?

RICHARD BOIES STARK

PROFESSOR EMERITUS OF CLINICAL SURGERY
COLUMBIA UNIVERSITY
NISS GOLD MEDALIST

AS AN INTERNATIONAL reconstructive plastic surgeon, I have seen a myriad of "before and after" emotional life stories that have brought cogent diplomacy to our country. One experience that lingers in my memory took place in the Dominican Republic. My host, an American-trained doctor, had scheduled the three lectures I was to give in the main hall of the autonomous university—well-known as a political hot bed. But when we got there, we found to our dismay that it was being painted.

In the only other auditorium, a large group of students was holding a political rally. My host interrupted, explaining that I would be lecturing there. We started to set up only to find that the projection screen was full of holes. The alternative was an oblique white side-wall which was plastered with political proclamations. The first one we took down and rolled up was a large pro-Castro poster. This met with a loud chorus of boos and catcalls. As angry students stormed out, one approached to within a few inches of my face and yelled, "What do you think you can teach us?" As he left, he scrawled on the wall, "YANKEE GO HOME."

"What an ominous beginning," I thought. These students were not only militantly anti-American, but more interested in politics than medicine—Mao and Fidel, rather than rebuilding the face and parts of the body. Although we had expected several hundred, there were only a few dozen in the audience when I began.

My lecture was largely visual with projections of "before" pictures and enough operative views to show how the "after" result came about. The cases were of reconstructions of almost every external part of the body—nose, ear, chin, cheek, breast, fingers, and by the time I came to the genital organs, I was aware of dark shapes quietly creeping in. When the lights went on, the hall was almost full.

Between the first and third lectures my host had arranged for me to perform three operations in the teaching hospitals for the residents to observe: the total reconstruction of the nose of a man who had lost it due to cancer; the repair in a single operation of a harelip and cleft palate restoring speech to a teenage boy; and the removal from a man's leg of a crippling tumor that had been growing for seventeen years.

Evidently word had spread that the Yankee doctor did have something to teach. The third lecture given to a standing-room only audience ended with prolonged applause and was followed by a question-and-answer period that went on for an hour. And to the graffiti on the wall, "YANKEE GO HOME," was added, "AND TAKE ME WITH YOU."

Well, I couldn't take him along, but indelibly imprinted in my memory were the before and after pictures of his face—hostile, flushed with anger in the beginning and smiling, friendly at the end. That I did take along.

Horrendous deformities exist uncommonly in our country but abound in emerging countries where expertise for repair is virtually non-existent. I was determined that my specialty of plastic surgery should extend its healing mission to suffering in other countries.

It was not a one-man job. A lot of support was needed. Not until 1961, when I became president of the Educational Foundation of the American Society of Plastic and Reconstructive Surgery, did it become possible when I met with the directors of Cooperative of American Relief Everywhere (CARE) to ask if they would be interested in giving logistical support. They said "Yes, we can use your specialty and use it now."

"Where?"

"Vietnam."

So in 1964, I felt since I had been responsible for this nexus of our two organizations, I had better go out and establish the program myself. I spent a total of eight years, January or February each year, in Vietnam instead of a vacation from my own practice. This became an extremely helpful effort since there was no expertise in reconstructive surgery in all of Vietnam. I found that the French-trained Vietnamese general surgeons were skillful but knew nothing about reconstruction. To insure a continuum of training, I was able to lure plastic surgeons from the United States and other free world countries to go to Vietnam for at least a month at their own expense.

How did I lure them?

I went up to a prospective candidate, or got him on the phone and asked invitingly, "How would you like to have an adventure?"

"A what?"

"How would you like to relinquish your vacation, abandon for a month or two your practice, your class, your family, and professional responsibilities, pay your own air fare and living expenses, give a dozen lectures and perform several dozen operations free of charge in some drastically under-equipped hospitals in dangerous, war-torn Saigon?"

And believe it or not, I persuaded twenty-five to go.

The training in reconstructive plastic surgery for Vietnamese general surgeons was on a par with that of the best United States teaching hospitals. They were given ongoing instruction that reflected techniques and procedures not merely of a single center but ones as widely divergent as those offered by the training programs from which the professors came.

In the program years (1964–73) over 1500 illustrative operations were performed along with over 100 slide lectures and nine Vietnamese general surgeons were trained to become competent reconstructive surgeons.

Now 30 plus years later, it is rewarding to know that the Plastic Surgery Educational Foundation continues to operate in a dozen or more countries, and the ever-increasing overseas volunteers continue to share the credo: An operation that helps the deformed to approach normalcy is love in action.

People still speak of man's "inhumanity" to man as if it were some unusual freakish behavior foreign to the species and love and generosity the norm to be found everywhere. It's really the other way around. We cannot rely on lovable traits exhibited en masse to salvage the human race, but rather on the few individuals who give altruistic love.

CHAPTER FORTY TWO

Breaking the Genetic Code

BEVERLY SILLS GREENOUGH

CHAIRMAN
LINCOLN CENTER FOR THE PERFORMING ARTS, INC.
NISS GOLD MEDALIST

SOME PEOPLE RECOIL when they hear the phrase "gene therapy." It conjures frightening images of scientists trying to play God. But the words actually hold great promise for doctors fighting to conquer crippling and lethal diseases.

Genes, units of DNA housed in human chromosomes, are the keys to heredity. They hold the codes that control individual characteristics such as our eye color and blood type. Genes can also determine our long-term health. Persons with damaged or missing genes are vulnerable to a wide range of serious illnesses. Through gene therapy, scientists have begun to restore or replace faulty or missing genes with healthy ones.

Obviously, all of this is not as simple as it sounds. Before researchers can replace a damaged gene, they have to locate it and determine its function. Thirty-five years ago, scientists knew the location of fewer than 100 of the estimated 100,000 genes that humans carry. By 1990, the number had risen to 1,850. That same year, researchers began a massive effort to map the rest. The Human Genome Project, funded by the Department of Energy and the National Institutes of Health, is the largest biological research effort ever undertaken. The work is painstaking. It could take 15 to 20 years to complete a genetic blueprint of the human body.

But there have already been breakthroughs. One involves a 4-year-old girl who, because of a missing gene, had been ill from birth with an inherited deficiency of her immune system. Like the "bubble boy" in Texas who suffered from a similar ailment, any minor infection could have been life-threatening. The condition made both the girl and her family virtual prisoners. Her mother and siblings seldom left home for fear they might bring back a potentially lethal infection.

Doctors removed some of the girl's white blood cells, treated them with copies of the missing gene, and reintroduced them into her body. Within a year, the child's immune system began to respond. She was well enough to take dancing lessons, swim, even go to a shopping mall. While the results are not conclusive, her prognosis is very promising. More than a happy ending for one little girl, the case marked the beginning of a new medical era. She was the world's first recipient of gene therapy.

Scientists have identified genes responsible for cystic fibrosis, Duchenne muscular dystrophy, Marfan syndrome, fragile X syndrome and certain cancers. The next step is the development of successful techniques to deliver corrected versions of genes to the cells of patients suffering from such disorders. Alzheimers, diabetes, and some forms of heart disease may be conquered by this technology.

Why should I care about all of this? One reason is that while I was national chairman of the March of Dimes Birth Defects Foundation, we learned that a large number of birth defects have a genetic origin. That is why the foundation devoted a sizable amount of its annual research budget to grants for the study of gene therapy.

There is a personal side for me as well. My daughter was born profoundly deaf. And my son, soon after birth, was found to be autistic, retarded, epileptic, and deaf. Unless you have been there, you cannot imagine how all this feels. Yet, during my pregnancies, I had the very best of prenatal care. I didn't smoke, drink, or use any sort of drugs. It didn't matter.

PUBLIC IGNORANCE

We still do not know all of the reasons why babies are born sick or with major disabilities. But we *do* know some. One baby, maybe more, out of one hundred is born with a serious genetic problem. Gene therapy offers a very real possibility of correcting many of these disorders. It could transform—indeed, it already has—lives that are doomed to the pain and anguish of chronic illness.

But scientific advances can also generate misunderstanding and fear. The Salk polio vaccine was one of the most important medical gains of our time. It was safe. It worked. But because earlier vaccines used "live" viruses that caused fatalities, researchers had to overcome public apprehension. (The Salk vaccine used a benign "dead" virus.)

Some critics are concerned that gene therapy will be abused to create "super" humans. Others are disturbed about possible disclosures of personally sensitive medical history. Still, the public seems to be giving this new technology the benefit of the doubt. A recent survey conducted for the Foundation revealed that 89 percent of Americans support gene therapy and favor continued research. Curiously, this same poll showed widespread public ignorance about this form of treatment. So the need for public education on a broad scale is self-evident. There is much yet for both scientists and lay people to learn.

The main thing is this: we *cannot* let our fears destroy our hopes. We cannot let myth and misinterpretation prevent us from seeking treatment for the thousands who suffer from genetic diseases. Let us continue to resolve the issues while moving onward to intensify the research effort.

From my own viewpoint, if gene therapy can spare *one* mother the anguish of knowing that her newborn will suffer throughout its whole life—if it can help sick little girls get well enough to dance—can we afford *not* to make the effort?

CHAPTER FORTY THREE

Scientists and Their Moral Authority in Government

WILLIAM C. SPRAGENS

RESEARCH DIRECTOR
SPRAGENS AND SKINNER ASSOCIATES

PROMINENT AMONG LEADERS who provide services to government and who help provide its moral authority are its scientists. These scientists are by definition discoverers of knowledge, inventors, and theoreticians. Because they are somewhat detached from the daily work of government in many instances, they are in some ways ideally situated to provide moral authority.

The term "moral" may be defined as having to do with matters of conscience—helping individuals to make choices between right and wrong. The term "authority" may be defined as having a suasive impact on its citizens. The authority of law requires citizens to follow certain behavior patterns. Law (both in statutory and constitutional enactments) requires patterns of behavior for the citizens. Moral authority leaders guide the citizenry in choosing the correct path, using influence rather than legal sanctions.

The role of scientists in this relationship with citizens is ideally one in which scientists set an example for citizens by using their talents for invention and theorizing to serve the nation and its citizens.

Three examples from World War II and its aftermath come to mind in which scientists performed necessary services for the citizens.

Dr. Albert Einstein recommended in 1939 to President Franklin D. Roosevelt that the United States begin research on the development of an atomic weapon. This was based on early laboratory work indicating that the splitting of the atom might be feasible and that it might lead to the development of a new and incredibly powerful weapon.

From the viewpoint of Dr. Einstein, the dilemma was a moral one. Either the United States could do nothing and allow Nazi-financed scientists to get the lead in this potentially significant field, or it could develop a new atomic weapon which, however, could be used to the detriment of mankind as well as for its defense.

In this instance, Einstein used his moral authority to recommend development of this weapon. He felt that to default on this responsibility might eventually plunge the world into a tyranny-dominated phase of its modern history. Einstein was named by Arthur M. Schlesinger, Jr. as sixth of the ten most influential people of the second millennium (1999 *World Almanac*, p. 498).

Another example of moral authority of a scientist, in this case a much more controversial example, was that of Dr. J. Robert Oppenheimer, termed by some "the father of the atomic bomb" and the director of the Manhattan Project of World War II. The Princeton physicist led the effort to develop the Hiroshima-Nagasaki bomb. Later on, he was opposed to the development of the hydrogen bomb. In this position, he was supported by President James B. Conant of Harvard University, but the opposing position of Dr. Edward Teller, an advocate of the hydrogen weapon, prevailed in government.

In his book on President Conant, James Hershberg details how on March 2, 1950, President Conant was asked to assist in a major policy review which resulted in the production of National Security Council 68 (NSC-68), a policy document recommending a buildup of American nuclear weaponry in defense against the Soviet Union. Conant engaged in a sharp debate with Dr. Paul Nitze, George Kennan's replacement as State Department Director of Policy Planning,[1] which eventually resulted in the removal of Dr. Oppenheimer's security clearance. Oppenheimer's foes maintained he was a "security risk" while his backers claimed he was ungratefully cut off from using his talents to assist the government.

The professional career of Dr. Edward Teller brings into relief the conflict existing between purely moral concerns, such as that of fearing use of nuclear and thermonuclear weapons, and political and diplomatic concerns such as the desire to have "state of the art weapons" which can be used to oppose systems deemed to be immoral. Teller's advice prompted the so-called "Star Wars" (Strategic Defense Initiative, or SDI) program developed during the Reagan Administration as a defense against nuclear weapons.

William J. Broad, a scholar who in essence opposed the Star Wars approach, gave this assessment of Teller's career:

> A review of Teller's life that focuses on shortcomings needs perspective lest sight be lost of his positive accomplishments over a long career. These were considerable. Teller understood the tyranny of communism and succeeded like no other individual in forging weapons to fight it. His decades of building bombs, of blasting boulders into the sky, of causing the planet to shudder, of doing everything in his power to frighten the Soviets, of going to the brink of war in a metaphorical sense, clearly succeeded in intimidating his foes. He played an important role in challenging Stalin's ambitions for the subjugation of Europe. His tireless militancy, occurring over a large part of the twentieth Century, made pivotal contributions to peace and freedom in the western world. . . .[2]

These three examples show how great is the moral authority or moral suasion of American scientists—backed up by the extensive facilities for "hard science" research and by the expertise of the American scientific community.

Another debate lies in the controversy over classification systems. In a democracy, which relies on public information about government, leaders must consider the status of sensitive information. They must ask what it is moral to withhold from the public—at least in terms of timing of this release.

What, then, should be the basic principles of a classification system, and what kinds of information ought to be protected from widespread public release? Certainly new weapons systems and other information that would be the object of foreign espionage would be covered. Also, the intelligence community would argue that methods of collection of such information should be protected.

Conversely, it may be argued that coutervailing factors such as the public's need to know where tax dollars are being spent should place limitations on the classification system. A balancing and weighing process seems to take place when governments make such decisions.

When is it permissible to release classified information to the public? When is such information no longer sensitive, perhaps because the political or diplomatic context has changed?

Still another distinction made in this question is that of government employees as opposed to members of the news media.

News media members are not subjected to the same kinds of restraints that government employees must follow. The legal restraints are greater on government employees who sometimes must take an oath to protect the secrecy of information that is protected by classification.

This raises the question of "leaks" and how they should be handled by journalists in their contacts with government sources. Should journalists get the opinions of government sources before releasing "leaked" information? Much more freely in the habit of disclosing "leaked" information than in earlier times, members of the news media must nevertheless deal with the question of whether unauthorized leaks, or unchecked leaks, might jeopardize their future access to government sources. Competitive pressures also enter into this equation.

A moral question remains for the members of the news media—should they press for the release of the story when the legality of their actions is in question? The controversy over when leaks may occur is a running controversy and one not likely to be settled anytime in the near future. But these are questions both those in government and those in the media must consider.

Also, apart from the moral constraints on rank-and-file government employees and rank-and-file journalists, we must look at the responsibilities of governmental leaders (e.g., cabinet and sub-cabinet officials) and also the responsibilities of leaders in the news media (specifically, editors and publishers, and executive producers of news programs in broadcasting). What guidelines should these leaders follow in the media–government relationship?

A further responsibility lies with members of the public in a democratic system. How accountable should members of the public hold government officials and members of the news media? Should actions considered offenses against shielding of secrets be punishable at the polls? The public is not held to some of the same constraints faced by those in government and the press. Nevertheless, there are moral constraints as to what the public considers proper behavior by government officials and journalists.

Scientific organizations, too, can play a role in setting down professional codes of conduct for their members. Some sanctions or forms of discipline are possible for scientific organizations. There is also a good deal of responsibility placed on individuals in the scientific community to apply their own personal moral standards in this relationship.

Institutional factors can weigh on individuals in such situations. The expectations of those in the different branches of government, apart from legal requirements, can play a major part in decisions made by individuals in those institutions. Such extra-governmental institutions as political parties, professional organizations, and, to some degree, social organizations, can all play a part in the choices made by their members. In each institution, the expectations of fellow members and the past behavior of members can play a part in the way choices of moral behavior are dealt with.

The moral authority of scientists is great. However, it is difficult, if not impossible, to predict in what directions this moral authority may take national policymakers.

This is in part because the context of decisions made by individuals and groups may be quite different. For example, decisions made in wartime may be different from decisions made in peacetime.

Suffice it to say that innovation and refinement of existing scientific products, in the final analysis, have overshadowed the darker side of innovation and weapons development. Scientists have indeed contributed greatly to the advancement of civilization by their contributions from the laboratory, even when their moral judgments may have differed.

Notes

CHAPTER ONE

1. Between 1973 and 1993, the public's confidence in people running public institutions (executive branch, Congress, courts) was lower than its confidence in the people running corporations. See surveys of the National Opinion Research Center, February–April, 1973–93, reprinted in *Public Opinion*, November–December 1993, pp. 94–5. Confidence in the federal government has taken a tumble: percentage of respondents answering "a great deal" or "some" declined from 74 percent in 1972 to 42 percent in 1992. The national government went from the highest- to the lowest-rated level of government according to polls conducted for the Advisory Commission on Intergovernmental Relations, reprinted in "Fig. 2: Confidence in Federal Government in Sharp Decline," *The Public Perspective* (January–February 1993): 4.
2. Contrast extensive presidential immunity in *Nixon v. Fitzgerald* 457 U.S. 731 (1982) with more limited staff immunity in *Harlow v. Fitzgerald* 457 U.S. 800 (1982); on the lack of civil immunity for the president, see *Jones v. Clinton*, 869 F. Supp. 690 (1994) and 72 F. 3d 1354 (1997), *Clinton v. Jones* 117 S. Ct. 1644 (1998).
3. *U.S. v. Nixon* 418 U.S. 683 (1974).
4. *In re Bruce R. Lindsey*, 158 F. 3d 1263 (1998).
5. The legality of such trust funds was upheld in *Judicial Watch Inc. v. Hillary Clinton, et al.*, 76 F. 3d 1252 (1996). For a general discussion, see Kathleen Clark, "Paying the Price for Heightened Ethics Scrutiny: Legal Defense Funds and Other Ways Government Officials Pay Their Lawyers," *Stanford Law Review* 50, no. 1 (November 1997): 65–138.
6. On the impact of true believers, see J. Patrick Dobel, *Compromise and Political Action: Public Morality in Liberal and Democratic Life* (Savage, Md.: Rowman and Littlefield, 1990), 2–3.
7. On the attitude of the White House, see Gerald Ford, "The War Powers Resolution: Striking a Balance between the Executive and Legislative Branches," reprinted in "War Powers Resolution," *Hearings before the Committee on Foreign Relations*, U.S. Senate, 95th Cong., 1977, 325-31; on the congressional attitude, see Clement Zablocki, "The War Powers Resolution: Its Past Record and Future Promise," *Loyola of Los Angeles Law Review* 17 (1984): 579–98.
8. "Judicial Restraint and the War Powers Resolution: Lowry V. Reagan," *Harvard Journal of Law and Public Policy* 11 (Summer 1988): 849–54.
9. Clinton Rossiter, *The American Presidency*, 2d ed. (New York: Harcourt Brace and World, 1960), 43.

10. Charles Perrow, *Normal Accidents: Living with High Risk Technologies* (New York: Basic Books, 1984).
11. On the concept of resiliency, see Aaron Wildavsky, *Searching for Safety* (New Brunswick, N.J.: Transaction Books, 1988), 15–18.
12. See, generally, Erwin Hargrove, *The President as Leader* (Lawrence, Kans.: University of Oklahoma, 1998), 46–48.

CHAPTER TWO

1. Walter Lippmann, "A Theory About Corruption," *Vanity Fair* XXXV (November 1930): 61.
2. *Jones v. Clinton* 36 F. Supp. 2d 1118 (E.D. Ark. 1999).
3. Louis Harris, *The Anguish of Change* (New York: W.W. Norton, 1973), 8.
4. Suzanne Garment, *Scandal: The Crisis of Mistrust in American Politics* (New York: Times Books, 1991), 2.
5. Harris, *The Anguish of Change*, 73.
6. Roger Morris, *Uncertain Greatness: Henry Kissinger and American Foreign Policy* (New York: Harper and Row, 1977), 249.

CHAPTER THREE

1. Isaiah Berlin, *Two Concepts of Liberty* (Oxford: Clarendon Press, 1958).

CHAPTER FOUR

1. *The New York Times*, 16 September 1998, Wednesday, final, sec. A, p. 1.
2. A search on the topic of morality was conducted by using the American Reference Library CD-ROM, published by Western Standard Publishing Company, 1997. The CD contains all the volumes in the three major series that have compiled presidential writings and public papers. The first of these sets is *Messages and Papers of the Presidents*, by James Richardson, Bureau of National Literature, 1911. This first series covers Presidents Washington through Calvin Coolidge. The second series is the *Public Papers of the Presidents*, containing the public messages, speeches and statements of the presidents, published by the Federal Register Division, Archives and Records Service, General Services Administration. This second collection covers Presidents Herbert Hoover, beginning in 1929, through William Jeffer-

son Clinton. The third series is *The Presidential Papers of Franklin D. Roosevelt* and covers only FDR.

3. George Washington's Farewell Address, 17 September 1796, *Messages and Papers of the Presidents*, 1:212.

4. George Washington, *Messages and Papers of the Presidents*, 1:212.

5. Ibid., 44.

6. Ibid., 47.

7. Ibid., 212.

8. Ibid., 518.

9. *The Mind of the Founder: Sources of the Political Thought of James Madison*, ed. Marvin Meyers (Hanover, N.H., and London: University Press of New England, 1981), 6.

10. Fourth Annual Message, 24 February 1813, *Letters and Other Writings of James Madison*, 1:507.

11. Research and analysis on Abraham Lincoln's moral view of slavery is taken from *Abraham Lincoln, Speeches and Writings*, 2 vols. (Library of America, 1989).

12. Ibid., 1:74.

13. Ibid., 1:512.

14. Ibid., 2:213.

15. Ibid., 1:328.

16. Ibid., 1:398.

17. Ibid., 1:315.

18. Ibid., 1:426.

19. George Washington, *Messages and Papers of the Presidents*, 1:212.

20. Ronald Reagan, *Messages and Papers of the Presidents*, 3 November 1984, 1741.

21. Ibid., 8 March 1983, 364.

22. Ibid., 28 April 1987, 425.

23. Ibid., 12 April 1982, 468.

24. Ibid., 23 May 1983, 755.

25. Ibid., 15 June 1983, 871.

26. Theodore Roosevelt, *Messages and Papers of the Presidents*, 5 December 1905, 7371–74.

27. Ibid., 3 December 1906, 7433.

28. Jeffrey K. Tulis, *The Rhetorical Presidency* (Princeton, N.J.: Princeton University Press, 1987), 102.

29. Jimmy Carter, *Messages and Papers of the Presidents*, 18 February 1978, 376.

30. Ibid., 16 June 1978, 1117.

CHAPTER SIX

1. James Davidson Hunter, *Culture Wars: The Struggle to Define America* (New York: Basic Books, 1993).

2. Paul DiMaggio, et al., "Have American Attitudes Become More Polarized?" *American Journal of Sociology* 102:3 (1996): 690–755. See also Alan Wolfe, *Marginalized in the Middle* (Chicago: University of Chicago Press, 1996); and more recently, Alan Wolfe, *One Nation After All* (Chicago: University of Chicago Press, 1998).

3. J. D. Hunter, *Culture Wars: The Struggle to Define America* (New York: Basic Books, 1993); J. D. Hunter, "Reflections on the Culture Wars Hypothesis," in *The America Culture Wars: Current Contests and Future Prospects*, ed. James L. Nolan, Jr. (Charlottesville, Va.: University of Virginia Press, 1996), 243–56.

4. D. Reisman with N. Glazer and R. Denny, *The Lonely Crowd: A Study of the Changing American Character* (New Haven, Ct.: Yale University Press, 1950).

5. Ms. Taxman, who is white, brought suit against a board of education which fired her to maintain diversity. President Bush originally entered the case on the side of Ms. Taxman. When he became president, Mr. Clinton reversed that position and had the Justice Department enter on the side of the board and against Ms. Taxman. Then, after two lower courts decided in favor of Ms. Taxman, the administration changed course again, this time submitting a brief urging the Supreme Court not to hear the case because its circumstances made it unusual and a poor vehicle for fashioning an important decision in this area. The court decided to take the case anyway, and the Clinton administration then submitted its third brief in the same case—this time on Ms. Taxman's side, but with a twist. The administration now argued that only in case of a proven history of discrimination could the desire to increase diversity be a legitimate standard to use, but it also argued that it might also be used in the absence of such a proven history when there was a tangible purpose for doing so—like a police or corrections department that might wish more diversity to better accomplish its mission.

6. "Presidential Debate in San Diego" (16 October 1996), *Weekly Compilation of Presidential Documents*, 21 October 32: 42, 2091–92.

7. *The Washington Times*, 31 August 1997, national edition, p. A1.

CHAPTER SEVEN

1. Our research on "Leadership and Citizenship" has been supported by the Pew Charitable Trusts; the responsibility for the interpretations offered here is our own.

This essay draws on the following works:

Robert M. Eisinger and Jeremy Brown, "Polling as a Means Toward Presidential Autonomy: Emil Hurja, Hadley Cantril, and the

Roosevelt Administration," *International Journal of Public Opinion Research* 10 (fall, 1998): 238–56.

Douglas C. Foyle, *Counting the Public In: Presidents, Public Opinion, and Foreign Policy* (New York: Columbia University Press, 1999).

John G. Geer, *From Tea Leaves to Opinion Polls: A Theory of Democratic Leadership* (New York: Columbia University Press, 1996).

Thomas Graham, "Public Opinion and U.S. Foreign Policy Decision Making," in *The New Politics of American Foreign Policy* ed. David A. Deese (New York: St. Martin's Press, 1994).

Erwin Hargrove, *Jimmy Carter and the Politics of the Public* (Baton Rouge: Louisiana State University, 1988).

Diane Heith, "Staffing the White House Public Opinion Apparatus, 1969–1988." *Public Opinion Quarterly* 62 (Spring, 1998): 165–89.

Diane Heith, "Presidential Polling and the Potential for Leadership," in *Presidential Power: Forging the Presidency for the 21st Century*, ed. Robert Y. Shapiro, Martha J. Kumar, and Lawrence R. Jacobs (New York: Columbia University Press, forthcoming).

Barbara Hinckley, *The Symbolic Presidency* (New York: Routledge, 1990).

Ronald H. Hinckley, *People, Polls, and Policymakers: American Public Opinion and National Security* (New York: Lexington Books, 1992).

Lawrence R. Jacobs, *The Health of Nations: Public Opinion and the Making of American and British Health Policy* (Ithaca, N.Y.: Cornell University Press, 1993).

Lawrence R. Jacobs and Robert Y. Shapiro, *Politicians Don't Pander* (Chicago: University of Chicago Press, forthcoming).

Lawrence R. Jacobs and Robert Y. Shapiro, "The Rise of Presidential Polling: The Nixon White House in Historical Pespective," *Public Opinion Quarterly* 59 (1995): 163–65.

Lawrence R. Jacobs and Robert Y. Shapiro, "Lyndon Johnson, Vietnam, and Public Opinion: Rethinking Realists' Theory of Leadership," *Presidential Studies Quarterly* 29 (fall 1999), in press.

Lawrence R. Jacobs and Robert Y. Shapiro, "Issues, Candidate Image, and Priming: The Use of Private Polls in Kennedy's 1960 Presidential Campaign," *American Political Science Review* 88 (September 1994): 527–40.

Samuel Kernell, *Going Public: New Strategies of Presidential Leadership*, 2d ed. (Washington, D.C.: Congressional Quarterly Press, 1993).

Everett Carll Ladd, *The Ladd Report* (New York: Free Press, 1999).

Benjamin I. Page and Robert Y. Shapiro, *The Rational Public: Fifty Years of Trends in Americans' Policy Preferences* (Chicago: University of Chicago Press, 1992).

Research/Strategy/Management, Inc., *National Credibility Index Surveys*, 1999.

Robert Y. Shapiro and Lawrence R. Jacobs, "The Public Opinion-Foreign Policy Linkage: U.S. Presidents and Public Opinion," in *Decisionmaking in a Glass House: Mass Media, Public Opinion, and American and European Foreign Policy in the 21st Century*, ed. Brigitte L.

Nacos, Robert Y. Shapiro, and Pierangelo Isernia (Lanham, Md.: Rowman and Littlefield, forthcoming).

CHAPTER EIGHT

1. I would like to thank Natasha Hagaman for her research assistance.
2. Richard L. Berke and Janet Elder, "Most in Poll Say President Should Remain in Office; Job Rating Still High But Public View of his Moral Character Sinks to a Low," *New York Times*, 16 September 1998.
3. Despite a tendency for the term "gender" to be used as a synonym for biological sex, it is not the same. Gender refers to the "meaning of being in the category of male or female." See Georgia Duerst-Lahti, "Reconceiving Theories of Power: Consequences of Masculinism in the Executive Branch," in *The Other Elites: Women, Politics and Power in the Executive Branch*, eds. Mary Anne Borrelli and Janet M. Martins (Boulder, Colo.: Lynne Reinner, 1997). Therefore, gender analysis examines how gender appropriate behaviors, traits, and roles are socially created and reinforced.
4. Appointments are a means for presidents to enhance their power by strengthening ties with constituencies, party activists, Washington elites, executive departments, and the general public. See Richard F. Fenno, Jr., *The President's Cabinet: An Analysis in the Period from Wilson to Eisenhower* (Cambridge, Mass.: Harvard University Press, 1959); Nelson W. Polsby, "Presidential Cabinet Making: Lessons for the Political System," *Political Science Quarterly* 93, no. 1 (1978): 15–25; James J. Best, "Presidential Cabinet Appointments, 1953–1976," *Presidential Studies Quarterly* 11 (1981): 62–65; James D. King, and James W. Riddlesperger, Jr., "Unscheduled Presidential Transitions: Lessons from the Truman, Johnson and Ford Administrations," *Congress and the Presidency* 22 (1984): 6–25.
5. See Janet M. Martin, "An Examination of Executive Branch Appointments in the Reagan Administration by Background and Gender," *Western Political Quarterly* 44 (1991): 173–84; Mary Anne Borrelli, "Gender, Credibility and Politics: The Senate Nomination Hearings of Cabinet Secretaries Designate, 1975–1993," *Political Research Quarterly* 51 (1997): 171–97; Janet M. Martin and Mary Anne Borrelli, eds., *The Other Elites: Women Politics and Power in the Executive Branch* (Boulder, Colo.: Lynne Reinner, 1997).
6. Nancy E. McGlen and Meredith Reid Sarkees, "Style Does Matter: The Impact of Presidential Leadership on Women in Foreign Policy," in *The Other Elites: Women, Politics and Power in the Executive Branch*, eds. Mary Anne Borrelli and Janet M. Martin (Boulder, Colo.: Lynne Reinner, 1997).

7. Thomas Cronin, *The State of the Presidency*, 2d ed. (Boston: Little, Brown and Company, 1980).

8. Kathryn Dunn Tenpas, "Women on the White House Staff: A Longitudinal Analysis, 1939–1994," in *The Other Elites: Women, Politics and Power in the Executive Branch*, eds. Mary Anne Borrelli and Janet M. Martin (Boulder, Colo.: Lynne Reinner, 1997).

9. Janet M. Martin, "Women Who Govern: The President's Appointments," in *The Other Elites: Women, Politics and Power in the Executive Branch*, eds. Mary Anne Borrelli and Janet M. Martin (Boulder, Colo.: Lynne Reinner, 1997).

10. *Ibid.*, 113.

11. McGlen and Sarkees, "Style Does Matter," 114.

12. Tenpas, "Women on the White House Staff," 93.

13. Mary Anne Borrelli, "Gender, Credibility and Politics: The Senate Nomination Hearings of Cabinet Secretaries Designate, 1975–1993," in *The Other Elites: Women, Politics and Power in the Executive Branch*, eds. Mary Anne Borrelli and Janet M. Martin (Boulder, Colo.: Lynne Reinner, 1997).

14. Virginia Sapiro and David Canon, "Race, Gender and the Clinton Presidency," in *The Clinton Legacy*, eds. Colin Campbell and Bert A. Rockman (New York: Chatham House Publishers, 1999).

15. Mifepristone is a postcoital nonsurgical means to terminate a first trimester pregnancy. If taken early, the drug halts the implantation of the fertilized egg in the uterine lining. If taken later in a pregnancy, it induces a miscarriage.

CHAPTER NINE

1. On the bully pulpit quote and the use of that rostrum by subsequent presidents, especially Wilson for the League of Nations and FDR in his fireside chats, see, Sam Kernell, *Going Public* (Washington, D.C.: Congressional Quarterly Press, 1993), 2. Each was given as a variation on the theme of giving moral messages.

2. Erwin C. Hargrove uses this reference from Abraham Lincoln which is cited in Erwin C. Hargrove, *The President as Leader: Appealing to the Better Angels of our Nature* (Lawrence, Kans.: University of Kansas Press, 1998), 1.

3. Michael Lerner, *The Politics of Meaning* (Reading, Mass.: Addison Wesley, 1996), 309.

4. John F. Harris, "A Celebratory Clinton Finally Declares Victory," *Washington Post*, 11 June 1999, p. A01.

5. Carter, writing in his autobiography in 1975, *Why Not the Best*, wondered aloud on the first page of the book why our government

couldn't be as honest, decent, fair and compassionate. See Jimmy Carter, *Why Not the Best* (New York: Bantam Books, 1976), 1.

6. Stephen Skowronek, *The Politics Presidents Make: Leadership from John Adams to George Bush* (Cambridge, Mass.: Harvard University Press, 1993), 17.

7. On the basis for presidential leadership, see Richard E. Neustadt, *Presidential Power and the Modern Presidency* (New York: Free Press, 1990), 8–9.

8. Skowronek, 18.

9. Michael Genovese and Thomas Cronin, *The Paradoxes of the American Presidency* (New York: Oxford University Press, 1998), 152–60.

10. On the debates over the role of the single executive, see Charles Thach, *The Creation of the Presidency* (Baltimore, Md.: Johns Hopkins University Press, 1923; paper 1969), 121. See also Frank Kessler, *Dilemmas of Presidential Leadership* (Englewood Cliffs, N.J.: Prentice-Hall, 1982), 34–40. For more on the single executive concept, see Lyn Ragsdale, *Presidential Politics* (Boston: Houghton-Mifflin, 1993), 85–87.

11. *Pastoral Constitution on the Church in the Modern World*, Vatican Council II (1965), Gaudium et Spes, Part II: "Some Problems of Spiritual Urgency," ch. IV, *The Life of the Political Community*, sec. 73–78, pp. 1–2.

12. Hargrove, 39.

13. Ross J. Hoffman and Paul Levack, *Burke's Politics* (New York, 1949), p. 15 as cited in Charles O. Jones, *The Trusteeship Presidency: Jimmy Carter and the United States Congress* (Baton Rouge: Louisiana State University Press, 1988), 2–3. On the heroic model see James McGregor Burns, *Presidential Government: The Crucible of Leadership* (Boston: Houghton-Mifflin, 1965).

14. There are a number of excellent sources to examine when looking at Presidential uses of rhetoric: See Jeffrey Tullis, *The Rhetorical Presidency* (Princeton, N.J.: Princeton University Press, 1987); George C. Edwards III, *The Public Presidency: The Pursuit of Popular Support* (New York: St. Martin's, 1983); Robert E. Denton, Jr. and Dan F. Hahn, *Presidential Communication: Description and Analysis* (New York, Praeger, 1986). For an excellent discussion of presidential rhetoric, see Mary E. Stuckey and Richard Morris, "The Other Side of Power: Who is Left Out of Presidential Rhetoric?" in *Presidential Frontiers: Unexplored Issues of White House Politics*, ed. Ryan J. Barilleau (New York: Praeger Series in Presidential Studies, 1998), 179ff.

15. For a thirty-year analysis of individual confidence in government (1952–1988) see Harold W. Stanley and Richard G. Niemi, *Vital Statistics on American Politics*, 2d ed. (Washington, D.C.: Congressional Quarterly Press, 1990), 155.

16. For Carter's take on handling the hostages, see "AFL-CIO remarks," *Public Papers of the President*, 15 November 1979, 2122–26. For a dis-

cussion of the crisis and its impact on the campaign, see: Jack W. Germond and Jules Witcover, *Blue Smoke and Mirrors: How Reagan Won and Carter Lost the Election of 1980* (New York: Viking Press, 1981), 8, 9, 11, 15, 19, 85–88, and also the final watch 10.

17. Nixon's lessons were well chronicled by Arthur Schlesinger, Jr., *The Imperial Presidency* (New York: Houghton Mifflin, 1973). Public opinion related to Watergate then compared to 1997 can be found in Lydia Sand, "Americans' Faith in Government Shaken but Not Shattered by Watergate," Princeton, N.J., *Gallup News Service Press Releases*, 19 June 1997, pp. 1–6 from http://www. gallup.com/poll/releases/pr970619.asp.

18. On Clinton's problems with "moral authority" after the Lewinsky affair and the Starr Report, see: "Clinton's Moral Authority Slips," *Pew's Poll Numbers*, pp. 1–2, The Pew Research Center for the People & the Press based on polling by Andrew Kohut of two telephone surveys done Sept. 9–13 and 11–15 (1,006 adults by phone and 1,012 adults by phone) with an error rate of ±3.5% from http://www.people-predss.org/starrpt.htm.

19. On Reagan and his ability to communicate, see Hargrove, 133–59. In his farewell address, Reagan denied that he was really a Great Communicator saying, "I wasn't a great communicator, but I communicated great things," from "Farewell to the Nation," 11 January 1989, *Public Papers of the President*, p. For an insightful analysis of the Reagan use of rhetoric, see: Mary E. Stuckey, *Playing the Game: The Presidential Rhetoric of Ronald Reagan* (New York: Praeger Series in Political Communication, 1990).

20. Instructive on religious principles and moral values would be "Washington Post/Henry J. Kaiser Family Foundation/Harvard University Value Study," 4 October 1998, a report based on random telephone interviews with 2,023 adults on 29 July–18 August 1998. the margin of error is a ±2.19 percentage points. These specific issues are addresses on pages 7 and 8 from http://www.washintonpost.com/wp-srv/politics/pollss/vault/stories/data 100498.htm.

21. See "Media Mogul Ted Turner Apologizes after Insulting Catholics, Poles," which refers to a 16 February 1999 speech in which Turner was addressing the National Family Planning and Reproductive Association in Washington, D.C. Turner said that the "Ten Commandments are a little out of date . . . if you are going to have ten rules, I don't know if prohibiting it [adultery] should be one of them." On the Pope, he said, "Ever see a Polish mine detector?" as he showed the crowd his foot. He then suggested that the Pope "get with it" and said "welcome to the twenty-first century." As reported in: *The Christian Culture News*, 26 February 1997 as from: http://www.ctr.org/newstopic7.htm.

22. For one of the best available discussions of morality in action, see

Barbara Hinckley, "Politics and Morality: The Action" in *The Symbolic Presidency* (New York: Routledge, 1990), 65–88. See also on the development of moral values within a society, Richard W. Wilson and Gordon J. Schochet, *Moral Development and Politics* (New York: F.A. Praeger, 1980). To examine ways in which government, including presidents, can restore the public's trust in government, see Peter G. Brown, *Restoring the Public Trust* (Boston, Mass.: Beacon Press, 1994). On the need for ethical leadership from the White House, see Louis W. Koenig, *The Chief Executive*, 6th ed. (Fort Worth, Texas: Harcourt Brace 1996), 14–16. For a broader based discussion of the president as communicator of values, see Mary E. Stuckey, *The President as Interpreter in Chief* (Chatham, N.J.: Chatham House, 1991).

23. James Q. Wilson, *The Moral Sense* (New York: Free Press, 1993), 1.
24. Op. cit., 3.
25. On Reagan as a cultural leader, see Hargrove, 154–56. For an excellent overview of the president's ability to lead public opinion, see George C. Edwards III, *The Public Presidency: The Pursuit of Popular Support* (New York: St. Martin's Press, 1983), esp. chap. 2, "Presidential Leadership of Public Opinion," 38–103.
26. As quoted in Tullis, 135.
27. Hargrove, 51.

CHAPTER TEN

1. Aristotle's conception of prudence, according to Dan Sabia ("Prudence," unpublished ms., July 1999) is manifest in the statesman's attention to detail, the broad experience that he brings to bear upon an issue, his ability to deal with complex value dilemmas, and an ability to empathize with others. The central importance of the latter quality is stressed in Aristotle's *Nicomachean Ethics* (1143a, 19–20); "we say the equitable (i.e., the just) man is above all others a man of sympathetic (i.e., empathic) judgement."
2. Minutes of the 302d Meeting of the National Security Council, 1 November 1956, Dwight David Eisenhower Library, Ann Whitman National Security Council files, Abilene, Kansas. Cited hereafter as DDE Library.
3. Evan Thomas, *The Very Best Men: Four Who Dared: The Early Years of the CIA* (New York: Simon and Schuster, 1995), 146; John Ranelagh, *The Agency: The Rise and Fall of the CIA* (New York: Simon and Schuster, 1986), 306–307.
4. Ann Whitman diary, Box 8, Whitman files, DDE Library.
5. Milton Eisenhower, *The President is Calling* (Garden City, N.Y.: Doubleday, 1974), 355. For Milton Eisenhower's role as Dwight Eisen-

hower's confidante, see pages 308–16. The White House was Milton Eisenhower's weekend home for eight years.

6. Emmet John Hughes, *The Ordeal of Power: A Political Memoir of the Eisenhower Years* (New York: Atheneum, 1962), 223; Ambrose, 368.

7. Eisenhower saw the risks he took at the time of the landing on the Normandy beaches as a requisite for any success in an extremely difficult enterprise that was justified by the importance of the goals at stake. For the risks, see "With Weather Still Risky, Ike Called for Invasion," *Washington Post,* 8 June 1964, p. A3; and "Extreme Security Measures Kept Invasion Secret," *Washington Post,* 11 June 1964, p. A3. Both are edited versions of Eisenhower's interview with Cronkite on CBS, 5 June 1964.

8. Eisenhower, *Waging Peace, 1956–1961* (Garden City, N.Y.: Doubleday, 1965), 466.

9. The quote is taken from Merle Miller, *Ike the Soldier: As They Knew Him* (New York: G.P. Putnam's Sons, 1967), 618–19. The conversation with Walter Cronkite was rebroadcast on CBS on 5 June 1984, on the 40th anniversary of D Day.

10. William E. Colby, and Peter Forbath, *Honorable Men: My Life in the CIA* (New York: Simon and Schuster, 1978), 134. See also Ranelagh, *The Agency: The Rise and Fall of the CIA,* 307.

11. "Memorandum of Conference With the President, Secretary Hoover and Colonel Goodpaster present, November 19, 1956." Lous Golambos, *The Diaries of Dwight David Eisenhower 1953–1961* (Washington, D.C.: University Publications of America, 1980), 1956.

12. Cook, *The Declassified Eisenhower,* 203, 371, n. 106.

13. Cook, *The Declassified Eisenhower,* 199.

14. The Joint Chiefs in a document dated 31 October 1956, recommended that the United States inform the Soviet Union that an "immediate military action would follow any Soviet use of military force to reimpose its control in Poland." Joint Chiefs of Staff "Memorandum for the Secretary of Defense on U.S. Policy Toward Developments in Poland and Hungary," 31 October 1956. From the Whitman National Security Council files, DDE Library. For details of other hawkish position papers of the Joint Chiefs, see Kenneth Kitts and Betty Glad, "Presidential Personality and Improvisational Decision Making: Eisenhower and the 1956 Hungarian Crisis," *Reexamining the Eisenhower Presidency,* ed. Shirley Anne Warshaw (Westport, Conn.: Greenwood Press, 1993). For a detailed description of Eisenhower's subtleties in maintaining support for his policies and his presidency, see Fred Greenstein, *The Hidden Hand Presidency: Eisenhower as Leader* (New York: Basic Books, 1982), 57–99.

15. For earlier pressures from the Hungarian National Council to move the issue to the General Assembly, see the discussion in Kenneth Kitts and Betty Glad, "Presidential Personality and Improvisational

Decision Making: Eisenhower and the 1956 Hungarian Crisis," loc. cit., 186.

16. The argument that Eisenhower frequently relied on his own expertise in his strategic choices in the military arena is made by Douglas Kinnard in his *President Eisenhower and Strategy Management: A Study in Defense Politics* (Lexington: University of Kentucky Press, 1977), 123–27.

17. James G. Blight, ed., "October 27, 1962: Transcripts of the Meetings of the Ex-Comm," *International Security* (winter, 1987–88), 30–92, McGeorge Bundy, transcriber.

18. James G. Blight, Joseph S. Nye, and D.A. Welch, "The Cuban Missile Crisis Revisited," *Foreign Affairs* (fall 1987), 170–88.

19. In addition to the works of Blight et al., the details of Kennedy's handling of the missile crisis and the Russian responses to the U.S. in this essay are from James Nathan, ed., *The Cuban Missile Crisis Revisited* (New York, St. Martin's Press, 1991). Particularly useful are the following chapters: Barton Bernstein's "Reconsidering the Missile Crisis: Dealing with the Problems of the American Jupiters in Turkey"; Laurence Chang's "The View from Washington and the View from Nowhere: Cuban Missile Crisis Historiography and the Epistemology of Decision Making"; and Elizabeth Cohn's "President Kennedy's Decision to Impose a Blockade in the Cuban Missile Crisis: Building Consensus in the Ex Comm After the Decision."

20. Actually, the later evidence suggested that Moscow had delegated decision making as to the firing of the Soviet missiles to local commanders in Cuba. See Chang, "The View from Washington," loc. cit., 145–46. Had the United States engaged in air attacks on bases in Cuba, Moscow would no longer be in control and local commanders, acting in accord with their training and traditional practices, would have been even more likely than Moscow to attempt to shoot down United States planes.

CHAPTER ELEVEN

1. Philip Young, personal interview, 15 June 1977, Van Hornesville, N.Y.; Eisenhower to Leonard Gerow, 10 October 1942, cited by Stephen E. Ambrose, "Eisenhower's Legacy," in *Eisenhower: A Centenary Assessment*, ed. Gunter Bischof and Stephen E. Ambrose (Baton Rouge, 1995), 255; Dwight D. Eisenhower, *At Ease: Stories I Tell to Friends* (New York, 1967), 350–51.

2. Young, interview; William Zinsser, "Columbia Confront Eisenhower With a Complex, Difficult Job," *New York Herald-Tribune*, 6 June 1948; Allan Nevins, review of *Eisenhower Speaks*, in *The New York Times*

Book Review, 16 May 1948; Ira Henry Freeman, "Eisenhower of Columbia," *The New York Times Magazine,* 7 November 1948.

3. "Notes of the Remarks," Box 34, Lewis L. Strauss Papers, Herbert C. Hoover Library, West Branch, Iowa; "Convocation," The Jewish Theological Seminary of America, 27 September 1948.

4. "Text of Eisenhower's Speech," *The New York Times,* 13 October 1948.

5. Edward R. Murrow, "With the News," 12 October 1948, Dwight D. Eisenhower Library, Abilene, Kansas (DDEL); Felix Frankfurter to Eisenhower, 15 October 1948, *The Papers of Dwight David Eisenhower: Columbia University* (PDDE), Vol. X (Baltimore, 1984), ed. Louis Galambos, 250.

6. Eisenhower, *Diary,* c. 1 January 1950, *PDDE,* XI, 882–89; "The Individual's Responsibility for Government," delivered at the New York Herald-Tribune Forum, *New York Herald-Tribune,* 25 October 1949; Eisenhower to Milton Stover Eisenhower, 16 October 1947, *PDDE: The Chief of Staff,* Vol. IX (Baltimore, 1978), ed. Louis Galambos, 1986–87.

7. Henry F. Graff, "Two Who Like Ike," *Columbia* (February, 1985): 18.

8. Eisenhower, "World Peace—A Balance Sheet," Gabriel Silver Lecture, 23 March 1950, Eisenhower MSS., DDEL; *The New York Times,* 24 March 1950.

9. Eisenhower to W. Averell Harriman, 30 November 1949, *PDDE,* X, 843–45; Eisenhower, *At Ease,* 349–50; Eisenhower to Leonard Franklin McCollum, 12 September 1950, *PDDE,* XI, 1305–10.

10. *Ibid.;* Eisenhower to Robert Cutler, 13 and 31 December 1950, *ibid.,* 1476–78.

11. *Ibid.;* Robert H. Ferrell, ed., *The Eisenhower Diaries* (New York, 1981), 29 November 1950, 182; Harriman to Eisenhower, 22 May 1951, DDEL.

12. *Public Papers of the Presidents of the United States: Dwight D. Eisenhower, 1960–1961* (Washington, D.C., 1961), 1036–40.

CHAPTER THIRTEEN

1. *Address Before the Young Men's Lyceum of Sringfield,* 27 January 1838.

2. *A Speech in Reply to Douglas,* Chicago, 10 July 1858.

3. *The House Divided Speech,* Springfield, 16 June 1858.

4. *Corner-Stone Speech,* 21 March 1861, in Henry Cleveland, *Alexander H. Stephens* (Philadelphia: National Publishing Co. 1866), 721.

5. *Speech on the Dred Scott Decision,* Springfield, 26 June 1857.

6. *Address Before the Young Men's Lyceum,* Springfield, 27 January 1838.

CHAPTER FIFTEEN

1. J. S. Mill, *On Liberty*, ed. David Spitz (1975), 18.
2. Aristotle, *Nicomachean Ethics*, in 9 Great Books of the World, eds. Robert M. Hutchins et al., and trans. W. D. Ross (1952), 339, 382.
3. John Milton, *Tetrachordon*, 1644–45.
4. Soliloquy by Tom Joad, *The Grapes of Wrath* (1940).
5. See Plato, *The Apology*, passim. and *The Crito*, passim.
6. Henry David Thoreau, *Civil Disobedience and Other Essays* (1963) passim.
7. Martin Luther King, Jr., "Letter from a Birmingham Jail," in *Why We Can't Wait* (Dover ed., 1993), passim.
8. Carl Cohen, *Civil Disobedience: Conscience, Tactics, and the Law* (1971), 131ff.
9. Anti-Slavery Examiner, September, 1836.
10. Thoreau, n. 6 supra, 259.
11. Id.
12. King, n. 7 supra, passim.
13. Charles DiSalvo, "The Fracture of Good Order: An Argument for Allowing Lawyers to Counsel the Civilly Disobedient," 17 *Ga. L. Rev.* 109 (1982).
14. Id.
15. Bruce Ledewitz, "Civil Disobedience, Injunctions, and the First Amendment," 19 *Hofstra L. Rev.* 67 (1990): 82.
16. Anti-Slavery Examiner, September, 1836.
17. Thomas R. Flynn, "Collective Responsibility and Obedience to the Law," 18 *Ga. L. Rev.* 845 (1984).
18. Daniel J. Boorstin, *The Genius of American Politics* (1953), 88–89. Boorstin looks to the work of Professor Charles H. McIlwain.
19. Norman P. Barry, *Modern Political Theory* (1995), 57–58.
20. David A. J. Richards, "Jurisprudence at the Crossroads: Steering a Course Between Positivism and Natural Law," 97 *Harv. L. Rev.* 1214 (1984).
21. Ledewitz, n. 28 supra, 82.
22. 5 December 1955, as cited by Randall Kennedy, "Martin Luther King's Constitution: A Legal History of the Montgomery Bus Boycott," 98 *Yale L. J.* 999 (1989): 1000, n. 10.
23. Alfred J. Sciarrino, "Civil Rights: Religion in the Public Sphere," 1987 *How. L. J.* 835 (1987): 840.
24. Id., 841.
25. King, n. 7 supra, 78.
26. Id., 79.
27. Id.
28. Id., 81.
29. Id.

30. I. F. Stone, *The Trial of Socrates* (1988), 100.
31. King, n. 7 supra, 81–82.
32. Id., 84.
33. Id., 85.
34. Id.
35. Id., 85–86.
36. Id., 86.
37. Id.
38. Id.
39. Letter to J. B. Colvin, 20 September 1780.

CHAPTER SIXTEEN

1. "Poll Update—Harris: 76% Say Washington Out of Touch with Rest of Nation," *The Hotline* (National Journal Group), 4 January 1999.
2. National Association of Secretaries of State, New Millennium Project, "Survey on Youth Attitudes," March 1999 (see http://www.nass.org/nass99/execsum.html).
3. Francis Fukuyama, *Trust* (New York: Free Press, 1995), 10–11.
4. Clinton Rossiter, ed., *The Federalist Papers* (New York: Penguin Books, 1961), 322.

CHAPTER EIGHTEEN

1. *USA: Verfassung und Politik* (Vienna: Bohlau, 1987).
2. *The Civil Law Tradition* (Stanford: Stanford University Press, 1969), 3.
3. Speech in the House of Representatives, 1795. Ames contrasted "monarchy" and "republic." Replacing these terms with "dictatorship" and "democracy" merely modernizes the statement; the latter terms had not yet attained currency.

CHAPTER NINETEEN

1. Walter Lippmann, *A Preface to Morals* (New York: Macmillan, 1929; reprinted 1960), 275.
2. *Ibid.*, 276.
3. Article I, sec. 5, clause 3.

4. Article I, sec. 7, clause 2.
5. Article II, sec. 2, clause 1.
6. Article II, sec. 3.
7. See, for example, 1 Stat. 68, 443, 519, and 724; 2 Stat. 302; 3 Stat. 145, 439, and 576.
8. See 1 Stat. 168.
9. See 1 Stat. 28, 49, and 65; these and similar provisions were consolidated in the *Revised Statutes of the United States* (1878) at section 161, which is presently located in the United States Code at 5 U.S.C. 301.
10. See 3 Stat. 140.
11. See 13 Stat. 460.
12. See 17 Stat. 510.
13. See 9 Stat. 113.
14. 12 Stat. 117.
15. 28 Stat. 601.
16. 11 Stat. 379.
17. 15 Stat. 292.
18. 3 Stat. 140.
19. 11 Stat. 253.
20. 28 Stat. 610; current authority for the depository library program may be found at 44 U.S.C. 1901–15.
21. 33 Stat. 584.
22. 42 Stat. 541.
23. John A. Fairlie, "Administrative Legislation," *Michigan Law Review*, vol. 18 (January 1920): 199.
24. Erwin N. Griswold, "Government in Ignorance of the Law—A Plea for Better Publication of Executive Legislation," *Harvard Law Review* 48 (December 1934): 199.
25. *United States v. Smith*, 292 U.S. 633 (1934), *appeal dismissed on the motion of the appellant without consideration by the Court.*
26. *Panama Refining Company v. Ryan*, 293 U.S. 388 (1935).
27. 49 Stat. 500.
28. 50 Stat. 304.
29. See U.S. Department of Justice, Committee on Administrative Procedure, *Administrative Procedure in Government Agencies*, S. Doc. 8, 77th Cong., 1st sess. (Washington, D.C.: U.S. Govt. Print. Off., 1941).
30. 60 Stat. 237.
31. 60 Stat. 238.
32. See note 9.
33. See 5 U.S.C. 552.
34. See 5 U.S.C. 552a.
35. See 5 U.S.C. App.
36. See 5 U.S.C. 552b.
37. Letter to William Charles Jarvis (28 September 1820) in *The Writings of Thomas Jefferson*, vol. 15, eds. Andrew A. Lipscomb and Albert

Ellery Bergh (Washington, D.C.: Thomas Jefferson Memorial Association, 1904), 278.

CHAPTER TWENTY

1. Ronald Dworkin, *Freedom's Law: The Moral Reading of the American Constitution* (Cambridge, Mass.: Harvard University Press, 1996), 2.
2. 163 U.S. 537, 544.
3. 347 U.S. 483.
4. *Green v. County School Board*, 391 U.S. 430 (1968).
5. 402 U.S. 1.
6. Excellent coverage of this dispute can be found in Herman Belz, *Equality Transformed: A Quarter-Century of Affirmative Action* (New Brunswick, N.J.: Transaction Publishers, 1991), chap. 1, passim; and Alfred W. Blumrosen, *Modern Law: The Law Transmission System and Equal Employment Opportunity* (Madison, Wis.: The University of Wisconsin Press, 1993), chap. 8, passim.
7. *Griggs v. Duke Power*, 401 U.S. 424 (1971).
8. *Sheet Metal Workers v. EEOC*, 478 U.S. 421, 448 (1986).
9. 438 U.S. 265 (1978).
10. 109 S. Ct. 2115.
11. Dworkin, *Freedom's Law*, 156–58.
12. 488 U.S., 469.
13. 132 L.Ed. 2d 158.
14. *Hopwood v. Texas*, 78 F. 3d 932 (5th Cir 1996), cert. denied, 518 U.S. 1033.
15. See the remand in *U.S. v. Fordice*, 112 S. Ct. 2727 (1992).
16. *Coalition For Economic Equity v. Wilson*, 122 F. 3d 692 (9th Cir 1997), cert. denied, 139 L.Ed. 2d 310 (1997).
17. "Is Affirmative Action Doomed," *New York Review* (5 November 1998), 56–60.
18. *Shaw v. Reno*, 125 L.Ed. 2d 511.
19. Robert G. McCloskey, *The American Supreme Court*, 2d ed., revised by Sanford Levinson (Chicago: University of Chicago Press, 1994), 212–13.

CHAPTER TWENTY ONE

1. Kirk Porter and Donald Bruce Johnson, comps., National Party Platforms, 1840–1956 (Urbana, Ill.: University of Illinois Press, 1956), 76, 80.
2. *Wabash, St. Louis & Pacific Railway Co., v. Sate of Illinois*, 118 U.S. 557 (1886).

3. 15 U.S.C. §1-11 (1890).

4. *U.S. v. E.C. Knight Co.*, 156 U.S. 1 (1895).

5. *United States v. Trans-Missouri Freight Assn.*, 166 U.S. 290 (1897); *United States v. Addyston Pipe and Steel Co.*, 175 U.S. 211 (1898).

6. *Northern Securities Company v. United States*, 193 U.S. 197 (1904).

7. *Standard Oil Company of New Jersey v. United States*, 221 U.S. 1 (1911); *U.S. v. American Tobacco Company*, 221 U.S. 106 (1911); *U.S. v. Swift & Co.*, 196 U.S. 375 (1905).

8. *History of the Standard Oil Company* (New Jersey), vol. 1, Ralph W. and Muriel E. Hidy, *Pioneering in Big Business: 1882–1911* (New York: Harper, 1955); and vol. 2, George Sweet Gibb and Evelyn H. Knowlton, *The Resurgent Years* (Boston: Houghton Mifflin, 1956), esp. chap. 1.

9. *An Economic History of the United States* (1965), 535.

10. David Burner, *Herbert Hoover: A Private Life* (1979), 171–73.

11. Robert F. Himmelberg, *The Origins of the National Recovery Administration: Business, Government and the Trade Association Issue: 1921–1933* (New York: Fordham University Press, 1976), 4.

12. *Schechter Poultry Corp. v. United States*, 295 U.S. 495 (1935).

13. For a full discussion on this, see Alan Brinkley, "The Antimonopoly Ideal and the Liberal State: The Case of Thurman Arnold," *The Journal of American History* 80 (September 1993), 557–58.

14. Public Law 457, 78 Cong. 2d sess., and 58 Stat. 765 (1944).

15. Good treatment of the entire action can be found in Simon N. Whitney, *Antitrust Policies: American Experience in Twenty Industries* (New York: Twentieth Century Fund, 1958), 85–118.

16. The decision making in the case was highly complicated. As four of the Supreme Court Justices had had to recuse themselves due to prior involvement with the case or industry, Congress passed a statute allocating final authority in civil antitrust actions absent a Supreme Court quorum of six to the three senior judges of the Circuit Court of Appeals which had the jurisdiction. As a result, Judges Learned Hand, Augustus N. Hand, and Thomas W. Swan heard the case and gave its opinon.

17. Whitney, *Antitrust Policies*, 116.

18. *The Report of the Attorney General's National Committee to Study the Antitrust Laws* (Washington, D.C., 1955); for a treatment of the choice of personnel, their deliberations and recommendations, see Theodore Kovaleff, *Business and Government During the Eisenhower Administration* (Athens, Ohio: 1980), chapter 2.

19. 1958 Trade Cases ¶ 69, 189; see also 168 F. Supp. 576.

20. *Brown Shoe v. United States*, 370 U.S. 294 (1962).

21. Robert Bicks (AAG) to William Rogers (Attorney General), 29 September 1959, Antitrust Papers Acc. 70A4771, file 60-0-37-302. The files of the Anti-trust Division are housed in the Federal Records Center, Suitland, Maryland.

22. For a more detailed coverage of the "Electrical Cases," see Kovaleff, *Business and Government*, 118–34.

23. As prophesied by Lee Loevinger in "Private Action—The Strongest Pillar of Antitrust," III: *The Antitrust Bulletin* (March–April 1958), 167–77.

24. 374 U.S. 220 (1966).

25. The complete text of all the Guidelines issued from this date onward can be found in ABA, *Horizontal Merger Law and Policy* (Monograph No. 12, 1986); also see 2 Trade Reg. Rep. (CCH) ¶ 44,510.

26. After a preliminary injunction was issued, the companies abandoned their plans (*United States v. Northwest Industries*, 310 F. Supp. 1066).

27. *United States v. International Telephone and Telegraph Corp.*, 1971 Trade Cases ¶ 73,619 (D. Conn. 1971).

28. *United States v. International Telephone and Telegraph Corp.* 324 F. Supp. 19 (D. Conn. 1970).

29. *United States v. International Telephone and Telegraph Corp.* 306 F. Supp. 766 (D. Conn.).

30. PL 95-504; 49 U.S.CS § 1,301.

31. Edwin Meese III to author (quote his); Martin Anderson to author; James Watt to author, 22 April 1993 at the Hofstra Presidential Conference, Ronald Reagan's America. The author wishes to express his appreciation for the efforts of the conference organizers who facilitated access by scholars to the persons who were indeed "primary sources."

32. *United States v. American Telephone and Telegraph Company*, CA No. 74-1698 (D.D.C.); also see 524 F. Supp. 1336 and 552 F. Supp. 131 (D.D.C.)

33. For an evaluation of the Reagan antitrust policy, see Theodore Kovaleff, *The Reagan ℝEvolution*, in Theodore Kovaleff, *The Antitrust Impulse: An Economic, Historical and Legal Analysis*, vol. 1 (Armonk, N.Y.: M. E. Sharpe, 1994), 193–278.

CHAPTER TWENTY FOUR

1. James Bennet and Janet Elder, "Despite Intern, President Stays in Good Graces," *The New York Times*, 24 February 1998, A16.

2. Ibid., A1.

3. Ben A. Franklin, "The National Jury Says the Starr Chamber May Be Sleazier Than the President," *The Washington Spectator*, 1 March 1998, 1–3.

4. Anthony Lewis, "Sex and Leadership," *The New York Times*, 23 February 1998, A19.

5. Alan Ryan, "Anything but Ridicule," *The New York Times*, 8 February 1998, WK15.

6. Peter J. Riga, "Lesson of a Scandal," *The New York Times*, 24 January 1998, A14.

7. Katharine Q. Seelye, "Conservatives Quietly Find Ways to Talk of Scandal," *The New York Times*, 30 January 1998, A12.

8. Gregor H. Riesser, "Once a Liar?" *The New York Times*, 12 March 1998, A26.

9. Herbert S. Marmet, "Fidelity Above All?" *The New York Times*, 20 March 1998, A22.

10. Howard Park, "On Both Sides of Broder," *The Washington Post National Weekly Edition*, 25 May 1998, 26.

11. Robert C. Solomoln, "Is It Ever Right To Lie? The Philosophy of Deception," *The Chronicle of Higher Education*, 27 February 1998, A60.

12. Janny Scott, "Covering Their Eyes With Parted Fingers," *The New York Times*, 4 April 1998, B13.

13. Gerard Hauser, *Introduction to Rhetorical Theory* (Palisades, Ill.: Waveland Press, 1986).

14. David S. Broder, "No Veils of Secrecy or Decency," *The Washington Post National Weekly Edition*, 2 February 1998, 4.

15. Anthony Lewis, "Sex and Leadership," *The New York Times*, 23 February 1998, A19.

16. Janny Scott, "Covering Their Eyes With Parted Fingers," *The New York Times*, 4 April 1998, B13.

17. Laura Kipnis, "Dangerous Liaisons: Public and Private," *Harper's Magazine* (April, 1998): 19–25.

CHAPTER TWENTY FIVE

1. James Madison, Alexander Hamilton, and John Jay, *The Federalist Papers*, 1787–1788 (many publishers have contemporary editions of this work).

2. Christopher Lasch, *The Revolt of the Elites and the Betrayal of Democracy* (New York: W.W. Norton, 1995).

3. Samuel P. Huntington, *The Clash of Civilizations and the Remaking of World Order* (New York: Simon & Schuster, 1996).

4. Lester C. Thurow, *The Future of Capitalism: How Today's Economic Forces Shape Tomorrow's World* (New York: William Morrow, 1996).

5. Peter F. Drucker, *Post-Capitalist Society* (New York: Harper Business, 1993).

6. Mary Ann Glendon, *Rights Talk: The Impoverishment of Political Discourse* (New York: The Free Press, 1991).

7. Reinhold Neibuhr, *The Children of Light and the Children of Darkness* (New York: Charles Scribner's Sons, 1944).

8. Jeffrey M. Berry, *The Interest Group Society*, 3d ed. (Washington, D.C.: Congressional Quarterly Press, 1996).
9. Seymour Martin Lipset, *American Exceptionalism: A Double-Edged Sword* (New York: W.W. Norton, 1996).

CHAPTER TWENTY SIX

1. Elliot L. Richardson, *Reflections of a Radical Moderate* (New York: Pantheon Books, 1996), 189.
2. Hugh Heclo, "The Future of Merit" in *The Future of Merit: Twenty Years After the Civil Service Reform Act*, ed. James P. Pfiffner and Douglas A. Brook (Washington: Woodrow Wilson Center Press, forthcoming).
3. Richardson, *Reflections of a Radical Moderate*, 211.
4. Cited by Heclo in *The Future of Merit*.

CHAPTER TWENTY SEVEN

1. Sissela Bok, *Lying, Moral Choice in Public and Private Life* (New York: Pantheon Books, 1978).

CHAPTER TWENTY EIGHT

1. *American Foreign Policy* (London: Methuen & Co. Ltd., 1952), 229.
2. Aaron Wildavsky, *The Beleaguered Presidency* (New Brunswick, N.J.: Transaction Books, 1991).
3. As quoted in Miroslav Nincic, *Democracy and Foreign Policy* (New York: Columbia University Press, 1992), 130–31.
4. For trenchantly critical, detailed commentary of FDR's maneuvers in the run up to the entry of the United States into World War II, see Charles A. Beard, *President Roosevelt and the Coming of the War 1941: A Study in Appearances and Realities* (New Haven: Yale University Press, 1948) passim.
5. For evidence that others shared Reagan's concerns, see the report of the blue ribbon bipartisan Kissinger Commission which noted that "The use of Nicaragua as a base for Soviet and Cuban efforts to penetrate the rest of the Central American isthmus, with El Salvador the target of the first opportunity, gives the conflict there a major strategic dimension. The direct involvement of aggressive external forces makes it a challenge to the hemispheric security and, quite specifically to the United States. This is a challenge to which

the United States must respond." As quoted in Lou Cannon, *President Reagan: The Role of a Lifetime* (New York: Simon and Schuster, 1991), 379.

6. *Decision-Making in the White House* (New York: Columbia University Press, 1963), 83–84.

SECTION FOUR, INTRODUCTION

1. R. Gordon Hoxie, *Frontiers for Freedom* (Denver, Colo.: University of Denver Press, 1952), 161.

CHAPTER THIRTY THREE

1. Anne O'Hare McCormick, *The New York Times*, 14 April 1945.
2. Public Papers of President Harry S. Truman, San Francisco Speech, 26 June 1945.
3. Ronald Reagan Presidential Library, Speech at Oxford University, 6 December 1992.

CHAPTER FORTY THREE

1. James Hershberg, *James B. Conant: Harvard to Hiroshima and the Making of the Nuclear Age* (New York: Alfred A. Knopf, 1993), 483, 484.
2. William J. Broad, *Teller's War: The Top-Secret Story Behind the Star Wars Deception* (New York: Simon & Schuster, 1992), 288, 289.

Index